OUTSIDE
AMERICA

REENCOUNTERS WITH COLONIALISM:
NEW PERSPECTIVES ON THE AMERICAS

Dartmouth College Series Editors
Marysa Navarro
Donald E. Pease
Ivy Schweitzer
Silvia Spitta

Frances R. Aparicio and Susana Chávez-Silverman, eds.,
Tropicalizations: Transcultural Representations of Latinidad

Renée L. Bergland, *The National Uncanny: Indian Ghosts and American Subjects*

Michelle Burnham, *Captivity and Sentiment:*
Cultural Exchange in American Literature, 1682–1861

Colin G. Calloway, ed., *After King Philip's War: Presence and Persistence in Indian New England*

John R. Eperjesi, *The Imperialist Imaginary: Visions of Asia and the Pacific in American Culture*

Jennifer L. French, *Nature, Neo-Colonialism, and the Spanish American Writers*

C. L. R. James, *Mariners, Renegades and Castaways:*
The Story of Herman Melville and the World We Live In,
with an introduction by Donald E. Pease

John J. Kucich, *Ghostly Communion:*
Cross-Cultural Spiritualism in Nineteenth-Century American Literature

Ruth Mayer, *Artificial Africas: Colonial Images in the Times of Globalization*

Dan Moos, *Outside America: Race, Ethnicity, and the Role of the American West in National Belonging*

Carla Gardina Pestana and Sharon V. Salinger, *Inequality in Early America*

Susana Rotker, *The American Chronicles of José Martí:*
Journalism and Modernity in Spanish America

Irene Ramalho Santos, *Atlantic Poets: Fernando Pessoa's Turn in Anglo-American Modernism*

Carlton Smith, *Coyote Kills John Wayne:*
Postmodernism and Contemporary Fictions of the Transcultural Frontier

DAN MOOS

OUTSIDE AMERICA

RACE, ETHNICITY,

AND THE ROLE OF THE AMERCIAN WEST

IN NATIONAL BELONGING

DARTMOUTH COLLEGE PRESS
Hanover, New Hampshire

PUBLISHED BY UNIVERSITY PRESS OF NEW ENGLAND
Hanover and London

Dartmouth College Press
Published by University Press of New England,
One Court Street, Lebanon, NH 03766
www.upne.com
© 2005 by Dan Moos
Printed in the United States of America

5 4 3 2 1

Library of Congress Cataloging-in-Publication Data
Moos, Dan.
Outside America : race, ethnicity, and the role of the
American West in national belonging / Dan Moos.
      p.   cm. — (Reencounters with colonialism—
new perspectives on the Americas)
Includes bibliographical references and index.
ISBN-13: 978-1-58465-506-0 (alk. paper)
ISBN-10: 1-58465-506-2 (alk. paper)
ISBN-13: 978-1-58465-507-7 (pbk. : alk. paper)
ISBN-10: 1-58465-507-0 (pbk. : alk. paper)
  1. West (U.S.)—Race relations. 2. West (U.S.)—Ethnic relations.
3. West (U.S.)—Civilization. 4. Acculturation—West (U.S.)—
History. 5. Assimilation (Sociology)—History. 6. National
characteristics, American. 7. United States—Race relations.
8. United States—Ethnic relations. I. Title. II. Series.
F596.2.M66   2005
305.8'00978—dc22   2005015532

FOR ZUBEDA

The nation was rushing forward with giant strides toward colossal wealth and world-domination, before the exigencies of which mere abstract ethical theories must not be permitted to stand.

—CHARLES CHESNUTT, *The Marrow of Tradition* (1901)

CONTENTS

ACKNOWLEDGMENTS

Writing a book so often feels like a lonely and solitary endeavor, yet such a project is never undertaken alone. Many people have helped me with the production of *Outside America*, from reading drafts, to tracking down sources, to providing intellectual support when my own seemed lagging. I would like to thank Carrie Bramen, Mike Frisch, Bruce Jackson, and Don Pease for their work guiding me through the project as both a dissertation and then later as a manuscript. I would also like to thank those who gave me valuable feedback on particular chapters: Kathleen Boardman, Scott Casper, Jim O'Loughlin, Charlene Regester, and Gioia Woods, as well as the anonymous readers at *African American Review* where a version of chapter 2 appeared. I probably would never have gone down this road if not for the initial prodding of Anne Butler to undertake the study of Western American History; she has been an invaluable guide—and friend—along the way. During my years at the University at Buffalo, the friendship and intellectual guidance and camaraderie of people like Ricky Baldwin, Chris Barnes, Joseph Conte, Kris Dykstra, Mark Frankel, Catharine Gray, Jim Holstun, Julie Husband, Joy Leighton, Imre Szeman, and Neil Schmitz helped shape the final outcome of this project.

Much of this study involved poring over books (obscure and otherwise), films, photographs, and rather mundane business prospectuses. None of this work would have been possible without the help of Myra Blank at the Interlibrary Loan office of Adams Library at Rhode Island College; Wallace Dailey at the Theodore Roosevelt Collection at Houghton Library, Harvard University; Coi Drummond-Gehrig at the Denver Public Library; Shelley Howe, Museum Collections Manager at the Buffalo Bill Museum and Grave; Jessica Lemieux at the Bancroft Library at the University of California, Berkeley; and Vyrtis Thomas at the National Anthropoligical Archives.

John Landrigan, Jessica Stevens, and others at University Press of New England have provided invaluable assistance in the reworking and the production of this book, and I would like to acknowledge their intellectual, administrative, and editorial efforts—without their attention, *Outside America* would be a lesser book. I would also like to thank the Faculty Resources Committee at Bowdoin College for providing funds to offset the costs of the photographs and other figures used in this book. Also along these lines, I heartily thank Jon Langford for the wonderfully apt cover art.

With sincere gratitude, I want to acknowledge my parents, Warren and Doris Moos, who believed in my ideas and allowed me the space—and the means—to pursue my academic career.

The last word: Nothing here could have been possible without the intellectual, emotional, and editorial support of my wife, Zubeda Jalalzai. To her I dedicate this book.

* * *

A version of chapter 2, "Reclaiming the Frontier: Oscar Micheaux as Black Turnerian," appeared under the same title in *African American Review* (36.3 [Fall 2002]). A version of chapter 3, "Recasting the West: Frontier Identity and African American Self-Publication," appeared as "African American Autobiography and Self-Publication" in *Western Subjects: Autobiographical Writing in the North American West*, edited by Kathleen Boardman and Gioia Woods (University of Utah Press, 2005).

INTRODUCTION

THE AMERICAN WEST AND U.S. NATIONAL CULTURE

ON SEPTEMBER 17, 2001, just six days after anti-American hijackers crashed four planes into the World Trade Center towers, the Pentagon, and a west Pennsylvania field, U.S. President George W. Bush declared Al-Qaeda leader Osama bin Laden public enemy number one by invoking tropes of Old West justice and cowboy vigilantism. A reporter asked President Bush, "Do you want bin Laden dead?" to which the president replied, "I want him—I want justice. And there's an old poster out West, as I recall, that said 'Wanted: Dead or Alive.'" Perplexed by the president's allusion, another reporter asked for clarification: "Are you saying you want him dead or alive, sir? Can I interpret your . . ." President Bush cut this reporter off brusquely and reiterated, "I just remember—all I'm doing is remembering when I was a kid, I remember that— they used to put out there in the Old West a wanted poster. It said 'Wanted Dead or Alive.' All I want, and America wants him brought to justice. That's what we want" ("Excerpts" A10).

Born in Texas in 1946, Bush likely saw a "Wanted" poster only on a flickering screen in a darkened theater. Yet this president felt that he could reach an American audience (if not Al-Qaeda itself) through his transparent reference to American West imagery. Bush's words reveal an American affinity for western mythologies that has not yet disappeared, even as that region looks more and more like the many other American public spaces covered with Wal-marts, McDonald's restaurants, and Starbucks shops, no less the now standard fast-food chains. Certifying his cultural connections to the West (though he was educated in the East at Andover Academy and Harvard and Yale Universities), President Bush regularly dons cowboy boots for public appearances. While on the campaign trail in 2000, his boots were festooned with the Texas state flag; as president, he transferred this regional allegiance to the nation at large, sporting monogrammed boots emblazoned with the presidential seal. But George W. Bush is certainly not the first U.S. cowboy president. Presidents as recent as Ronald Reagan (who, while no cowboy himself, occasionally played one in film) have used the imagery of the American West and its frontier mythos to justify U.S. foreign and domestic policies. Theodore Roosevelt looms the largest as a western figure, peppering his speeches with references to the rugged men with whom he worked during his short tenure as a cattleman in South Dakota. Lyndon B. Johnson, who also hailed from Texas, was often photographed in a cowboy hat and sought the refuge of his cattle ranch when escaping from politics. Through their allusions and words, the American West exemplified U.S. history; its imagery—the cowboy hat, the boots, the cattle ranch, the sixshooter, the "Wanted" poster—became representative of American character. The West has provided ample material for proving the special nature not only of U.S. history but of the United States's place as a world power. By invoking the American West, these politicians have given life to its fabled history and set it to work for their political agendas.

Western narratives of adventurous mountain men, self-sufficient pioneers, and honest, hardworking cowboys (as well as suspect Chinese, lascivious Mormons, and savage Indians) provided the building blocks for a story of American exceptionalism and bolstered the immanence of a distinctly masculinist American Manifest Destiny. But the construction of this western identity demanded a careful navigation of the racial, ethnic, and religious difference so prominent in these vast western spaces. Over the course of the last decades of the nineteenth century, the federal government enacted a series of laws regimenting the ways in which difference could—or could not—be incorporated into American culture. While American political leaders sought a kind of unity, both political and social, the complete cohesion of ideals (no less races or classes) could never completely be achieved. But the restriction of access to avenues of power in American society could be implemented so as to corral Americanness into a more tightly controlled and codified social system. The American West in particular became a place where difference was suppressed for the sake of an imagined national cultural cohesion.

After the Civil War, American political leaders endeavored to build a unified country through violent, legislative, and hegemonic means. The attacks on Fort Sumter on April 12, 1861, began the violent rupture of a nation defined by difference. But almost exactly four years later, General Lee's surrender clearly pointed America toward a union, a joining together of differences to form a United States of America. But this project of the confederation of ideals became a mission of oppression and silencing throughout the course of the rest of the nineteenth century and into the twentieth, much of it centered in the American West. While Lincoln's government and the Union army emancipated southern slaves, issues of difference arising from the free intercourse of white America with peoples of other colors and other creeds only became increasingly problematized within this new national space of union and unity. While union implies togetherness and unity implies homogeneity, the nation during the last half of the nineteenth century (no less the entire twentieth century) undoubtedly displayed neither of these qualities.

After the Civil War, Reconstruction put the nation into a state of apparent solidarity, though at the local levels, the realities of Reconstruction regularly fell short of its ideals. With the end of Reconstruction in 1877 and the return of Democratic control to the South, many of the short-lived freedoms for newly freed slaves disappeared into racist laws and bureaucracies. In 1882, the federal government passed the Chinese Exclusion Act, which effectively kept Chinese immigrants out of the country. With the establishment of dissociative laws regarding communal Native American property ownership through the 1887 Dawes Act, Indian land was now open for easy and unthreatened settlement and Native Americans became excluded from the nation and relegated to reservation—that is, separate—lives. In 1890, the federal government ended violent Native American resistance to federal control with the massacre at Wounded Knee. Also in 1890, the Mormon Church issued the Woodruff Manifesto, which declared that the church did not and would not sanction plural marriages. This capitulation to the demands of gentile society occurred after two decades of federal legal persecution and a suspended military campaign against Utah Mormons that involved the largest peacetime mobilization of the U.S. Army to that date. Six years later, in 1896, the Supreme Court decision in *Plessy vs. Ferguson* effectively alienated African Americans and placed them outside of U.S. national culture. And finally, the Frontier Thesis, elaborated by historian Frederick Jackson Turner in an address at the Chicago World's Fair in 1893, became a definitive document in organizing the boundaries for the American national consciousness. With the close of the frontier, American identity could become conceivable through its clarified geographic boundaries; to be American was, at minimum, to be inside this perimeter.

Outside America locates the place of the American West in the national culture of the turn-of-the-twentieth-century United States and considers the ways this narrative was appropriated by those Americans who resided structurally outside of that story. Looking at writers who did not fit into the terms of national unity because of structural differences such as race or religion, I examine how these writers embraced or found themselves caught within the web of that dominant national story that excluded their presence. Many of the writers addressed in *Outside America* pursued the ideals of American culture—here, the mythic narratives of the American West—in the belief that its broad terms could include their own voices. By writing within these tropes, such writers often dissociate their literary worlds and their everyday ordinary lives, revealing the limits of the myths as well as the constraints set upon these outsiders by both political and civil society.

While Raymond Williams has argued that culture is ordinary and contested, this ordinariness of everyday life becomes distilled as heroic in the narratives of the American West and transferred to an "official" culture of the nation. Thus American culture—the narrative of the nation—appears simultaneously exceptional and ordinary; the heroic myths of the West become the everyday terms for understanding the limits of American cultural nationalism. The official culture of U.S. nationality has shifted regularly over the last 150 years as the nation struggled for self-definition. It has mutated according to the presence of people or groups with varying ideological perspectives who hold public offices, sit on industrial or corporate boards, maintain sway in popular culture, or have other avenues to ideological power. Official culture is the culture—the "whole way of life," as Raymond Williams writes (*Culture and Society* xviii)—of the nation writ large. Lauren Berlant writes in *The Anatomy of National Fantasy* that "'America' is an assumed relation, an explication of ongoing collective practices, and also an occasion for exploring what it means that national subjects already share not just a history, or a political allegiance, but a set of forms and the affect that makes these forms meaningful. . . . We are bound together because we inhabit the *political* space of the nation, which is not merely juridical, territorial (*jus soli*), genetic (*jus sanguinis*), linguistic, or experiential, but some tangled cluster of these" (4–5). This "National Symbolic" (5) leads citizens to an understanding of national belonging by linking that "tangled cluster" of national identifications to locally precipitated ideals of the nation itself. Official culture is the hegemonic narrative of the nation given credence through citizens' acceptance of that National Symbolic. While the ideological space of official culture remains frequently contested by various voices seeking recognition, if not dominance, within the nation, this singular ideological space called "American" houses the momentary "whole way of life" necessary for any particular political or social project. Culture in this sense is a shell filled by competing nationalist discourses, its terms and boundaries repositioned by representatives of U.S. political and social power.

I concur with Priscilla Wald's understanding of official culture's associative powers in *Constituting Americans*, her analysis of American identity in the nineteenth and early twentieth centuries. She succinctly declares, "Official stories constitute Americans" (2), arguing that the narrative of the American nation fashions the identity of its citizens. In *Constituting Americans*, Wald searches for discomfort among American literary citizens as they work to build national narratives; she seeks the places where the constitution of their national identity has misfired. In these imperfections of Americanness, Wald discovers "an uneasy awareness of a larger story controlling their stories" and "an oscillation between conformity and incomprehensibility" (3). These larger stories to which she refers are the narratives of official culture. This official culture, then, is very much the cultural arm of hegemonic nationalism, seemingly disconnected from nationalist strategies but ultimately providing the engine for national consensus and apparent unity. In *Outside America*, I complicate Wald's reading of constituted Americans by examining the ways certain culturally segregated Americans embraced the terms of a national narrative that was fundamentally oppressive to them. I ask what advantages such an endorsement offered to these marginalized citizens as well as how this narrative might have affected their own sense of identity as outsiders.

Antonio Gramsci's concept of hegemony helps to unpack the dynamics of power in official culture and to see the connection between its artifacts—novels, advertising, letters, speeches, art—and nationalism. In Gramsci's concept of hegemony, the State maintains power through a combination of coercion and consent within the national community. Specifically, hegemony is the construction and maintenance of social relations advantageous to the preservation of the State, operating through governmental structures, such as laws, justice, and policing, but also through less direct avenues, particularly education and popular culture. Gramsci divides societal superstructure into "civil society," which reflects the hegemony of a dominant group, and "political society" (the State), within which the dominant group manipulates social forms and structures to maintain its existence. For Gramsci, a dominant group maintains power through "the 'spontaneous' consent given by the great masses of the population to the general direction imposed on social life by the dominant fundamental group" in combination with "the apparatus of state coercive power which 'legally' enforces discipline on those groups who do not 'consent' either actively or passively" (12). Hegemony, then, does not involve forced acquiescence but rather the construction of a politics through which those members of society who reside outside of the dominant ideology appear in need of realignment. Coercion, when necessary, brings antagonistic elements of civil society into concert with the ideology of the present dominant group. But coercion must operate within the limits of the consent given by civil society; otherwise, such force appears oppressive and will lose the sanction of a nation's citizens. Hegemony operates by asking members of the nation to live within the boundaries of the ideology of its rulers, provided that those rulers (as members of political society) provide models of behavior and ideals for the members of civil society. Gramsci claims that the "spontaneous consent" of civil society occurs when its members "[modify] their own habits, their own will, their own convictions to conform to those directives and with the objectives which [political society] propose[s] to achieve" (266). Given the relationship between civil and political society, hegemony consists of a "combination of force and consent which form variable equilibria, without force ever prevailing too much over consent" (80, n. 49). Tipping the balance too far to either side tears the relationship between the segments so as to disrupt a careful balance of ideological power.

Official culture, then, is the narrative or historically grounding story of a nation attained through the terms of hegemony. Official culture has no police force, no coercive apparatus that forces citizens' bodies or thoughts into line, but it does inscribe limits to the stories allowed in the construction of this national narrative. As a hegemonic narrative, official culture projects the desires of a dominant group onto the "whole way of life" of the nation's citizens to form a cohesive and unified account of national life. (This unity may be a narrative of cultural homogeneity or of cultural variability and difference; either sense still demands a singularity of ideals.) In order to maintain consent, official culture must appear to speak to the entire nation, thus allowing all citizens to feel empowered and included in the national narrative in at least a peripheral fashion. Thus many of those people barred from entering political society still participate in the construction of the dominant narrative by identifying with that story of the nation that fundamentally keeps them marginalized. As demonstrated within *Outside America*, numerous western African Americans, Mormons, and Native Americans embraced this structure, identifying with a fundamentally alienating national narrative while effectively remaining barred from the privileges such an ideological attachment offered.

With the end of the short-lived and much celebrated cowboy era in the late 1880s, the "closing" of the frontier West by the 1890 United States Census, the curtailment of Mormon polygamy with the issuance of the Woodruff Manifesto, and the disruption of Native American resistance at Wounded Knee, American politicians, historians, and culture makers turned to the West to find the exceptional qualities of the nation and to construct from this ideologically significant region a history appropriate to the conditions of the early twentieth century. The West became a locus for this new Americanness: cowboys became righteous American heroes, western railroads signified American unity (corporate and political), and the grand vistas of mountains and deserts typified the epic sweep of the United States's (brief) history of conquest and rise to global power.[1]

Painters such as Frederic Remington and authors such as Owen Wister celebrated a colorful West of cowboys, Indians, Indian fighters, and frontier towns now gone from their turn-of-the-century vantage points. Remington constructed visual tapestries that evoked the heroism of western cowboys and soldiers—always rough, ready, and white—and deliberately ignored the drudgery of these labors and the contributions of non-white participants. He consistently sought to present an image of the American West as a historical moment now passed, an exceptional period in the formation of the United States. Owen Wister produced similar western myths by creating cowboy heroes who acted righteously, played fair, understood natural social hierarchies, and, of course, always got the girl. His heroes, like the Virginian, Lin Mclean, or Scipio Le Moyne, seemed to grow directly from the open spaces of the Rocky Mountain West, comfortably traversing its expanse in self-sufficient and cautious movement. Like Remington in his paintings, though, Wister always wrote nostalgically, claiming that these knights on horseback—whose lineage stretched "from the tournament at Camelot to the round-up at Abilene" (Wister, *Owen Wister's West* 39)—"will never come again. He rides in his historic yesterday" (Wister, *Virginian* x). In these mythologies rests a narrative of masculine individuality as well as national success and a desire to strive forward from this base of personal and geographic conquest. By proving their affinity with this narrative and by adopting the terms of western triumph, marginalized westerners sought inclusion in these heroic stories, removing their peculiarity in favor of western values.

Within an American memory often built on the speeches of cowboy presidents, the prose of Wister, and the paintings of Remington, western culture—particularly the mythic West presented by these men—is generally overdetermined. But over the last two decades, historians have questioned the legitimacy of this pioneer narrative, which has come to be known as Old Western History. Their new western narrative, appropriately entitled New Western History, challenges a prescriptive chronicle of the West that insists on an American exceptionalism rooted in the western soil. Old Western History, also called Triumphalist History by New Western Historians, grew from Frederick Jackson Turner's perception of a progressive, evolutionary, westward-moving frontier line that generated a unique American culture, politics, and social character. The contributions of New Western Historians are manifold: they challenge grand narratives of western progress; they confront the traces of Manifest Destiny in contemporary popular history and textbooks; they dispute the Eurocentric ideals of vacant wilderness, free land, and aboriginal peoples as nature; and they add to the standard formulas of western history the experiences and voices of those traditionally outside entrenched grand narratives.[2]

Two historians, Patricia Nelson Limerick and Richard White, have become the leading theoreticians of New Western History. Building from the tenets of social history, they seek to overturn the prescriptions of Old Western History by calling into question the motives and assumptions of earlier historians and by valorizing the impact of those historical actors lost in more traditional narratives. Condensing her critiques of earlier western historians, Limerick rather playfully calls Old Western History "happy face history" in that its outcomes are always fortuitous for its actors ("What Raymond Chandler Knew" 31).

In 1987, Patricia Nelson Limerick published *The Legacy of Conquest: The Unbroken Past of the American West*, a groundbreaking book in western history that Limerick claims cost her many academic friends. Her title itself set the stage for a new paradigm in thinking about the American West. As she writes rather bluntly in her introduction, "Conquest forms the historical bedrock of the whole nation . . . [and] was a literal, territorial form of economic growth. Westward expansion was the most concrete, down-to-earth demonstration of the economic habit on which the entire nation became dependent" (27–28). For

Limerick, the narrative of the American West was one of ongoing conquest—a mastery of the land and its peoples. It was also a continual history, not one mystically concluded at the end of the nineteenth century, as more traditional narratives of the West would have it. By 2000, Limerick reduced the principles of New Western History to four interlocking concepts: "continuity, convergence, conquest, and complexity" (*Something in the Soil* 18). According to Limerick, New Western Historians assume (1) that western history was not radically broken by the mythical end of the frontier; (2) that the West was "one of the great meeting zones of the planet . . . [where] people from all over the planet met, jockeyed for position, and tried to figure each other out" (*Something in the Soil* 19–20); (3) that the violent subjugation of land and people informed the very real day-to-day lives of westerners as well as the historical narrative of this region; and (4) that in the complex narrative of the West, "good intentions could lead to regrettable outcomes, and the negative aspects of life wove themselves into a permanent knot with the positive aspects" (*Something in the Soil* 21).

The work of this first generation of New Western Historians is generally informed by strong materialist and anti-imperialist politics. Limerick claims New Western History as a revolutionary scholarship in which "it is OK for scholars to care about their subjects, both in the past and the present, and to put that concern on record" ("What on Earth" 86–87). Limerick's awareness of the subjects of history, that is, the warm-blooded people who populate historical narratives, allows her to better write history with an eye toward the effects of large, faceless social and economic structures such as industrialism, capitalism, or institutional racism on the lives of western individuals, communities, or ecological locales. Traditional western history, based on Turner's Frontier Thesis, seeks the forces of individual will and determination that ultimately produce the exceptional brand of American democracy. But these institutions celebrated by Old Western Historians became those faceless structures that affect the lives of Limerick's historical actors. Thus, in caring about her subjects Limerick gives credence to the subjective experiences of individuals as she finds them in the historical record, presenting history from the perspective of people manipulated by the forces of capitalism and national expansion.

In 1991, Richard White furthered Limerick's call to unseat western mythologies in his western history textbook *"It's Your Misfortune and None of My Own": A New History of the American West* by refusing to use the word "frontier" or to even mention Turner.[3] White does not explain this strategy, but presumably, by removing these markers of conquest-centered narratives, White believes he can undo the triumphant ideology that has masked a "true" Western history. New Western History claims to be nonprescriptive and does not insist on historical templates that match ideologically driven outcomes, as New Western Historians claim Old Western History demands. In fact, White connects these two competing brands of scholarship with the literary genres of comedy and tragedy. He claims that Triumphalists, that is, Old Western Historians, tend to "write comedy, in the sense that they provide a happy resolution" ("Trashing the Trails" 31). For them, western history "is the story of a journey, and challenge, and a . . . transformation" ("Trashing the Trails" 32). New Western Historians, though, write tragedies. Their narratives do not focus on "the qualities of any single set of occupants" (that is, triumphant white pioneers) and often "find people attempting one thing and very often achieving another" ("Trashing the Trails" 33). In these tragedies, which distinctly oppose those cheery narratives of Old Western success, White dryly writes, "Things don't end well" ("Trashing the Trails" 33).

New Western History has opened up doors for the evaluation and celebration of voices and stories from the West that have traditionally been ignored. It has broadened the expanse of historical discourse and helped to create narratives of the United States that more closely reflect its demographic make-up and its violent history of conquest. Besides undertaking fresh histories of traditionally marginalized western subjects such as western Native Americans, African Americans, Latino/as, and Asian immigrants, New Western Historians have produced new scholarship on western women's experiences, western children, and western environmental history.[4] But lacking within the critical perspective of New Western History is an awareness of the power of the cultural capital embedded in the western mythologies they debunk. Historian William G. Robbins writes in *Colony and Empire: The Capitalist Transformation of the American West*, "To the degree that the West became the archetype for the triumphalist and exceptionalist ideology of the nation-state, it marked a retreat from history [and] . . . an escape from the material base of things" (6). New Western Historians generally see as their mission the removal of this nationalist ideology to show the "material base of things," and thus they often set up traditionalist narratives against the silenced narratives of marginalized people. But New Western Historians such as Limerick and White (among others) often disallow the empowerment that western mythologies offered (and sometimes delivered) even for those people for whom the myths were not originally intended—sometimes those very outsiders that the myths sought to subdue. New Western Historians such as Limerick and White endeavor to claim the "real" West (the West of warm-blooded subjects) from the mythic West, believing that this conquest will dissolve the power of false mythologies. But as these historians try to undo the mythic West through the conscious rejection of its terms (clearly evidenced by White's abandonment of the word "frontier"), they disregard the reality of the myth itself. New Western Historians have overturned the Triumphalist narrative, but they have also lost sight of the enduring cultural power of a myth that continues to circulate, even when emptied of content.

As reprehensible as the tenets of western pioneer identity may be (to New Western Historians), some western outsiders, such as African Americans, Mormons, or certain groups of Native Americans, espoused elements of western mythology in complicated ways that they believed might offer them the advantages of western subjectivity. By extension, in a turn-of-the-century nation whose identity rested heavily upon the narrative of western expansion and its attendant ideals of self-sufficiency, individualism, self-improvement, freedom, and unencumbered progress, recognition as an American westerner could potentially aid in the inclusion in the national body. This inclusion was especially important for westerners who for reasons of race or religion were otherwise neglected or even excised from the nation. Thus, along with learning from the expansiveness of the New Western History paradigm, we should pay attention not only to those people left out of Triumphalist history, but to those ignored by New Western Historians, that is, those subjects who problematically endorsed western myths in their attempts at national inclusion. American narratives of success as well as narratives of failures—both comedies and tragedies—contribute to the construction of American culture. To simply ignore one story, prescriptive or not, in favor of another that fits a new paradigm more neatly will produce only another carefully bound set of stories.[5] The cultural narrative of the American West sits centrally within the ideology of American exceptionalism and within official culture. Thus we need to turn to both the people who populate New Western History as well as the myths of the region that drove the Triumphalist story and seek the points of contestation and conflict that link regional identification with national citizenship.

Most contemporary scholars writing about the turn-of-the-twentieth-century United States saw a nation with deep internal conflicts, not, as some contemporary American spokespersons claimed, a nation of unity.[6] As the United States struggled to conceive of itself from the ashes of the Civil War, its official spokespersons proposed to unify the nation through a process of exclusion and amalgamation. That is, certain people could never become American (anarchists, polygamists, and, for a period, the Chinese); some citizens presented difficult visible problems, such as dark skin, while others, such as Mormons, required reconstruction and absorption into the larger political and social body. In some instances, the official culture demanded a group's adherence to cultural norms, as in the case of the Mormon concession to federal law. As for others, notably African Americans after 1896 and Native Americans under a reservation system, the official culture demanded domestic separation within the nation. Thus, while America had been created from contesting stories of identity from many competing cultural narratives, its emergence as a culturally, politically, and geographically unified nation rested primarily on a rhetorical dialectic between the culture of its powerful elite—white Protestant men—and the various constituent parts of America's complex demography.

Donald Pease has argued in "National Identities, Postmodern Artifacts, and Postnational Narratives" that the fundamental character of American culture—the originary building blocks of national identity—rests on the necessary exclusion of groups and peoples who are seemingly alien to the foundational concepts of an American nation based on the American colonies' severance from England's imperious rule. He claims that the nature of American culture at any moment in its history rests on the psychological/cultural establishment of Others who provide the binary opposite for the appellation "American." Pease writes, "When understood from within the context of the construction of an imagined national community, the negative class, race, and gender categories of these subject peoples were not a historical aberration but a structural necessity for the construction of a national narrative whose coherence depended upon the internal opposition between Nature's Nation and peoples understood to be constructed of a 'different nature'" (4). Thus certain citizens remain outside of the boundaries implicitly set for being "American" or, to use Wald's term, for attaining "personhood" within the nation. But the terms of these boundaries are generally intangible and constructed within the social fabric—indeed, within the political unconscious—of the nation and are prone to rupture and reorganization when those people of a "different nature" demand a place within the national narrative. For Pease, it is precisely these ruptures that "expose national identity as an artifact rather than a tacit assumption, a purely contingent social construction rather than a meta-social universal" (5). In that sense, *Outside America* locates sites of contest that lead toward a reformulation of American identity based on various principles held in tension with each other, rather than on a simple modification of foundational myths.

While this study defends the place of the American West (as a region and as an ideological construct) in the formation of American national identity, I do not argue here for the primacy of western mythology in the construction of national culture. There are categories that operate equally as profoundly, namely racial unrest, North-South regional tensions, increasing immigration, women's suffrage agitation, and the shift from national expansion to global imperialism. Narratives about the American West, however, remained deeply enmeshed in a matrix that involves all of these discourses. Thus *Outside America* is meant to add to an understanding of American material culture at the turn of the century by introducing the varied ideologies associated with the American West into discussions of race, gender, class, consumerism, imperialism, and nativism, among others, in this period. As such, *Outside America* looks at certain individuals who saw their placement as westerners as a key avenue toward national cultural citizenship or national belonging when other avenues seemed closed. For example, some black frontiersmen and frontierswomen found more affinity with their situation as individuals on a leading edge of American continental expansion than as children of freed slaves seeking the rights guaranteed to them after the Civil War. Mormons found it more useful to recast themselves as hardworking pioneers subduing western lands and native peoples than to press for their religious rights under the First Amendment. And many Native Americans who found employment in Indian shows or Wild West exhibitions discovered that they could wield more power in the national story by transforming themselves into images of their own subtle making rather than fight—martially or legally—for their rights as members—or wards—of the nation.

The myth of the West called to Americans to seek their fortunes on the lands of the open frontier and to leave behind the squalor and inequalities of the East (as well as the depleted soil of its farms). While this summons was not designed for all Americans, certain westerners realized that they could, with varying degrees of success, write themselves into these regional and national narratives. *Outside America* examines the role of the West in nineteenth- and early-twentieth-century American official culture in order to trace the enduring power of those regional myths of individuality and self-sufficiency as well as their role in nation formation at this time. I examine how those members of the nation who necessarily occupied cultural space outside of the national narrative through structural considerations such as race or religion appropriated the terms of identity that sprouted from the West and its mythologized history. Rather than being constant victims of these western tropes, these unlikely subjects of western identity tried to capitalize on the roles available to them, either as pioneers, cowboys, or noble savages, in order to attach themselves to American national identity. Native Americans were by definition *not* frontiersmen; neither were Mormons or African Americans, regardless of their actual roles in settling the West. Native Americans in the West were savage threats to expansion; Mormons were seen as lustful and heretical outsiders; and African Americans in the West seemed mere aberrations. By invoking their connections to the West, these western outsiders sought the establishment of "personhood" within the American nation.

Chapter 1, "Rough Riding Across America: Mythologizing the West, Constructing the Nation," situates the American West as central to the formation of an official national culture in the turn-of-the-century United States through the figure of Theodore Roosevelt. As a cattleman and hunter in the West in the 1880s, Roosevelt believed that the masculinist culture of western frontier laborers and cattle entrepreneurs represented the fundamental characteristics of American culture and American nationalism. As a politician less than ten years later, Roosevelt turned these beliefs toward policy as he molded the United States into an imperial global power. But Roosevelt's theories connecting western identity and American national character distinctly excluded westerners such as African Americans, Native Americans, and Mormons; he did not provide theoretical possibilities for these Others to adopt the mythic vision of the West that provided opportunity for all people. Roosevelt's embracing of the West allowed him to place white male pioneer westerners at the center of his vision of American culture without consideration for the place of others. This chapter turns primarily to Roosevelt's narrative of the First Volunteer Cavalry in Cuba (the Rough Riders) to determine the boundaries for inclusion in the national body for people outside of Roosevelt's vision and then links Roosevelt's vision of the United States to Turner's theories of frontier identity.

Chapter 2, "Reclaiming the Frontier: Oscar Micheaux as Black Turnerian," examines the autobiographical novels of South Dakota homesteader and pioneer of African American film Oscar Micheaux. Micheaux presents himself (and his fictional proxies) as the embodiment of the spirit of self-sufficiency supposedly inherent to the West. Micheaux brought Booker T. Washington's theories of vocational development to the Great Plains, advocating the ideals of self-help and agricultural pursuit in the interest of racial uplift. Emulating the ideas of Turner's Frontier Thesis, Micheaux sought rejuvenation along the frontier. Behind a plow, Micheaux embodied Turner's ideals, if not the racial identity of his historical actor. Within Micheaux's fiction, though, we can locate his frustration at the conflict between the western myth and racist reality. Nonetheless, Micheaux continued to embrace the supposed regenerative properties of life on the plains, and over time his fiction turned toward fantasies of black agricultural colonies and the racial metamorphoses of his forbidden white lover. Like Roosevelt, Micheaux's attachment to the mythic narratives of the West increased with his distance, both spatially and temporally, from that space. For Micheaux, the western strenuous life—though one particularly directed at production rather than Roosevelt's strenuous leisure of camping and hunting—gave rise to the possibilities of racial uplift.

Many other western African Americans produced similar narratives of their lives. Chapter 3, "Recasting the West: Frontier Identity and African American Self-Publication," examines the self-published and primarily autobiographical writings of western African Americans Robert Ball Anderson, Thomas Detter, and Nat Love (as well as Micheaux with particular reference to his self-publication). These narratives—of two homesteaders, a barber, and a cowboy—rest between the opposing poles of race identification and American nationalism. By self-publishing their memoirs, autobiographies, and fictions, these authors reinforced the western ideals of self-sufficiency and self-determination. Collectively these authors sought out both African American and western audiences in order to weave their narratives of western success, thus evincing their belief that as westerners, even as black westerners, they belonged within the mainstream of American national identity. Too often, though, the cast of their narratives, which generally advocated self-sufficiency and the inherent meritocracy of the West, collided with racial inequalities that refused to disappear west of the Mississippi River.

Chapter 4, "The Making of Americans: Assimilation and Mormon Literature of the Mid-Twentieth Century," focuses on early-twentieth-century fiction by members of the Church of Jesus Christ of Latter-day Saints. In late-nineteenth-century popular culture, Mormons shared the stage in cartoons, sensational novels, and theater with other seemingly troublesome racial minorities. Though Mormons have been drawn as the epitome of frontier peoples, they in fact did not move west to seek frontier opportunity or rejuvenation. Rather they were hounded west by U.S. citizens incensed at Mormon theology and their rumored polygamy. The ideal of Mormon frontiersmen (and frontierswomen) who embodied western values of self-determination derives primarily from mid-twentieth-century narratives that equated Mormons' westward struggles with the mid-nineteenth-century expansion of the United States. Novels by Mormon authors such as Vardis Fisher, Ardyth Kennelly, George Dixon Snell, Virginia Sorensen, and Maurine Whipple sought to dispel the unpalatable aspects of Mormon history while also presenting images of heroic pioneers who sought refuge from injustice in the opportunistic West. According to the narratives of these authors, the frontier allowed Mormons the opportunity to erase difference and prepare themselves for inclusion in a national cultural narrative. In fact, in an unusual switching of western gender roles, it was primarily female women authors who paved the way for Mormon men to become—at least mythically—ideal westerners. This construction of Mormons as the apotheosis of frontierspeople became so ingrained that by the mid-twentieth century many Mormon authors manifested a belief that Mormon assimilation was near complete and their identity would soon fold into a larger national character.

The final chapter, "Buffalo Bill's Object Lessons: Native American Survivance in the Arena," turns to one of the most ironic appropriations of Western identity positions, that of the defeated—though noble—Native American in Buffalo Bill's Wild West. Here I focus on a marginalized group who, unlike African Americans and Mormons, actually played a role in the development of the mythologies of the West and who assumed within that narrative their function as the vanquished and vanishing antagonists of the United States's westward expansion. Native American leaders such as Sitting Bull, Black Elk, and Luther Standing Bear, as well as individual warriors and sometimes whole families, joined Buffalo Bill's Wild West and played out their parts as the enemy—conclusively defeated, of course, with a flourish by the charming William F. Cody himself. Native Americans in the Wild West played only two roles: they were savages or they were dead, and generally these theatrical postures coincided. Outside the arena, many Native Americans sold photos and autographs, establishing a kind of historical identity through trinkets and memorabilia. Some participants, like Sitting Bull, maintained the rights as well as the cash gained from these sales, thus providing a flourishing side business in identity production. Both Luther Standing Bear and Black Elk discuss their experiences with the Wild West in their autobiographical narratives *My People the Sioux* and *Black Elk Speaks*, to which we can turn to understand the divisions between their role as entertainers in a scripted melodrama of U.S. history and their sense of effacement within the very real West of intolerance and inequality. Effectively postcolonial subjects, these Native Americans manipulated the terms of western identity and history to enable their "survivance," to use Gerald Vizenor's term, within the American nation. But in this not-quite-authentic survival we see the constructedness of both Native American and U.S. national identities, each equally indebted to the history of the West and its particular retellings.

The analysis of the fiction and the autobiographies of these various western outsiders reveals the relevance of the western mythologies of self-definition and economic freedom to national identity. The drive toward American identification through regional ideological affiliation also demonstrates the limits to cultural as well as political citizenship as these individuals butted against social prejudices that proved more powerful than western identity. Nonetheless, individual African Americans and Native Americans, as well as the great collective of the Mormon Church, did attain varying degrees of empowerment insofar as they could fully replicate the American ideals located in western mythology. Mormons may have had an easier time of exorcizing polygamy than African Americans or Native Americans had of erasing race, but all benefited from the myth when their markers of difference were made secondary to westernness. Unfortunately, simply embracing the West as a great leveler of racial, class, or religious conflict in American society was rarely enough to completely sublimate those differences.

1

ROUGH RIDING
ACROSS AMERICA

MYTHOLOGIZING THE WEST,
CONSTRUCTING THE NATION

IN STEPHEN CRANE'S SHORT STORY "A Man and Some Others," published in *The Century Magazine* in 1897, a group of Mexicans attack a white shepherd named Bill on the plains of Texas after warning him, "We want you geet off range. We no like" (*Complete* 328). Bill, who has a violent history and a penchant for fights, has refused to leave and, though an Anglo stranger helps to fend off the attackers, Bill does not survive their assault. The story closes with the stranger waving his gun threateningly at the "limping and staggering" Mexicans before he "[stoops] to loosen Bill's gray hands from his throat" (339). After reading a manuscript of "A Man and Some Others," Theodore Roosevelt, then New York City police commissioner, wrote to Crane, declaring that "Some day I want you to write another story of the frontiersman and the Mexican Greaser in which the frontiersman shall come out on top; it is more normal that way!" (Crane, *Correspondence* 1: 249).[1]

Beyond the simple racism imbedded in the term "Mexican Greaser" and Roosevelt's mandate for the "natural" superiority of the American shepherd, Roosevelt creates a historical situation that does not appear in Crane's story. By turning Crane's shepherd into a "frontiersman," Roosevelt invests Bill with a history dear to his heart. Roosevelt's "frontiersman" evokes an image of the hardy western pioneer (cowboy, rancher, trapper, forty-niner) pushing forward the American frontier through his dedication to hard work, self-sufficiency, and individualism while taming the land for other less adventurous Americans to follow. But Crane's character, "a tattered individual with a tangle of hair and beard, and with a complexion turned brick-color from the sun and whiskey" (*Complete* 332), established his present livelihood only after a Bowery fight in which three sailors at the far end of a piece of scantling "landed him in Southwestern Texas, where he became a sheepherder" (331). Bill, in fact, had very little to do with being a "frontiersman." Before starting his latest career, Bill had owned and lost a mine in Wyoming and worked as a cowboy, a brakeman, and a Bowery bar bouncer, but his numerous professions were dictated by the frequency and gravity of the various fights and killings he left in his wake. By tending sheep, he engaged in work generally relegated to loners, often Mexican or Basque, and categorically despised by cattlemen.[2] This "frontiersman" engaged in neither nation-building activities nor frontier improvement. By setting up a hierarchical dichotomy between "frontiersman" and "Mexican Greaser," Roosevelt proffers a template for narratives—both historical and future—of U.S. expansion; these formulaic stories demand that Americans "come out on top" because, as Roosevelt so effortlessly declares, "it is more normal that way." In Roosevelt's version, the central character must defeat the Mexicans, thus mutating him from a mere shepherd into the necessary western model of American exceptionalism: the "frontiersman."

By the date of his letter to Crane (August 1896), Roosevelt was ascendent. Within four years, Roosevelt would hold the second highest office in the United States, with his accession to the presidency only nine months away. Between the time of his letter to Crane and his appointment to the U.S. presidency, Roosevelt was selected as the assistant secretary of the navy, caught the American public's imagination by leading his volunteer regiment to victory in Cuba, and won the New York governor's election in 1898. Over the course of the first decade of the new century, Roosevelt would then prove himself a favorite politician among the American people and an admirable adversary of overstuffed late-nineteenth-century monopolies. Not always embraced by his peers, Roosevelt was designated "that cowboy in the White House" by industry barons and Republican party foes alike (quoted in DiNunzio 13). McKinley's advisor Mark Hanna, who irritably referred to Roosevelt as "that damn cowboy" (Morris, *Theodore Rex* 30, 36), feared Roosevelt's nomination as vice president, apparently quipping quite presciently, "Don't you realize that there's only one life between this madman and the Presidency?" (quoted in DiNunzio 12).

Roosevelt molded American ideals into new patterns at the beginning of the twentieth century, validating the connection between power, politics, and the embodied life. His love of the West (and all of its myths), his attempt at ranching (albeit a financial failure), his profound appreciation of wilderness (and its attendant sport of hunting), and his veneration of adventure, virility, and personal danger made Roosevelt a marker of a new America whose leaders sought the strenuous life so important to American identity. Roosevelt, as the leader of a burgeoning imperial power, offered to the world an American spirit, a masculinist culture of machismo, control, and autonomy with its roots located deep in the American soil rather than in European governments or the tattered threads of Europe's aristocracies. We might sketch Roosevelt's sense of himself as an ideal American from his symptomatic book titles; he saw himself as a *Ranchman*, a *Wilderness Hunter*, an *American Hunter*, a *Rough Rider*, a *Book Lover [. . .] in the Open*, and an advocate for *The Strenuous Life*. At the turn of the twentieth century Roosevelt defined American culture, projecting outward to the rest of the world and inward back to the American populace an image of the nation as exceptional, with a distinctive history, society, and politics that set it apart from all other nations.

Even as a local municipal official, Police Commissioner Roosevelt felt entitled to rebuke, albeit as a friend, a popular author's construction of the American West and the narrative of its history. Stephen Crane's stories and journalistic writings provided access to places and events that his readerly public often dared not venture (urban slums, rowdy bars, western deserts), thus simultaneously playing upon and creating Americans' imaginations about themselves. As an antidote to the parts of Crane's cultural formation that jarred with Roosevelt's vision, the police commissioner simply advised altering the story to fit the imagination. Furthermore, as an established (though not professional) historian who had recently published a four-volume history of the United States's westward impulse, Roosevelt demanded that Crane's narratives fit his own historical designs.[3] Roosevelt's divination of American culture invoked an American objective and nationalist teleology of progress—"it is more natural that way"—while Crane's story, at least according to Roosevelt, demonstrated an unfortunate misapprehension of ideals. Roosevelt demanded that American prose directly reflect the ideals necessary for the establishment of U.S. imperial power; American culture needed to step in line with American politics and reflect the drives of the nation.

THE RANCH LIFE AND THE AMERICAN LIFE

Theodore Roosevelt, as a rising politician, and later as a U.S. president, worked hard to solidify the conceptualization of the United States as a post-frontier nation. Using America's pioneer heritage as guiding its ideals, Roosevelt turned his sights to the global arena, setting an imperial agenda that would last to this day. Roosevelt brought with him to the White House (as well as to most of his politics) ideals cemented in the myths of the American West: individual self-sufficiency, American exceptionalism, the right to easy land acquisition, and, perhaps most importantly, the necessary and transparent implementation of these myths into political policies.

As a child of well-to-do New Yorkers who traced their lineage to seventeenth-century Dutch settlers, Roosevelt's initial contact with the West came through his reading of juvenile adventure tales, such as those written by Thomas Mayne Reid, R. M. Ballantyne, and Captain Marryat, as well as his father's readings aloud of James Fenimore Cooper (see Roosevelt, *Theodore Roosevelt* 14–19, and Morris, *The Rise of Theodore Roosevelt* 45; see also Bederman 172–74). His fascination with the outdoors led him west immediately after his graduation from Harvard University in 1880 for a five-week hunting trip with his brother Elliot in Minnesota near the Dakota Territory border. In 1883, Roosevelt ventured west again, this time to Little Missouri, a desolate town on the edge of the Badlands in the Dakota Territory. He went at the invitation of Commander Henry H. Gorringe, a naval officer who purchased an abandoned army camp there with an eye toward creating a hunting preserve (Collins 12). Arriving in Little Missouri, Roosevelt hoped to bag a bison (which he did), but by the time he left he had arranged a $14,000, seven-year contract with two of his hunting guides that authorized the acquisition of four hundred head of cattle for the Chimney Butte Ranch, his guides' present operation outside of town (Collins 21). Three years earlier, Roosevelt and a Harvard classmate had invested $10,000 in a Wyoming cattle company; this venture provided a meager 5 percent return over the next three years. Though Roosevelt's initial interest in the West seemed to be for sport, he clearly had turned his attentions toward business as he glimpsed his potential future as a cattleman. With the privilege of eastern money, Roosevelt could not only buy cattle at will but could also develop land significantly faster than most other people living locally. With his initial purchase of stock, Roosevelt bought the Chimney Butte ranch and used it as his headquarters; he soon built another ranch, Elkhorn, with a relatively comfortable lodge forty miles downriver.

Roosevelt journeyed west again in June of 1884, just five months after the death of his wife and mother on the same day. He wrote to his sister from Medora in Dakota Territory, discussing his future ranching plans, "the cattle have done well, and I regard the outlook for making the business a success as being *very* hopeful. . . . I shall put on a thousand more cattle and shall make it my regular business" (*Letters* I: 73). Roosevelt played cowboy/cattleman for the next two years, buying more stock, building a new ranch, and, as the myth goes, turning himself from a four-eyed, tenderfoot easterner into a seasoned ranchman.[4] But Roosevelt had not remained in the West the entirety of those last two years; he traveled between New York and Dakota Territory to attend to family business and political encouragements, even electing to miss the dreary cold of the Great Plains winter in favor of New York's relatively balmy climate. By 1886, Roosevelt had formally put his cowboying days behind him. The unrelenting frigid and snowy winter of 1886–87 proved disastrous for the cattle industry across the northern plains; hundreds of thousands of under-fed cattle died on overstocked ranges in what has been called the "Great Die-Up." Roosevelt himself lost half of his cattle in the winter blizzards that year.[5] Roosevelt spent the bulk of the following summer hunting and completing his biography of Thomas Hart Benton, his cattle operation in shambles. Leaving Dakota Territory in the fall of 1887, Roosevelt turned his attention from the land of the West to the narrative of the West as he began his intellectual creation of this region in his multivolume history *The Winning of the West.*

Roosevelt never returned to the day-to-day life of ranching, and his regular western pilgrimages stopped. As Collins points out in *That Damned Cowboy,* "His trips became fewer and shorter. But his love for the American West, if anything, grew stronger" (111–12). I would add to Collins's assessment that as Roosevelt's love for the West waxed, so did his overdetermination of that region; with an increasing distance from the actual geographic space of the West came Roosevelt's increased celebration of its mythical qualities. Over the next ten years, Roosevelt turned his attention to intellectual activities, producing numerous books on hunting in the West as well as historical texts.[6] Implicit in these texts lie Roosevelt's assumptions that the American frontier produced particularly American individuals and that frontier life—including cowboying—defined U.S. national and social characteristics.

Roosevelt's first book from the American West, *Hunting Trips of a Ranch-man* (1885), consists primarily of hunting sketches and presents the West as a sportsman's paradise, focusing little on its potential for business, agriculture, or municipal evolution. In fact, the subtitle to *Hunting Trips of a Ranchman* is *Sketches of Sport on the Northern Cattle Plains.* Roosevelt's first chapter, how-ever, illustrates ranch and cowboy life around his property in South Dakota.

Here he discusses not only the day-to-day work of ranch life, but also the inherent characteristics of westerners that in later books Roosevelt claims define American social sensibility. Roosevelt asserts that life on the frontier converts individuals of varying ethnicities, classes, and temperaments into representatives of a single people. He writes, "The cowboys form a class in themselves and are now quite as typical representatives of the wilder side of Western life, as were a few years ago the skin-clad hunters and trappers. . . . [T]hese plainsmen are far from being so heterogenous a people as is commonly supposed. On the contrary, all have a certain similarity to each other; existence in the West seems to put the same stamp upon each and every one of them" (6). Thus ethnic or national origins disappear in the West when life there imbues each inhabitant with characteristics that override earlier sensibilities.

But Roosevelt's West does not merely manufacture types; instead, it enables a historical procession of which the cowboy is simply the most recent development in the struggle to wrest one's living from western lands. Within the same chapter on ranch life, Roosevelt laments the passing of earlier frontier specimens:

> [T]he true old Rocky Mountain hunter and trapper, the plainsman, or mountain-man, who for all his faults, was a man of iron nerve and will, is now almost a thing of the past. In place of these heroes of a bygone age, men who were clad in buckskin and who carried long rifles, stands, or rather rides, the bronzed and sinewy cowboy, as picturesque and self-reliant, as dashing and resolute as the saturnine Indian fighters whose place he has taken; and, alas, that it should be written! he in his turn must at no distant time share the fate of the men he has displaced. The ground over which he so gallantly rides his small, wiry horse will soon know him no more, and in his stead there will be plodding grangers and husbandmen. (31)

As of the publication of *Hunting Trips of the Ranchman*, Roosevelt himself appears unsure as to which of these frontier people he belongs. After the initial chapter, "Ranching in the Bad Lands," his book reads like a sportsman's sketchbook; indeed, the photograph facing the title page shows Roosevelt in full hunting garb, including the buckskin and long rifle he attributes to mountain men, thus alluding to his affinity with a quickly disappearing era (figure 1). Here a confused westerner, Roosevelt cannot distinguish himself from the patrician money that enabled these hunting trips, from the childhood stories of

FIGURE 1 Roosevelt posing in hunting garb.
Theodore Roosevelt Collection, Harvard
College Library.

FIGURE 2 Roosevelt posing in cowboy
outfit. Theodore Roosevelt Collection,
Harvard College Library.

daring deeds and mountain adventure, or from the cowboys and cattlemen
amongst whom he lived and worked (for at least part of the year). Roosevelt,
in fact, posed in two different outfits for the publicity photographs for *Hunting Trips of a Ranchman.* Besides the already noted picture of Roosevelt in the
fringed buckskin tunic and long rifle, he also posed in a showy cowboy outfit,
complete with embroidered flowers, carefully fitted chaps, and a flat-brimmed
hat (figure 2). Here the requisite sixshooter and cartridge belt replaces the
long hunting knife seen in the earlier photograph. Both photographs were
taken in a New York studio.

Roosevelt's adoration of the cowboy life appears in his next western book,
Ranch Life and the Hunting Trail (1888)—a text fully illustrated by celebrated
western painter Frederic Remington—and continued to inform all of his
subsequent analyses of both the American West and the nation more generally. *Ranch Life and the Hunting Trail* more clearly presents Roosevelt's observations and anecdotes concerning life as a cattleman, though he does include

hunting sketches in the last third of the book. Roosevelt again repeats his theory that cowboys are replacing hunters and that even this present western livelihood will disappear. But he makes his contempt for the approaching and imminent agricultural phase even more clear. In a discussion of the open range, where he depicts cattlemen as inherently cooperative and neighborly (at least with each other), Roosevelt techily writes, "Of course, in the end, much of the ground will be taken up for small farms. . . . [W]e are inclined to welcome the incoming of an occasional settler, if he is a decent man, especially as . . . he is obliged to fence in his own patch of cleared ground, and we do not have to try to keep our cattle out of it" (22). Roosevelt closes this particular chapter by asserting the imminent end of ranch life: "In its present form stockraising on the plains is doomed, and can hardly outlast the century. . . . [W]e have seen, what is perhaps the pleasantest, healthiest, and most exciting phase of American existence" (24). Thus the future of the American West lies with the farmer, who carries none of the heroics of Roosevelt's hunters or cattlemen. The farmer, Roosevelt's "plodding granger," may enable stability in this new American region, but it is the ideals embodied in the frontiersmen that define the characteristics of the nation.

Roosevelt quite transparently—and not altogether incorrectly—assumes that those pioneers who paved the way for the "plodding grangers" were necessarily male, but he builds from this gendered pioneering a mythic West that remains masculine throughout all frontier phases and places. In most of his public references to the West as a geographic locale, to his time in the West, or to people he associates with the West, Roosevelt refers only to men. In a 1901 address in Colorado Springs to mark the twenty-fifth year of Colorado statehood, Roosevelt directs his comments to "You and your fathers who built up the West," succinctly highlighting a western patrilineage and excising all women from their roles in conquering and settling the region (*Strenuous Life* 252). In the same speech Roosevelt outlines the traits he saw as definitive of those pioneer sons and fathers: daring, hardihood, iron endurance, resolution, courage, indomitable will, and perseverance (252, 257). Certainly Roosevelt's masculinist vision was not relegated solely to the American West. From the moment of his entry into public life, he consistently concerned himself with the establishment of manly virtues, particularly of the stripe noted at the 1901 Colorado celebration.[7] Roosevelt's 1897 collection of articles, *American Ideals*, literally brims with the celebration of tough male ideals. For example, "The Manly Virtues and Practical Politics," explains to potential (male) politicians the necessity of masculine virtues for effective politics. Later in *American Ideals*, Roosevelt concludes a book review of Charles H. Pearson's pessimistic *National Life and Character: A Forecast* with this seeming non sequitur: "But be this as it may, we gladly agree that the one plain duty of every man is to face the future as he faces the present . . . to play his part manfully, as a man among men" (292). Certainly this manly part necessarily was one of strength, hard work, and virility. Admonishing attendees at the 1901 Minnesota State Fair, Roosevelt assailed men who sought pleasure instead of national progress and women who chose lives other than as mothers and wives: "the wilfully idle man, like the wilfully barren woman, has no place in a sane, healthy, and vigorous community" (*Strenuous Life* 281). For Roosevelt, manliness, in all its vigor (and in its attachment to willing childbearers), was the only option for creating a rugged, hearty, and salubrious nation.

Roosevelt published *Ranch Life and the Hunting Trail* two years after he had left his ranch life behind. Satisfied with his own performance as both a hunter and a rancher, Roosevelt seemed content to leave the West to its inevitable agricultural changeover. But the individual traits he believed grew from the frontier became the baseline for this soon-to-be politician's world view. In *The Winning of the West*, Roosevelt's sweeping history of American westward expansion (through roughly 1807), Roosevelt declares that the backwoodsman, the prototype for the plainsman and cowboy, embodied specifically American traits that enabled him not only to become a true American but to establish distinctive institutions such as American democracy. Again hailing from varying national and ethnic backgrounds (though they were primarily European), these pioneers became Americans through frontier adversities: "Long before the first Constitutional Congress assembled, the backwoodsmen, whatever their blood, had become Americans, one in speech, thought, and character. . . . They resembled one another, and they differed from the rest of the world—even the world of America—in dress, customs, and in mode of life" (1: 108–109). Roosevelt claims that these backwoodsmen, who would soon move west for new opportunities, were defined by their strength, thrift, courage, industry, and penchant for "self-help" (see 1: 113, 116). In *Ranch Life and the Hunting Trail*, Roosevelt imbues his cowboys and cattlemen with these same characteristics: "shrewd, thrifty, patient, and enterprising, but he must also possess qualities of personal bravery, hardihood, and self-reliance. . . . Stockmen are in the West the pioneers of civilization, and their daring and adventurousness make the settlement of the region possible" (7). Frontiersmen bring civilization to the front line of the United States's westward movement and in the process establish the traits necessary for the rest of the country's citizens.

In 1886, Roosevelt opened the first volume of *The Winning of the West* with his claim that "During the past three centuries the spread of English-speaking peoples over the world's waste spaces has been not only the most striking feature of the world's history, but also the event of all others most far-reaching in its effects and importance" (1: 1). Just pages later he consequently asserts that the conquest of the American continent "was the crowning and greatest achievement of a series of mighty movements" (1: 7). Thus within the very first pages of his history, Roosevelt sets up the American West as an endpoint for the spread of European people; from the position of the frontier, one might look back to the mighty conquests and imperial adventures of England. Of course, in Roosevelt's West, albeit an endpoint for "English-speaking peoples," all manner of Europeans can reemerge as Americans through their wrestling with the frontier environment. By 1901, now established as the nation's vice president and with years of heroics in the public eye behind him, Roosevelt could manifest his theories of the connections between the American West, the nation's character, and his present movement toward imperial ventures. At the aforementioned quarter-centennial celebration of Colorado's statehood, Roosevelt, invoking both a transparently masculine West of the past and its connection to the United States's new global designs, told his audience:

> The men who founded these communities showed practically by their life-work that it is indeed the spirit of adventure which is the maker of common-wealths. Their traits of daring and hardihood and iron endurance are not merely indispensable traits for pioneers; they are also traits which must go to the make-up of every mighty and successful people. You and your fathers who built up the West did more even than you thought; for you shaped thereby the destiny of the whole republic, and as a necessary corollary profoundly influenced the course of the events throughout the world. (*Strenuous Life* 252–53)

Westerners—male Westerners—had become the true Americans; the back-woodsman and the cowboy embodied American ideals and the character necessary for a successful nation. With the establishment of America's boundaries, partially defined by Roosevelt as the decline of cattle ranching, the rising politician could look elsewhere to continue, if not the spread of English-speaking peoples themselves, at least the expansion of their temperament. As the ranch life had shaped the American life, Roosevelt saw the American life as the template for the world at large.

COWBOY SOLDIERS: ROOSEVELT'S ROUGH RIDERS

As a creator and arbiter of official culture, no moment shines brighter in the popular mythology of Roosevelt than his years immediately preceding his assumption of the vice presidency. In 1898, a decade after he had abandoned his western ventures (business and otherwise), Roosevelt once again turned to the raw material of the West to provide examples of "True Americanism."[8] In April of 1898, Secretary of War Alexander Alger asked then Assistant Secretary of the Navy Roosevelt to lead one of the three volunteer regiments authorized by Congress for the U.S. fight in Cuba against Spain. Roosevelt modestly turned down the colonelship but agreed to be second in command if his friend and colleague Leonard Wood could assume the leadership. Wood had little formal military experience (he was officially Mrs. McKinley's doctor), though he received the Medal of Honor for helping to capture the Apache chief Geronimo.[9] Regardless of his secondary leadership role, Roosevelt became the media star as well as the hero of the regiment, with Wood generally tending to its managerial details. The First Volunteer Cavalry was to be drawn from Arizona, New Mexico, Oklahoma, and the Indian Territories, though Roosevelt did add an east coast troop (Troop K) that consisted of friends and associates from Harvard and other well-to-do circles. The members of the other two volunteer cavalry regiments hailed from the northern plains. In the contemporary press, the First Volunteer Cavalry came to represent a spirit of the United States's now disappearing frontier. The media apparently christened the First Volunteer Cavalry the Rough Riders, but numerous other western-tinged appellations abounded in the press, such as Teddy's Tarantulas, Teddy's Cowboy Contingent, Roosevelt's Rough 'Uns, Roosevelt's Wild West, the Cowboy Cavalry, and even Wood's Wild Westerners (Samuels and Samuels 17; Walker 102).[10]

Roosevelt presented his volunteers as "true" Americans within *The Rough Riders*, his serially published narrative of the life of the First Volunteer Cavalry.[11] These generally newly minted soldiers hailed from the West, especially the Southwest, and were primarily cowboys, miners, part-time sheriffs, trappers, and mountain men, though a number of the recruits came from Ivy

League colleges. In Roosevelt's description, most of the Rough Riders hailed from "the Four Territories which yet remained within the boundaries of the United States; that is, the lands that have been most recently won over to white civilization, and in which the conditions of life are nearest those that obtained on the frontier when there still was a frontier" (Roosevelt, *Rough Riders* 11[12]). Roosevelt viewed these men as particularly American in that they were hewn from the harsh environs of life on the frontier. They could withstand cold, discomfort, and hunger and feared neither violence nor death. This collection of men was hardened by "Voyages around Cape Horn, yacht races for the America's cup, experiences on foot-ball teams which are famous in the annals of college sport; more serious feats of desperate prowess in Indian fighting and in breaking up gangs of white outlaws; adventures in hunting big game, in breaking wild horses, in tending great herds of cattle, and in wandering winter and summer among the mountains and across the lonely plains" (Roosevelt, *Rough Riders* 149). The single thing that brought these men together in unity was not political ideology (the defense of Cuba, for example), but adventure and sport, two necessary elements within "strenuous" masculinity of the turn of the century. In fact, according to Roosevelt, these shared traits allowed the various Rough Riders to transcend potentially problematic categories such as class, regional affiliation, or education in favor of a common masculinity. Roosevelt writes in *The Rough Riders,* "All—Easterners and Westerners, Northerners and Southerners, officers and men, cow-boys and college graduates, wherever they came from, and whatever their social position—possessed in common the traits of hardihood and a thirst for adventure. They were to a man born adventurers, in the old sense of the word" (14). Roosevelt's vision of America as embodied in the Rough Riders included only men strengthened by the adverse conditions of the American continent or those from positions of privilege who had transcended that entitlement to embrace the strenuous life.

Though the majority of the Rough Riders hailed from the West, Roosevelt celebrated his regiment as typically and broadly American. On May 25, 1898, Roosevelt wrote Henry Cabot Lodge from San Antonio (en route to Cuba):

> It is as typical an American regiment as ever marched or fought. I suppose that 95 per cent of the men are of Native birth, but we have a few from everywhere, including a score of Indians, and about as many of Mexican origin from New Mexico; then there are some fifty Easterners . . . and almost as many Southerners; the rest are men of the plains and the Rocky

Mountains. Three fourths of our men have at one time or another been cowboys or else small stockmen. (*Letters* 2: 832–33)

Thus of the almost one thousand men in the regiment, which consisted of twelve different troops, 2 percent were Native American or of Mexican origin; Troop K was primarily from the East, though only thirty-three of its ninety-nine members proved to have definitive eastern addresses (White, *Eastern Establishment* 153). Using Roosevelt's arithmetic, then, roughly 750 of his volunteers were cowboys, stockmen, or ex-range hands. In actuality, only 160 men listed their occupation as "cowboy" and fourteen as "cattleman" (Jones 342). Roosevelt's formulation—2 percent Native or Mexican American, zero percent African or Asian American, 5 percent foreign born, 5 percent wealthy college graduate, 13 percent indeterminate, and 75 percent cowboy—hardly presents a typically American company.

Though Roosevelt's vision seemed to seek a commonality of men in action, he actively denied places to African and Asian Americans within a regiment that served to house men of dubious backgrounds who might be denied acceptance into other portions of the United States military. However, Roosevelt had no qualms about Native American volunteers, though he tempered their presence by declaring, "Only a few [Indians] were of pure blood. The others had shaded off until they were absolutely indistinguishable from their white comrades" (*Rough Riders* 15). The typical Americanness of the regiment rested on its racial boundaries, which, if not maintained in blood and lineage, at least were solidified through physical appearance. Underlining the impossibilities of blackness in the regiment, some members dubbed a near albino volunteer with the incongruous nickname "Nigger" (Walker 122). Other unsavory and ironic names abounded—the only Jew in the regiment was given the unfortunate nickname "Pork-Chop" (*Rough Riders* 31). A definitive marker of the Rough Riders was not only their westernness but also their essential whiteness, be that of faded Indians, darkened albinos, or non-kosher Jews.

AFRICAN AMERICANS AT SAN JUAN HILL

The racial composition, the Americanness, of the Rough Riders was also set against the two black cavalries of regular soldiers fighting in Cuba. Both the Ninth and the Tenth Regular Cavalries saw action alongside Roosevelt's Rough Rider volunteers, though in the history of the definitive fight in Cuba, the Battle of San Juan Hill, their roles have been obfuscated, if not completely obliterated. The Ninth and Tenth Cavalries, as well as the African American Twenty-fourth and Twenty-fifth Infantries, were called to fight in Cuba in early April of 1898, a full two to three weeks before Congress had even authorized what would become the Rough Riders. Though Roosevelt and his volunteers presided over the popular image of the war in Cuba, African American regular soldiers were a central and stable cog in the war machine to which Roosevelt and his men had only recently become attached.[13] In *The Rough Riders*, Roosevelt praises the actions of the Ninth and Tenth Cavalries, though he rather paternalistically claims that they were "peculiarly dependent upon their white officers" and easily lost their direction with the absence of these commanders (92). Allowing his own troops a kind of race-based autonomy, Roosevelt remarks, "With the colored troops there should always be some of their own officers; whereas, with the white regiment, as with my own Rough Riders, experience showed that the non-commissioned officers could usually carry on a fight by themselves if they were once started, no matter whether their officers were killed or not" (92).

While the Rough Riders's charge of San Juan Hill is generally seen as evidence of the continued success of the American frontiersman—the transfer of an ideology of determined rugged individualism onto U.S. military might—the actual events of the day point to a more clearly mixed and definitively confused action. The division of the troops during the assault on San Juan Hill, even by Roosevelt's account, is murky at best. Numerous soldiers, black and white, had become separated from their troops and joined the fight with whichever troop was nearby; Roosevelt found himself in charge of at least "a score of colored infantrymen" as well as numerous other soldiers from other regiments (*Rough Riders* 92). The volunteer Rough Riders fought alongside both white and black regular U.S. soldiers in this battle, though Roosevelt himself, backed by his volunteers, took the glory for capturing the hill. Looking past the presence of both black cavalrymen and infantrymen at other positions near the hill as well as the actions of that score of black soldiers under his command, Roosevelt claims that the African American regulars "began to get a little uneasy" in the face of the violence and "drift[ed] to the rear, either helping wounded men, or saying that they wished to find their own regiments" (*Rough Riders* 93). Incensed by this black retreat under fire, Roosevelt drew his revolver and threatened to "shoot the first man who, on any pretence whatever, went to the rear" (93).

According to numerous accounts, these soldiers may not have been beating a hasty retreat but rather were aiding wounded soldiers or withdrawing to acquire supplies for the front line. Also, some of the less confident soldiers did not necessarily retreat from the line of fire but rather sought their own regiment with whom to continue the battle.[14] According to Presley Holliday, a black soldier in the Tenth Cavalry who fought at San Juan Hill, Roosevelt visited the Tenth Cavalry the day after the battle and apologized for his assumptions of cowardice concerning the retreating black soldiers. Holliday writes that Roosevelt "had seen his mistake and found [the black soldiers] to be far different men from what he supposed" (quoted in Gatewood, "*Smoked Yankees*" 94). But in Roosevelt's published memories of that day, he effectively enervates or erases those black soldiers so important to his victory, thus bleaching the story that becomes definitive of the American spirit in Cuba. Holliday's May 11, 1899, letter to the *New York Age* confronts Roosevelt's account of the actions of the black troopers in the serial version of *The Rough Riders* that had been recently published in *Scribner's*. Rather than trying to refocus the valiant actions at San Juan Hill on African American soldiers, Holliday instead voices his dismay at Roosevelt's excision of his apology from his narrative. Holliday writes, "I thought he was sufficiently conscious of his error not to make a so ungrateful statement about us at a time when the Nation is about to forget our past service" (quoted in Gatewood, "*Smoked Yankees*" 94). Responding to the official culture machine—the narrative of the battle at San Juan Hill validated in print by the self-appointed hero of the battle—Holliday laments, "I could give many other incidents of our men's devotion to duty, of their determination to stay until the death, but what's the use?" (96). Clearly, a "typical an American regiment" was whatever Roosevelt deemed typical, and, as in his criticism of Crane's story, he demanded its construction and memorialization in print, regardless of the facts.

In her essay "Black and Blue on San Juan Hill," Amy Kaplan argues that Roosevelt's depiction of African American troops in Cuba works to maintain a domestic ideology of racial separation and black inferiority. She claims that, although politicians and the press represented the war in Cuba fundamentally as a conflict with an external and foreign enemy, the subtext of these depictions "reestablishes the reassuring order of the domestic color line in a foreign terrain" (222). By looking at Roosevelt's narrative in *The Rough Riders* and at the portrayals of the war by American journalists, Kaplan finds that both Cubans and African Americans become demonized, emasculated, comically

infantilized, or, at best, are absent. The primary rhetoric surrounding the entrance of the United States into the war with Spain was one of domestic
unification, a "splendid little war" (as John Hay called the U.S. expedition to
Cuba) that might heal the wounds of a nation torn in two only four decades
earlier. Support for the war seemed generally shared in both the North and
the South, an irony not lost on Booker T. Washington, who found the South's
support for a revolution inspired primarily by Cuba's black population "inex-
plicable" (*A New Negro* 24). The nation, looking toward the southern island
for its own national unification and reconstitution, played out its domestic
battles on the Cuban landscape. Kaplan finds that within the depictions of the
war "the narrative shifts from conflict with an external enemy, Spain, to internal struggles with reputed allies" (226). Indeed, as Roosevelt turns his revolver, which had been rescued from the wreckage of the *Maine*, onto those
black soldiers momentarily under his command, he turns the critique of national loyalty away from the front line and back to domestic racial relations.
According to Kaplan, these African American soldiers—as representatives of
black America—"are forced into the body politic at gun point, Americanized
by keeping their place" (230). Continuing his ideological attention to the
Maine revolver, Roosevelt tells us just a few pages later that he used this same
renowned weapon to kill a fleeing Spanish soldier who had fired on him from
the trenches.

Even the Cubans themselves, whom Stephen Crane believed to be "the
worst thing for the cause of an independent Cuba that could possibly exist"
(quoted in Kaplan, "Black and Blue" 226), effectively disappeared from Roosevelt's narrative, occupying only a few disparaging pages. Roosevelt has little
praise for Cuban soldiers. In fact, all of his references to Cubans (particularly
Cuban soldiers) in *The Rough Riders* are dismissive. He notes that upon arriving in Cuba, "we found hundreds of Cuban insurgents, a crew of as utter tatter-
demalions as human eyes ever looked on, armed with every kind of rifle in all
stages of dilapidation. It was evident, at a glance, that they would be no use in
serious fighting, but it was hoped that they might be of service in scouting.
From a variety of causes, however, they turned out to be nearly useless, even
for this purpose" (49). Roosevelt also disparagingly notes that both the soldiers and the aid promised by General Castillo, the commander of the Cuban
forces, for an engagement at Las Guasima did not appear "until the fight was
over" (53). Roosevelt then remarks that during this fight, "There was a Cuban
guide at the head of the column, but he ran away as soon as the fighting

began," unlike the two newspapermen there, Edward Marshall and Richard Harding Davis (56). In the heat of battle, when "something exploded over our heads," Roosevelt and his troops gallantly "sprung to our feet and leaped on our horses" to escape. But when the same shells exploded among a group of Cuban soldiers, Roosevelt claims that they "scattered like guinea-hens," likening them to fearful and feminized scatterbrains (76). Even after the fall of Santiago, Roosevelt notes of the fleeing noncombatant inhabitants, "we had to feed them and protect them from the Cubans" (134). The presence of people difficult to absorb into an American narrative demanded that their identity be manipulated—or erased—so as not to undercut the domestic racial balance struck by the arbiters of official culture, if not the shapers of official policy.

At the top of San Juan Hill, Roosevelt and the Rough Riders posed for a photograph. The best known picture from this session situates Roosevelt in the center of a cluster of his soldiers, some with their hats set rakishly, the U.S. flag stirring in the wind behind them (figure 3). Roosevelt stands just left of the flag so as not to be lost in its prominence in the top half of the photograph. He alone presents a full-frontal view; the other standing soldiers are partially blocked by the volunteers sitting or squatting in front of them. Just as Roosevelt takes center stage in his narrative, he holds the center of the heroic photograph of conquest (regardless of his position as second in command). But in the original 1899 edition of *The Rough Riders*, Roosevelt (or possibly *Scribner's*) chose to publish a slightly different photograph from the same session, likely taken only minutes before or after the more famous shot. In this more expansive picture (figure 4), Roosevelt again appears at the center, though now his visage has become blurred and he is primarily identified by the fleeting possibility of his spectacles and his rather characteristic stance—hands on his hips and his chest thrust out—in distinct contrast to his slouching confederates. While Roosevelt fades into the center of this heroic photograph, his body apparently no different from those surrounding him (here a soldier sits at Roosevelt's feet and blocks his legs from view), a figure emerges from the far right edge demanding the viewer's attention. Staring directly back at the camera is a black regular soldier, his gaze fixed squarely and deliberately on the camera. He is not posed for the camera like so many Rough Riders, nor is he inattentive, as are the soldiers around him. In fact, we might discern from the attitude of those soldiers around him that he and his immediate neighbors were not intended for inclusion in this historic photograph at all.

FIGURE 3 Roosevelt and the Rough Riders posing at San Juan Heights (narrow view). Library of Congress, Prints and Photographs Division. Photograph by William Dinwiddie, 1898, LC-USZ62-7626 DLC.

Nonetheless, this soldier's presence at the margin of the photograph demands that he be recognized for his service in this important battle. His place in the photograph, even if it be unintentional, underscores the importance of African American soldiers and their representation as victors at San Juan Hill. With the inclusion of this photograph in *The Rough Riders*, the black soldier's gaze confronts Roosevelt's narrative and demands that Roosevelt, as well as the viewer/reader, acknowledge the labors and sacrifices of African American soldiers. Roosevelt's fuzzy and indiscriminate presence becomes insignificant compared to the piercing gaze of the black soldier's casually turned head. Later editions of *The Rough Riders* did not include this photograph, and most secondary sources that use photographs of Roosevelt in Cuba favor the first, more focused photograph. Upon close examination of the broader photo-

FIGURE 4 Theodore Roosevelt, Rough Riders, and other soldiers at San Juan Heights (wide view). Photograph by William Dinwiddie (1898). Theodore Roosevelt Collection, Harvard College Library.

graph, however, one can discern still other African American soldiers, particularly the two men immediately left of the rightmost American flag as well as the soldier in the back line with his brim turned up, midway between Roosevelt and the left margin (figure 5). The tighter photograph of Roosevelt in front of the flag is distinctly cropped near these men. Likely the desires to present Roosevelt as a heroic figure rather than merely one soldier among many and to exclude black faces, and particularly the demanding gaze of the unaccounted black soldier, drove such decisions.

For all of Roosevelt's attempts at crossing certain racial boundaries, his racism remains apparent not only through his manipulation of the narrative of San Juan Hill but also in his general depiction of African American soldiers. In the narrative of *The Rough Riders*, after Roosevelt has quelled the supposed retreat of African American soldiers at San Juan Hill, he notes that the black soldiers "flashed their white teeth at one another, as they broke into broad grins, and I had no more trouble with them" (93). Almost two years later (May 1900), Roosevelt wrote to Robert J. Fleming, a black lieutenant from the Tenth Regular Cavalry who had ordered black soldiers away from the front line to replenish rations and supplies during the charge on San Juan Hill.[15] In

FIGURE 5 Detail of figure 4: African American soldiers at San Juan Heights. Theodore Roosevelt Collection, Harvard College Library.

this letter, Roosevelt describes the battle preparations on Kettle Hill (a mound just east of San Juan Hill) during which he engages both white and black troopers, working in shifts separated by race, to dig trenches at the front line. But while Roosevelt reports to Fleming that the black and white soldiers worked equally hard, the now New York state governor ascertained a race-specific difference in their labors. For an unexplained reason, upon returning from a shift the black troops exhibited a moment of panic in which "the rear-most men grew nervous, jumped forward and in a few seconds the whole body broke and came in like so many stampeded buffaloes, racing and jumping over the trench" (*Letters* 2: 1305). The white soldiers in the trench, Roosevelt told Fleming, "merely laughed and slouched out, did their two hours' work, and slouched back with entire unconcern" (1305). Finding his own white troopers at ease with whatever event had just passed, Roosevelt attributes the apparent panic of the black troopers to "the superstition and fear of the darkey" (1305). At a time when African American soldiers were fighting not only for the establishment of black officers but for simple respect from the U.S. public for their dedication to the country, Roosevelt only helped to perpetuate African American stereotypes and undercut their achievements.

ROUGH RIDERS, ROUGH CHARACTERS

Roosevelt claimed his men to be a cross-section of the United States or ideal Americans, yet the actions of many of his Rough Riders seem far removed from those of model citizens. During their mustering-in at San Antonio, for example, many of the Rough Riders attended a band performance in their honor at San Antonio's Riverside Park. The band director requested sound effects for a piece entitled "The Cavalry Charge" and multiple Rough Riders complied, firing enough bullets to panic the majority of the concert-goers and subsequently injuring a number of women there. The post–pistol volley mayhem also included cutting electrical lights and rushing the beer tent (Jones 42). In another incident in San Antonio, a group of Rough Riders attacked a Chinese restaurant owner and destroyed his business in retaliation for an unknown offense; the soldiers were convicted but paid no fines and served no jail time (Samuels and Samuels 55). Roosevelt's responses to these incidents are vague and unfocused. In a letter to President McKinley penned the day after the riot at Riverside Park, Roosevelt had the aplomb to write that his soldiers "are very intelligent, and, rather to my surprise, they are very orderly" (*Let-*

ters 1: 832). In *The Rough Riders*, Roosevelt refers vaguely to an incident in San Antonio where "a few of them went on a spree, and proceeded 'to paint the town red.'" In his only reflection on this unspecified "spree," Roosevelt rather glibly writes, "One was captured by the city authorities, and we had to leave him behind us in jail. The others we dealt with ourselves, in a way that prevented a repetition of the occurrence" (30).

Well after the disbanding of the regiment, many of its former members were jailed for various violent crimes, most notably murder. A few even turned to Roosevelt for help with their legal troubles, to which Roosevelt generally and politely refused. In one letter alone, Roosevelt (quoting correspondence with William H. H. Llewellyn, the captain of Troop G of the Rough Riders and later a New Mexico lawman) discusses three ex–Rough Riders who were either charged with or incarcerated for murder. In one celebrated case to which Roosevelt refered regularly, an ex–Rough Rider had killed his sister-in-law, though he apparently had been aiming at his wife at the time. Another ex-soldier named Ritchie killed a man in a poker game. The man had "called him very bad names, even going as far as to cast reflections on the legitimacy of our comrade's birth" (*Letters* 3: 556), for which Ritchie shot him. Roosevelt reports that upon seeing Ritchie he asked him, "'Had he drawn his gun, Ritchie?' . . . 'He didn't have time, Colonel,' answered Ritchie simply." Roosevelt reports to John Hay, the recipient of the letter, that Ritchie was acquitted (*Letters* 3: 556; see also 2: 1463). According to Dale Walker in *The Boys of '98*, Roosevelt wrote to Secretary of War Taft in 1906 concerning the appointment of an ex–Rough Rider from Yale to a government post, telling him, "I guess Yale '78 has the call, as there seems to be no Rough Rider available and every individual in the Southern District of the Indian Territory (including every Rough Rider) appears to be either under indictment, convicted, or in a position that renders it necessary that he should be indicted" (273). In an aside in *The Rough Riders*, Roosevelt mentions a "Cherokee half-breed" who had to return to the mainland to recover from injuries sustained in Cuba. Roosevelt notes, "Before he rejoined us at Montauk Point [at the mustering-out] he had gone through a little private war of his own; for on his return he found that a cow-boy had gone off with his sweetheart, and in the fight that ensued he shot his rival" (68).

Possibly the most telling of all are Roosevelt's jocular comments in an appendix to *The Rough Riders* entitled simply "Corrections."[16] After a long diatribe against the apparent inaccuracies of Stephen Brosnal's book *The Fight for*

Santiago, Roosevelt turns to the recent histories of some of his Rough Riders. He writes,

> It is difficult for me to withstand the temptation to tell what has befallen some of my men since the regiment has disbanded; . . . how Cherokee Bill married a wife in Hoboken, and as that pleasant city ultimately proved an uncongenial field for his activities, how I had to send both himself and his wife out to the Territory; how Happy Jack, haunted by visions of the social methods obtaining in the best saloons in Arizona, applied for the position of "bouncer out" at the Executive Chamber when I was elected Governor, and how I got him a job at railroading instead, and finally had to ship him back to his own Territory also; . . . In another letter Rowland tells of the fate of Tom Darnell, who rode the sorrel horse of the Third Cavalry: "There ain't much news to write of except poor old Tom Darnell got killed about a month ago. Tom and another fellow had a fight and he shot Tom through the heart. . . . Tom was sure a good old boy, and I sure hate to hear of him going, and he had plenty of grit too. No man ever called on him for a fight that he didn't get it." (296–98; 1905 ed.)

Though Roosevelt impassionedly celebrates his regiment as "typical an American regiment," the Rough Riders included a number of volunteers who were little more than bullies, criminals, racists, and rogues.

COWBOY IMPERIALISTS

At the mustering-out of the Rough Riders on September 13, 1898, the members of the regiment presented Roosevelt with a replica of the Remington statue *The Bronco Buster.* Supposedly with tears in his eyes, Roosevelt eloquently and emotionally responded to the gift by telling his regiment, "I am proud of this regiment beyond measure. I am proud of it because it is a typical American regiment. The foundation of the regiment was the cowpuncher, and we have got him here in bronze" (*Rough Riders* 157 n. 1). Not wanting to lay his accolades only on cowpokes, Roosevelt expanded the sweep of his praise by proclaiming, "It is primarily an American regiment, and it is American because it is composed of all races which have made America their country by adoption and those who have claimed it as their country by inheritance" (157 n. 1). Though African Americans were not a part of those who Roosevelt claimed could be American through "adoption" or "inheritance," he did praise the Ninth and Tenth Cavalries separately by declaring, "The Spaniards called them 'Smoked Yankees,' but we found them to be an excellent breed of Yankee" (157 n. 1). In this instance, the black soldiers, most of whom had significantly more battle experience than any of the volunteer regiments, could only be granted recognition through the rhetorical power of Colonel Roosevelt's words. The use of "we" implies the implicit authority of the Rough Riders to acknowledge the place of "Smoked Yankees" in a white world. As "an excellent breed of Yankee," the African American soldiers suddenly lost their tawny tinge and could officially settle, if only briefly, in the heroic shadow of the Yankee volunteers.

According to historian Michael Collins, Roosevelt had always dreamed of leading a mounted regiment into battle (8, 81); after his years on the northern plains, Roosevelt believed that cowboys would make the best soldiers for such an outfit. Painting these independent and often hard working laborers with a broad stroke (and echoing Owen Wister's vision of synchronic history), Roosevelt declared to his friend Henry Cabot Lodge, "The statesman of the past has been merged into the cowboy of the present" (quoted in White, *Eastern Establishment* 79). Roosevelt's depiction of diplomats in chaps may have been overly generous, but his desire to mix western cowboys with U.S. political strength and resolve never wavered. In the decade and a half before Roosevelt assumed the presidency, he was spoiling for a war. In 1886, prompted by strained relations with Mexico, Roosevelt wrote to Secretary of War William Endicott and personally offered his services in case of a military conflict. He wrote to Henry Cabot Lodge from South Dakota concerning his desires for war: "I have written on to Secretary Endicott offering to try to raise some companies of horse riflemen out here in the event of trouble with Mexico. Will you telegraph me at once if war becomes inevitable. . . . [A]s my chance of doing anything in the future worth doing seems to grow continually smaller I intend to grasp at every opportunity that turns up" (*Letters* 1: 108). Roosevelt even went so far as to urge the Dakota territorial governor to create these mounted regiments (Collins 81).

In another letter to Lodge just ten days later, Roosevelt wistfully describes his imagined mounted companies as an "utterly reckless set of desperados, as ever sat on a saddle" (*Letters* 1: 109). Only three months earlier, Roosevelt had envisioned these military desperados as vigilante lawmen when he wrote to his sister about the Haymarket incident: "My men are hardworking, labouring men, who work longer hours for no greater wages than many of the strikers. . . . I believe nothing would give them greater pleasure than a chance with

FIGURE 6 Frederic Remington, *The Charge of the Rough Riders at San Juan Hill* (1898). Courtesy Frederic Remington Art Museum, Ogdensburg, New York.

one of their rifles at one of the mobs" (*Letters* 1: 100). In the early 1890s, Roosevelt fumed over the killing of two American sailors in Chile and fiercely argued with his friends and his colleagues in Washington again for war instead of diplomacy in settling the matter (Morris, *The Rise of Theodore Roosevelt* 444). Thus the establishment of the First Volunteer Cavalry in April of 1898 was the realization of a longstanding military dream for Roosevelt: cowboy riflemen as the leading edge of U.S. imperial strength and military tenacity. (Ironically, few horses were ultimately transported to Cuba, as the U.S. military commanders believed a mounted campaign expensive and foolhardy in those tropical environs.)[17]

Roosevelt and his Rough Riders returned from Cuba as national heroes. Besides receiving merely journalistic praise, the Rough Riders were soon the objects of nationalistic poetry, popular songs, and even cigar advertisements (Jones figs. 82, 83). Not long after their return, Frederic Remington immortalized the heroics of the Rough Riders in *The Charge of the Rough Riders at San Juan Hill* and *The Scream of Shrapnel at San Juan Hill* (figures 6 and 7).[18] Lesser known—and less subtle—artists created cruder heroic images of Roosevelt in Cuba, sometimes planting him and his troops on wild-eyed horses galloping over cactus or short-grass prairie, thus distinctly connecting Roosevelt and the Rough Riders to the American West (figure 8). Immediately following the

FIGURE 7 Frederic Remington, *The Scream of Shrapnel at San Juan Hill* (1900). Yale University Art Gallery, Gift of the Artist.

FIGURE 8 Lithograph of Roosevelt leading charge at San Juan Hill (1899). Theodore Roosevelt Collection, Harvard College Library.

Battle of San Juan Hill, Roosevelt became, according to Edmund Morris, "the most famous man in America" (see *The Rise of Theodore Roosevelt* 662–87). And with the fame and the stories, the boundaries between reality and myth concerning Roosevelt's actions in Cuba soon blurred—for both the American public as well as for Roosevelt. With the celebration of Roosevelt's heroics by the American press, the image of cowboy imperialists became cemented in the American imagination and would soon be strengthened by the emergence of the cowboy president.

BRINGING CUBA HOME VIA THE WILD WEST

Throughout his career, Roosevelt turned to the frontier for his vision of America, lauding people like Owen Wister or Frederic Remington as artists whose occupation was merely to record the truth. He writes in his autobiography, "Half of the men I worked with or played with and half of the men who soldiered with me afterwards in my regiment might have walked out of Wister's stories or Remington's pictures" (*Theodore Roosevelt* 122). Just as Roosevelt believes that his cowboys and soldiers could have sauntered out of the realms of representation, so too these very real laborers and cavalrymen rode from Cuba directly back into the world of discursive invention by becoming the subjects of lyric, song, painting, and advertising. More significantly, though, some of these walking abstractions returned to their mythic roots by becoming participants in one of the most popular Western spectacles of the 1890s, Buffalo Bill's Wild West. After the disbanding of the First Volunteer Calvary, sixteen Rough Riders opted to join Buffalo Bill's Wild West and begin new careers in show business. William F. Cody, popularly known as Buffalo Bill, claimed throughout the production of his long-standing Wild West that everything presented was "All Genuine, All True, All Honest!" (from poster in Brooklyn Museum of Art 41); he employed ex-army scouts, "real" cowboys, and Native Americans to act out, as Cody's publicists wrote, "a series of original, genuine and instructive object lessons in which the real participants repeat the heroic parts they have played in actual life" (quoted in Slotkin, *Gunfighter Nation* 82).

Cody carefully hired various individuals who could draw a crowd. Some people he hired for their skills as entertainers, such as trick riders or sharpshooters like Annie Oakley, but others he engaged for their names alone, particularly people such as gunman Wild Bill Hickok, western scout Texas Jack

Omohundro, and Sioux chief Sitting Bull. Cody presented his pageant as mimetic, faithfully recreating events in western history for the consumption and edification ("object lessons") of his audience. He recreated generic events such as an attack on a settler's cabin, an Indian raid on the famous Deadwood stagecoach, and even a buffalo hunt, but he saved certain narratives to be showstoppers that portrayed for the audience a specific historical event. Most famously, Cody staged "Custer's Last Fight," a flamboyant reenactment (and reinterpretation) of the Battle of Little Bighorn. For this event, Cody engaged surviving members of the Seventh Cavalry who had not been with Custer's detachment at the Battle of Little Bighorn, as well as Rain-in-the-Face, the Sioux who supposedly killed Custer in that battle. Cody introduced "Custer's Last Fight" in 1886, and from 1893 to 1898 he used this spectacle to close his show. In this finale, the epitome of self-aggrandizement and historical manipulation, Cody rode slowly among the bodies of slain cavalrymen and Native Americans while above the arena hung a tapestry upon which was projected the simple fallacy, "Too Late."

Reflecting a shift in American politics away from the acquisition of western territory and toward the clear establishment of the nation as an international world power, Cody dropped "Custer's Last Fight" as his closing act in 1899 and replaced it with a reenactment of the Battle of San Juan Hill. Even before embarking on this new historical panorama, Cody had already primed his audiences for the nationalist fervor that America's presence in Cuba had wrought. By the beginning of the 1898 season, Cody had included in his show "A Squad of Cuban Insurgents Direct From The Field" (from poster in Rennert 90), thus championing support for the Cuban fight against Spain. With the inclusion of these "insurgents," Cody set the stage for the later jingoistic celebration of the U.S. victory at Santiago. By including sixteen Rough Riders who had fought at San Juan Hill in his reenactment of that battle, Cody helped to produce a narrative in support of U.S. imperialism, one not unlike the political work done by his earlier tragic depiction of the death of Custer and the men of the Seventh Cavalry and their connection with domestic expansionism.

Though a showman and not a politician or a Washington administrator, Cody presented himself as a willing participant in the Spanish-American War. In an interview in *World* on April 3, 1898, Cody illustrated how he could "Drive Spaniards from Cuba with 30,000 Indian Braves." Here he proposed to bring the recent enemies of U.S. expansion together under the national flag to fight an imperial war. Native Americans would be particularly eager to fight in Cuba because, as Cody put it, "Spain sent the first white man to America" (quoted in Kasson 249). Almost three weeks later, on April 20, 1898, Cody recorded a prowar statement for the Berliner Gramophone Company that advocated complete domestic support for a war with Spain (though he closed his message with a hurried signature advertisement: "Ladies and Gentleman, permit me to introduce to you a Congress of the Rough Riders of the World" [Rosa and May 164]).[19] Though urged to by his friend General Nelson A. Miles, Cody never actually took part in the Spanish-American War, ostensibly because he claimed he would lose $100,000 in closing his show. Following Cody's lead, one of his star performers, sharpshooter Annie Oakley, wrote to President McKinley on April 5, 1898 offering "fifty lady sharpshooters" in the event of war in Cuba; Oakley guaranteed that these sharpshooters would supply their own arms and that "Every one of them will be an American" (figure 9). For people like Cody and Oakley, a war in Cuba seemed merely an extension of their stories and their feats in the Wild West arena. When Roosevelt returned, his actions, along with those of the Rough Riders, became canonized within those very performances that Cody and Oakley believed could be transparently dispatched to the battlefields of Cuba. For Cody and Oakley, entertainers became soldiers as easily as returning heroes became star performers in arena shows when their martial duties ended.

Buffalo Bill's Wild West solidified the cultural myths surrounding the American West and its connection to national (and now imperial) ideology by engaging the very actors of this ideology in various political and historical dramas that were definitive of U.S. expansion. By presenting the feats of cowboys and sharpshooters (horses and guns being the primary signifiers of the West) and recreating memorable moments in U.S. history, Cody and his show cemented the idea of the American West as representative of American culture. Joy Kasson writes in *Buffalo Bill's Wild West: Celebrity, Memory, and Popular History* that "Buffalo Bill's showmanship *created* American memory through the medium of popular entertainment" (265, ital. in original), arguing that Cody not only shaped the ways that Americans thought about the American West, but that he also helped create an American memory in which "the content of national identity seems identical to its performance" (273). Thus, according to Kasson's reading, American national identity may be purchased, consumed, and recreated as authentic through the medium of spectacle; Buf-

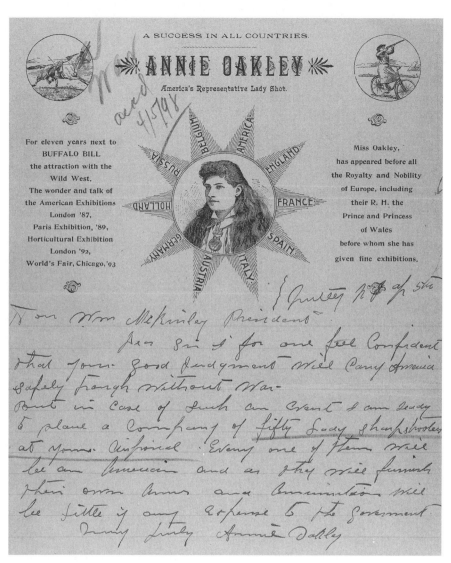

FIGURE 9 Annie Oakley's letter to President McKinley (April 4, 1898). National Archives, Washington, D.C.

falo Bill's Wild West, a spectacle that Richard Slotkin notes lacks the noun "show" or "exhibit" or "performance" to designate it as such (Slotkin, "Buffalo Bill's" 165), stands in for the place called the American West and the narrative of U.S. history itself. By bringing Roosevelt's Rough Riders and the narrative of San Juan Hill to the stage, Cody created the necessary heroics to match Roosevelt's vision of U.S. history as well as its imperial future.

While Theodore Roosevelt and Buffalo Bill worked to create national identity through politics and popular culture, the relatively new field of American history attempted to uncover and sanctify the national narrative through apparently objective and apolitical rhetoric. Specifically, historians such as Frederick Jackson Turner—and Roosevelt, in an earlier career—cemented the place of the American West in the official narrative of the nation through historical discourse. Turner is best known for his Frontier Thesis, the foundational argument of his 1893 paper "The Significance of the Frontier in American History." He argues in this essay that American character, ideals, and institutions were founded on the existence of "free land," the intrinsically American imperative to inhabit that land, and the principles that grow from the process of acquiring and cultivating it. Pithily, Turner writes, "The existence of an area of free land, its continuous recession, and the advance of American settlement westward, explain American development" ("Significance" 31). Turner finds in the American West the fundamental building blocks for American character and politics. For Turner, the West was not necessarily an outgrowth of the East; rather, he argues that the process of frontier life—from white fur traders following Indian trails to pioneer farmers building stable towns and cities—creates a collection of habits, laws, and activities that become definitive of American life in general. Ultimately, the character of the West, those aspects built through the process of pioneering, reflect back onto American identity and broadly inform the construction of American life.

For Turner, the frontier was the "meeting point between savagery and civilization . . . it lies at the hither edge of free land" ("Significance" 32–33). As white Americans moved across the continent from east to west, they experienced "a return to primitive conditions on a continually advancing frontier line" (32). Traveling west from the eastern seaboard, one could see successive historical evolutionary phases. Starting with established cities and towns in the East, one would travel first through permanent agricultural areas, then past pioneer farming settlements, and then past ranches. Further west, settlement of any kind disappears and one might find hunters, then trappers, and then one would finally pass into the realm of savagery, that is, a space occupied only by Indians and buffalo. With time, the frontier, just at "the hither edge of free land," moves west, and the corresponding evolutionary phases creep westward accordingly. Thus the "meeting point" in 1890 appeared significantly further west than it did in, for example, 1690.[20]

Turner's narrative primarily presents an American conquest of nature. Concerning the first contact with the ever-westward-moving frontier, he writes "the wilderness masters the colonist" ("Significance" 33), evincing an ideal that American exceptionalism rests in humans' fundamental relationship with nature and their constant struggle to maintain mastery over the anarchy of wilderness. Though Turner admits that "at the frontier the environment is at first too strong for the man," he soon tells us that through the frontiersman's sheer determination and tenacity, "Little by little he transforms the wilderness" (33). Fundamental to Turner's ideal of "free land" that the colonist transforms is the notion that Native Americans are a component of nature and not a part of the transformation. He claims that when a nation is involved in territorial expansion, "it has met other growing peoples who it has conquered. But in the case of the United States, we have a different phenomena" (32). Thus Native Americans do not appear as "peoples," growing or otherwise. Their stake in terms of both codified property and the use-value inherent in the earth itself does not fit into Turner's construction. In fact, he notes that "The first frontier had to meet its Indian question, its question of the public domain" (37), thereby sidestepping Native American property claims and ideologically settling all American landscape into the public sphere of the colonists alone. Turner completely ignores Native Americans as subjects in his writings, though in the notes of one of Turner's later students we find the pronouncement (attributed to one of Turner's lectures) that "we had conquered the Indians. Was this just? Failure to use resources will submit people to subordination of a superior type which *does*" (quoted in Bogue 378). Thus the Darwinian supremacy of white settlers naturally moves aside Native American claims to land and resources and, by extension, human rights, religion, self-determination, and even happiness, all ideals fundamental to American society. For Turner, the conquest of nature, a conquest that happened over and over again in each successive confrontation with the frontier, defined the culture of the United States. With this conquest came the subjugation of others—those not seen as active frontier participants—who might step in front of this steamroller of history.

Turner and Roosevelt shared an ideological stance, painting a picture of the United States as a rugged nation of white men who had wrested their identity from the soil. Both saw Native Americans as encumbrances to pioneer movement (Turner even used the telling phrase "Indian barrier" at one time; see Bogue 377) and connected them to the wilderness that pioneers needed to tame. Roosevelt, otherwise more generally sympathetic to Native American issues when compared to Turner's apathy, publicly joked in 1886 that "I don't go so far as to think that the only good Indians are dead Indians, but I believe nine out of every ten are" (quoted in Collins 61). Both men also celebrated specific qualities that the West seemed to imbue in its male citizenry. Roosevelt celebrated rugged and uncultivated cowboys, envisioning them as domestic antilabor vigilantes and figures on the forefront of U.S. imperial adventures. Turner argued that the frontier process produced American characteristics that became "called out elsewhere because of the existence of the frontier" (like Roosevelt's cowboy soldiers in Cuba). Specifically, he found that the frontier produced "coarseness and strength . . . that masterful grasp of material things, lacking in the artistic but powerful to effect great ends; that restless, nervous energy; that dominant individualism" ("Significance" 59). The strenuous life of Roosevelt found its historical justification in Turner's academic prose.

Unlike Roosevelt's heroic and imperial West of cowboy statesmen and "reckless set[s] of desperados" however, Turner's West centered on farmers and the rather tedious and mundane shift from wild to cultivated lands. While Turner's linear vision of Indians following buffalo trails, soon followed by fur traders, ranchers, and finally pioneer farmers, appears romantic in its sweep, ultimately the progression of Turner's events that formed the post-frontier West happened through little more than walking behind a plow and learning to rotate crops so as not to lose soil nutrients. The content of Turner's theory provides very little in the way of imperial justification, but the form, the mechanics, the necessary driving forces of history underneath his formulation support an ideal of American exceptionalism rooted in the western landscape and the narrative of its conquest. The farmers themselves may not be the picturesque heroes of Roosevelt's books or speeches, but the forces that allowed these farmers to settle in one place proved, according to Turner, the importance of the United States's pioneer heritage.

The convergence of these two historians happened on the occasion of Turner's review of Roosevelt's first two volumes of *The Winning of the West* in 1889. Roosevelt's first letter to Turner, however, does not appear until five years later, in 1894, when he wrote to the University of Wisconsin historian to praise his recently published "Significance" essay. Roosevelt congratulates Turner here on "[putting] into definite shape a good deal of thought which has been floating around rather loosely" (*Letters* 1: 363).[21] Roosevelt and Turner corresponded over the next few years, primarily concerning details of their historical endeavors, but the tone of the older Roosevelt remained flattering and even intellectually submissive. While Turner and Roosevelt never developed a personal relationship, their professional paths appear to have crossed fleetingly a few times, particularly after Turner began teaching at Harvard in 1904.[22]

Richard Slotkin argues that Roosevelt's and Turner's theories of frontier development grew from coinciding desires to explain systematically the importance of the western regions to U.S. history and national character as well as to respond to the crisis of national closure codified in the United States Census's 1890 declaration of the end of the frontier, a demographic announcement that Turner uses to open his famous essay. But beyond this foundation, Turner and Roosevelt diverge. Slotkin asserts that Roosevelt's frontier ideology becomes played out through race-defined struggles, such as white/Indian or Texan/Mexican, that allow for the emergence of a single powerful figure who is prominent as the ruling westerner, if only momentarily, before he is overthrown by a new master (*Gunfighter Nation* 39). Turner, on the other hand, envisioned a struggle primarily with the land and elaborated the consequent emergence of institutions and a distinctly American and egalitarian democracy. Both historians, in fact, believed in the necessity of American democracy, but, according to Slotkin, Turner saw democratic ideals "as good in themselves" while Roosevelt perceived democracy primarily as a handmaiden to "national power" (*Gunfighter Nation* 59, 60). Indeed, the leaders of these democracies and the ideological champions who precipitate from these theories differ accordingly. Slotkin writes, "While Turner locates the crucial dynamism [of the frontier] in a democratic collectivity, Roosevelt locates it in successive classes of heroes emerging from the strife of races to earn a neo-aristocratic right to rule" (*Gunfighter Nation* 35). Turner himself recognized this ideological difference in his review of volume 4 of Roosevelt's *The Winning of the West*, where he criticized Roosevelt for overt romanticism. Turner writes, "It is the dramatic and picturesque aspects of the period that most interest him," protesting precisely that Roosevelt favors dramatic personalities over "the development of institutions" ("Roosevelt" 171).

Nonetheless, Roosevelt's concern with historical heroes becomes bolstered by Turner's structural theories of American evolution. Together they form an ideological bulwark that places the American West and particular westerners at the center of the narrative of American development. Roosevelt's westerners were distinctly white and male but particularly individualistic, scrappy, and unique. His historical actors and representatives of "True Americanism" were subjects invested in specific narratives of conquest, action, and tenacity. Turner, however, built an ostensibly disinterested movement of history that nonetheless favored these same characters. Even through this more objective lens, Turner consigned all other possible western subjects—women, people of color, religious outsiders—to the landscape. In both Roosevelt's and Turner's visions, narratives that have held fast throughout the twentieth century, the West both reflects and shapes the formation of American culture and identity. Though Slotkin argues that Roosevelt's and Turner's theories are actually antitheses (*Gunfighter Nation* 32), he concludes that they unite to form a myth of the American West as a place where the specialized processes of the frontier produce uniquely American institutions and values as well as heroic individuals who embody those values. Slotkin emphasizes the concept of myth, where the physical space of the American West becomes transformed into idealized fictions that then pass over into a national historical memory. The myth of the West, the confrontations of plodding and progressive farmers and heroic and militaristic statesmen cowboys—played out in Buffalo Bill's arena—stands in for the land and its history itself. The official vision of the West, Turner and Roosevelt intertwined, becomes a national narrative and thus develops as a conspicuous engine of Americanization.

2

RECLAIMING THE FRONTIER

OSCAR MICHEAUX AS BLACK TURNERIAN

BORN IN 1884, the year Roosevelt established his short-lived ranching career in Dakota Territory, Oscar Micheaux became the most successful African American filmmaker of the first half of the twentieth century. In a highly productive career spanning from 1919 through 1948, Micheaux produced almost forty films, including the first sound film directed by an African American. But before Micheaux began his career in film production, he was a homesteader in South Dakota, arriving there in 1905 to farm on some of the last publicly distributed land in the nation. During Micheaux's thirteen years in South Dakota, which included two years of intense drought, foreclosure on his properties, and a broken marriage, Micheaux wrote three novels documenting his homesteading experiences with protagonists that were thinly veiled stand-ins for himself. Micheaux, like most other self-avowed "pioneers," displayed an affinity for the mythologies of the Old West: boundless opportunity, self-definition, and individual freedom. In true Turnerian fashion, he sought to establish "civilization" in a land of "savagery" and untapped resources. But he also engaged Booker T. Washington's principles of thrift, hard work, and vocational enterprise as a guiding framework within his South Dakota narratives—and, we can assume, within his life there—even dedicating his first novel to the Tuskegee educator. Micheaux combined the Turnerian narrative of western progress and opportunity with Washington's insistence on economic self-sufficiency to present a West that held unlimited promise for racial uplift. Turner's West provided the rhetorical raw materials within Micheaux's narratives, while Washington's principles provided the methodology. Linked together in Micheaux's fiction, these ideals produce an African American pioneer who insists that the frontier is raceblind and thus offers unique opportunities for African Americans. Micheaux believed that he could incorporate the "free land" of the West in a project of racial uplift, ultimately opting for the establishment of frontier, rather than black, identity as the endpoint of that project. Thus, by embracing frontier mythologies, Micheaux situates his narratives within the national stories—such as those of Roosevelt and Turner—that place the West as foundational to American national character in the early twentieth century. Carrying Booker T. Washington's principles to the Great Plains, Micheaux becomes a Black Turnerian.

Micheaux has received increased attention over the last two decades, especially with reference to his films. In fact, most Micheaux scholarship has centered on the discovery, canonization, and analysis of his films, particularly his pre-sound production, and has been fueled by the recent discovery of a number of film prints long thought lost.[1] There is very little scholarship on Micheaux's tenure in South Dakota, and those few articles dedicated to this portion of his life tend to celebrate Micheaux's pioneer heritage and offer little analysis of the content of Micheaux's novels (or his films) except insofar as they vouch for the veracity of his pioneer efforts.[2] Since 1996 Gregory, South Dakota, the town closest to Micheaux's homestead, has hosted the Oscar Micheaux Film Festival, an annual conference that attempts to bring together these two seemingly disparate areas of Micheaux scholarship. While this festival does screen Micheaux's films and invites the participation of film scholars, it is also dedicated to maintaining the history—as well as the mythology—of Micheaux's presence in the area. Many attendees live in Gregory or the surrounding areas and come to celebrate the pioneer history of this particular man. During my attendance in 1999, many roundtable discussions were punctuated with memories of someone's grandmother who had known "the black man outside of town"; presentations there often described Micheaux as "full of grit" or claimed him "more South Dakotan than African American." In the town itself, all aspects of Micheaux's persona and legacy fall under a pioneer motif. A mural near the center of town includes an image of Micheaux among buffalo, covered wagons, a drawing of his homestead, and a perspective painting of a steam train that looms out from the center. In the narrative created by Gregory and the Micheaux Film Festival, Micheaux's race simply strengthens the notion that the empty spaces and potential opportunities of the American West were a great economic and social leveler and that the West held an inherent potential for self-made success. Within this discourse, the West becomes a race-blind environment where dedication to hard work and a "pull yourself up by your bootstraps" philosophy keeps all pioneers, regardless of race, heading—like the mural's locomotive—toward a necessary prosperity.

As the scholarship on African Americans in the West grows, scholars have focused on the ways in which the African American experience in the West was defined racially rather than geographically, as might be considered under Turner's model. In 1957, Walter Prescott Webb, a historian who was attentive to the geographic peculiarities of the West that undid aspects of Turner's theory, defined the West by a dearth of "water, timber, cities, industry, labor, and Negroes" (30). Over the last two decades, New Western Historians have worked to undo just such a racial characterization of the American West. Certainly a figure like Micheaux adds to this project by providing narratives of African American homesteading on the Great Plains. Yet even with the recent republication of two of Micheaux's early novels, Micheaux does not figure prominently (if at all) in discussions of the African American West by New Western Historians. In general, New Western Historians have rejected the imagery of hardy western pioneers and instead constructed a narrative of western history as "an ongoing competition for legitimacy—for the right to claim for oneself and sometimes for one's group the status of legitimate beneficiary of Western resources" (Limerick, *Legacy* 27). Rather than a frontier, the West of New Western Historians is a "meeting ground" or a "common ground" where this contestation for resources occurs (27). Specifically concerning African Americans within this model, the older narrative of pioneers and frontier progress seemed to make little sense, for, as African American literary critic Houston Baker Jr. writes, "the legends of men conquering wild and virgin lands are not the legends of black America; . . . and tales of pioneers enduring the hardships of the West for the promise of immense wealth are not the tales of black America. . . . To black America, *frontier* is an alien word" (2). Yet the narrative that Baker claims is inaccessible and alien to African Americans and that New Western Historians reject as oppressive and whitewashing is precisely the narrative that Micheaux found so compelling. New Western Historians challenge the veracity—and the tenacity—of the Turnerian myth by showing that whites were not the only actors in the American West and that the myth of the frontier swallowed up the identities of nonwhites in its narrative. But the polyvocal and multicultural logic of the narratives of New Western History precludes the possibility of a minority figure who embraces the dominant white rhetoric of western expansion. As a Black Turnerian, especially one who tends to subordinate many issues of race to those of a progressive and civilizing frontier, Micheaux represents a presence in the grand narrative of New Western History that disrupts the idea of a West defined more by the multiculturalism of its inhabitants than by the supposed transcendence of Turner's theory of historical progress.

The frontier to which Houston Baker refers is not necessarily the leading edge of Turner's wave, a western land of mountain men or covered wagons. Rather it is a rhetorical and ideological space that is alien to African Americans because they cannot easily place themselves within the mythic narratives of western progress. Yet Micheaux displays quite the opposite affinity for this story, embracing the frontier in all of its permutations. With Micheaux as an example, we can see the importance of tracing the Turnerian myth through the lives of all westerners, regardless of race or ethnicity, for even if the concept of the frontier may not have been meant for nonwhites, its rhetorical power could be useful to those outside of the myth in establishing themselves as legitimate beneficiaries of cultural resources, particularly national ones. As an African American novelist and filmmaker who incorporates frontier mythologies into his work, Micheaux challenges the cultural dispossessions of both Turnerian narratives as well as New Western History. In either of these paradigms, Micheaux cannot be both black and Turnerian at the same time, yet he insists on this very construct within all of his western narratives. In Turner's narrative of Triumphalist history, the growth, progress, and development of the West are evidence of the success of both this region and a new American ideology spawned by the frontier. Micheaux's claim to Turnerian ideals and privilege illustrates the power and desirability of the myth's promises. In the spirit of New Western History, Micheaux's stories add a multicultural element to Great Plains homesteading history, but these narratives complicate the relationship between racial privilege and western identity offered by both an oppressive and whitewashing Old Western History and a liberatory and revisionist New Western History. As this seemingly contradictory character of a Black Turnerian, Micheaux embraced the myth of an ever-dynamic and enterprising West in an attempt to locate his identity within this progressive vision of American national culture. In doing so, he discounts race as a causal factor for failure or injustice and presents the frontier narrative as the paradigm for African American racial uplift.

There is no repository for Micheaux's papers (Micheaux's widow may have destroyed them after his death; see VannEpps-Taylor, 142), so any attempt at biography must be speculative.[3] But biographical information can be gleaned from his novels, particularly his fictional autobiography *The Conquest* (1913). Micheaux was born in 1884 near Metropolis, Illinois. After leaving home, he held numerous jobs, the longest being a train porter based out of Chicago. In 1904, convinced that urban life bred depravity, greed, sloth, and arrogance among black Americans, Micheaux sought rejuvenation by homesteading on a recently opened portion of the Rosebud Sioux Reservation in South Dakota. Though he did not succeed in the land lottery, in which filers' names were drawn at random for quarter-section allotments (160 acres), he did purchase a relinquishment (a sale of a claim originally acquired through the land lottery) later that year and settled on it in 1905.[4] After a severe drought in 1910–11 in which Micheaux lost all of his crops, Micheaux turned to writing novels that he sold door-to-door to his primarily white neighbors as well as to African Americans in the South. Micheaux remained in South Dakota (with some stints in Sioux City, Iowa) until 1918, when he turned his attentions to filmmaking and left South Dakota, apparently never to return.

Micheaux chose to homestead in South Dakota because he had little money with which to purchase already improved farmland elsewhere. He concluded that "one whose capital was under eight or ten thousand dollars . . . must go where the land was raw or new and undeveloped" (*Conquest* 53). Paraphrasing Horace Greeley's pronouncement to "Go west young man and grow up with the country," Micheaux felt that anyone with so little capital should "begin with the beginning and develop with the development of the country" (*Conquest* 53).[5] South Dakota, with its newly opened reservation lands, fit precisely Micheaux's ideal of "raw or new and undeveloped" land. Following the dominant mythology of westward expansion during the nineteenth century, Micheaux emigrated away from what he perceived to be depraved urban centers and toward a West that he believed promised boundless personal opportunities and immense tracts of tillable land, free but for the sweat of their improvement. But Micheaux's grand vision of free land and agricultural opportunity looked rather unlike western reality in that the 1904 opening of the Rosebud Sioux Reservation to homesteading proved to be one of the last offerings of public land in the United States.[6]

In 1910 and 1911, Micheaux wrote two articles for the *Chicago Defender* chastising urban African Americans for their lack of drive toward exploring new opportunities. Positioning himself as a pioneer and seasoned homesteader, Micheaux writes in his first article, "Where the Negro Fails," "I return from Chicago each trip I make more discouraged each year with the hopelessness of his foresight (the young Negro). His inability to use common sense is discouraging. . . . The Negro leads in the consumption of produce, and especially meat, and then his fine clothes—he hasn't the least thought of where the wool grew that he wears" (1). As a western booster Micheaux exhorts African Americans to seek this kind of material knowledge through homesteading self-sufficiency and the development of western agriculture. Micheaux opens his article with an anecdote about a young man, presumably black, who had drawn a number at a recent land opening not far from Micheaux's homestead in South Dakota. When Micheaux questions him as to his homesteading plans, the young man responds ambivalently, claiming an engagement to a "young society girl . . . [who] would not think of going out in the wilderness like that," as well as a general lack of support for such an endeavor from his Chicago friends. Micheaux curtly advises him, "I think you had better stay in Chicago. For any one [*sic*] with no more force had no business in South Dakota or any part of the northwest" (1). Micheaux also advises this young man not to ask the opinion of "the average colored man around Chicago, or . . . his brother porters or waiters," but rather to "Ask the president of the St. Paul [rail]road or the president of the First National bank or any other great man and see what they say" (1). As the model of a self-sufficient black man, Micheaux sets himself apart from urban African Americans and urges his companion—and his readers—to compare his success to that of other—likely white—"great" men.

In a second article for the *Chicago Defender*, "Colored Americans Too Slow," Micheaux again urges African Americans to seek western agriculture as a solution to the economic and social inequalities experienced by African Americans in the East and in large cities. Micheaux, identified in the byline as "Government Crop Expert for Rosebud County," tells his readers of the almost tenfold increase in land values since his arrival in South Dakota. He notes that when he arrived, the land was "raw and undeveloped" but has since become "an improved county, including railroads, several good towns, rural free delivery, Bell Telephone company operates all the phones; in fact all the improvements you find in countries 100 years old" (1). While in these articles Micheaux sought to increase the black agricultural population in the West and help build self-sufficiency among African Americans, his strategy relied primarily on chastising African Americans for their apparent lack of entrepreneurial drive, especially with regards to agrarian pursuits. In his second article, for example, Micheaux castigates a "presiding elder in the Methodist conference" who claimed he would register for a recent land opening but never followed through with the paperwork, thus leading Micheaux to declare that "It's not the individual, but it's the cause that follow [sic] such pretensions that is detrimental to our young people" (1). While Micheaux's attack on this particular elder (possibly his father-in-law) may be personally motivated, he again sets himself apart from those other urban African Americans who he claims cannot see the value of agricultural self-sufficiency.

Though Micheaux was quite possibly one of the only African Americans attempting to acquire an allotment from the Rosebud Sioux Reservation, African American homesteading in the West was by no means a rarity. In fact, Micheaux's establishment in South Dakota in 1905 was relatively late in the history of African American settlement west of the Mississippi River. Though individual African Americans moved west throughout the nineteenth century, the two most significant western settlements occurred in the 1880s and 1890s. With the end of Reconstruction and the subsequent narrowing of the ex-slaves' civil liberties, many African Americans felt that they would find less oppression outside the South. In 1879, under the urging of Benjamin "Pap" Singleton, an ex-slave who established the Edgefield (Tennessee) Real Estate and Homestead Association, roughly four thousand African Americans migrated to Kansas to homestead in and around a number of all-black towns. Though black settlers steadily streamed into Kansas throughout the 1880s, the much publicized Exodus of 1879 brought the largest single influx of black Southerners into the state (Painter 146–47). Escaping the injustices of the post-Reconstruction South, African Americans in Kansas acquired land, developed homesteads, and built a number of all-black towns in hopes of creating a refuge from race hatred. But within twenty years many of the black towns had, to use historian Robert G. Athearn's words, "withered on the vine" (75), and black Kansans became atomistically absorbed into the state, disrupting hopes of building political power within the state.

Though the Exodus to Kansas established successful African American settlements on the plains, Indian Territory to the south also proved to be fertile ground for African Americans fleeing the post-Reconstruction South. Initially, many African Americans arrived there as slaves of the Native American tribes who were relocated from the South in the early part of the nineteenth century. (After the end of the Civil War, the federal government negotiated treaties freeing black slaves from the tribes residing in Indian Territory.) In 1870, the U.S. census reported 6,378 African Americans in Indian Territory, or roughly 9.4 percent of the total population there (Taylor, *In Search of the Racial Frontier* 104). By 1890, this count had at least tripled (see Taylor, *In Search of the Racial Frontier* 135; see also Carney 148, whose figures are higher). Though the actual numbers of African Americans in Indian Territory were lower than in Kansas, African Americans in Indian Territory and parts of Oklahoma Territory founded more black settlements and vociferously advocated for greater African American roles in state politics. Between 1859 and 1907, the date of Oklahoma statehood, African Americans established roughly thirty all-black towns in the Twin Territories. Initiated by the famous "land run" in April of 1889, parts of present-day Oklahoma (then entitled the Unassigned Lands, as the Sac, Fox, Apache, and other tribes had been relocated west to Oklahoma Territory) opened to homesteading. By early 1891, seven all-black towns were firmly established in Oklahoma. During this period, E. P. McCabe, an active leader in the black town of Nicodemus, Kansas, in the 1880s, lobbied for the territorial governorship of Oklahoma Territory from President Benjamin Harrison, thus hoping to tip the balance of political power toward the Twin Territories' African American population. Though McCabe failed in his bid for territorial governor, he helped build Oklahoma Territory's reputation as a land of opportunity for black Americans seeking change.

By the turn of the century, roughly 765,000 African Americans lived in the West, about 80 percent of them in Texas.[7] Of the other 20 percent, 52,000 lived in Kansas (36 percent of this group) and 55,700 lived in the Twin Territories (39 percent of this group). One of the states with the least number of African Americans was South Dakota, with only North Dakota, Idaho, and Nevada having fewer black residents. Of the nearly 144,300 blacks living in the West outside of Texas, only 465 (0.03 percent) resided in South Dakota in 1900, a full five years before Micheaux arrived there (all figures are from Taylor, *In Search of the Racial Frontier* 135).

As these African Americans moved west, they focused on building towns and colonies as collective enterprises. Two successful and firmly established western black towns were Nicodemus, Kansas, a town built initially by Exodusters, and Boley, Oklahoma. In one of Booker T. Washington's few comments on African American settlement in the West, he called Boley "the youngest, the most enterprising, and in many ways the most interesting of the Negro towns in the United States" ("Boley" 28; see also *Story of the Negro* 2: 248–52).[8] Micheaux's tenure in South Dakota coincided with the presence of a number of all-black agricultural colonies in other areas of the Great Plains. Not far north of Micheaux's land lay the Sully Colony, founded in the late nineteenth century. At its peak population in 1920, Sully boasted thirteen black families (VannEpps-Taylor 53; Bernson and Eggers 251–52). To the east, along the Missouri River, lay the Yankton Colony. Though less of an agricultural establishment, the black population of Yankton in 1920 was 144, 17 percent of the entire black population statewide (Bernson and Eggers 253). Outside of South Dakota, the all-black agricultural colony of Dewitty, near Brownlee, Nebraska, and the all-black town of Dearfield, Colorado, focused on homesteading, agricultural improvement, and self-government. Dewitty, Sully, and Dearfield all peaked in their success in the early 1920s and then slowly disintegrated, as their new generations moved to cities or found farming too difficult or too uncertain an occupation.[9]

As Betti Carol VannEpps-Taylor has speculated, Micheaux could not have been ignorant of these other African Americans attempting projects of racial uplift and agricultural success not dissimilar to his own; Sully and the much larger Dewitty were both only one hundred miles from his homestead (53). Micheaux's silence arises possibly from his ideological need to present himself as a lone black man breaking the frontier prairie, a story quite different from the black colonies' narratives of collective resistance to white economic control. Also, Micheaux's clear adherence to the Turnerian ideals of American exceptionalism and a nation mastered by the western progression of individuals necessitated narratives of lone pioneers (of any race) preparing the wilderness for civilization.

Micheaux's depiction of the lone black homesteader drives his three autobiographical novels set in South Dakota, *The Conquest* (1913), *The Homesteader* (1917), and *The Wind from Nowhere* (1941), the first two written during Micheaux's homesteading years there. Micheaux develops three almost identical homesteaders—clearly fictional surrogates of himself—to people these nearly autobiographical stories: Oscar Devereaux in *The Conquest*, Jean Baptiste in *The Homesteader*, and Martin Eden in *The Wind from Nowhere*. All three novels recount essentially the same story of a black man born in southern Illinois who moves to Chicago to work as a porter. Inspired by stories he hears from passengers crossing the West, this man saves his wages and moves to

South Dakota to acquire land at the Rosebud opening. Purchasing a relin-quishment, the homesteader settles into improving his property and begins searching for a suitable, that is, black, wife. Eventually meeting and marrying a woman in Chicago, he amasses more property by having his wife homestead on a second section of Rosebud Reservation land (opened in 1908). In each story, the imperious father-in-law, a well-known Methodist minister, disap-proves of the homesteader's ideals and his interference eventually destroys the marriage. *The Conquest* closes with Devereaux's wife's decision to stay with her father in Chicago, thus rejecting her husband's homesteading ideals. In both *The Homesteader* and *The Wind from Nowhere*, Micheaux extends this narrative to include the homesteader's attempts to win his wife back from the control of her father. Torn between two strong male figures who vie for her attention, the homesteader's wife eventually kills her father and then commits suicide. With the death of the wife, Micheaux opens up the narrative for the return of an earlier white love interest who, in the last pages of both novels, discovers that she has a black heritage and can thus consummate her relationship with the homesteader. Micheaux writes *The Conquest* as an autobiography of Oscar Devereaux (the first edition is anonymous, written "by the Pioneer") and spends over half the novel discussing the politics of land openings and town building in South Dakota, particularly with reference to the possibilities of railroad extensions, while *The Homesteader* and *The Wind from Nowhere* read more like conventional melodramas.

Micheaux saw the opportunities to acquire agricultural land in the West as a great antidote to the social ills confronting turn-of-the-century urban blacks. By directly improving undeveloped western lands, Micheaux believed African Americans could better themselves individually, thus helping the race as a whole. By remaining in cities, though, Micheaux felt that African Amer-icans became distracted by idle concerns, especially by conspicuous consump-tion. Worst of all, Micheaux "found a certain class in large and small towns alike whose object in life was obviously nothing, but who dressed up and aped the white people" (*Conquest* 195). For Micheaux, only economic survival measured one's success, and he clearly believed that homesteading was a most expedient route to this success. The empty plains demanded a focus on self-improvement, or they would bring imminent failure. In fact, Micheaux be-lieved farming to be a great race-leveler, thus providing an exceptional op-portunity for African Americans. He writes in *The Homesteader*, "Only in the pursuit of agriculture can the black man not complain that he is discriminated against on account of his color" (430). For Micheaux, the land did not distinguish between its tillers, and it alone determined fortune or failure.

Micheaux credits many of his beliefs in the possibilities of racial uplift in the West to Booker T. Washington. Given the popular sense that the West was the place to make one's fortune or start a new life in the second half of the nineteenth century—and many African Americans did just that—Washington rather oddly writes almost nothing about this region. Washington's 1908 article in *The Outlook* on Boley, Oklahoma, is one of his few published statements on the possibilities of the West for African Americans. Washington writes on Boley that "behind all other attractions of the new colony is the belief that here negroes would find greater opportunities and more freedom of action than they would have been able to find in the older communities North or South" (31). Primarily, though, Washington presents Boley as a black town not unlike others of its kind in the East; his consideration of Boley's western locale seemed only useful in producing a few colorful stories about this town, "where, it is said, no white man has ever let the sun go down upon him" (30). His only other comments about the West are rather harsh words concerning the Exodus to Kansas, which he calls "an uprising" against "real or fancied oppression" that ultimately "created such embarrassment among the planters in the region from which the emigration took place" (*Story of the Negro* 1: 185–86). Only a few western personalities appear in Washington's writing, namely Mifflin Wistar Gibbs, who in Arkansas became the first African American municipal judge and later a federally appointed consul to Madagascar, and Junius P. Groves, who was known in Kansas as the "Potato King" (see *The Negro in Business* 218–21 and 29–37). Before moving to Arkansas, Gibbs opened a successful shoe store in San Francisco in the 1850s; soon thereafter he traveled to Victoria, British Columbia, to open the first coal mine on the Pacific Coast. Groves was an extremely successful potato grower in Kansas who moved there in the Exodus of 1879 with, Washington tells us, only ninety cents (*The Negro in Business* 29). Through thrift, hard work, and prudent business practices—that is, the essence of Washington's program—Groves expanded his potato farm to over five hundred acres and by 1906 was considered the most successful African American in Kansas, if not the entire West.[10] Washington lauds both of these figures for their success in business, but he does not speculate on the possibilities that the West specifically may have provided for each of these men.[11] The West, even at the turn of the century, still represented a land of opportunity in the public imagination. Yet Washington refused to support the mythology of western promise, possibly because such a narrative ran counter to his idea that African Americans, especially those in the South, should strive to improve their conditions locally.[12]

Despite Washington's relative silence on the West, Micheaux transfers Washington's belief in the importance of thrift, hard work, and vocational values over intellectual values into his narratives of the development of the South Dakota plains by each of his homesteaders. Washington advocates the "dignity of labor" and "self-reliance" (*Up from Slavery* 69, 70, for example), which Micheaux then translates into "common sense" (*Wind from Nowhere* 161). Micheaux's South Dakota novels present a way in which Washington's philosophy of racial uplift can be translated onto the apparently blank tableau of Turner's frontier. Through Micheaux, Washington's ideals set to work on the Great Plains become a call for African American pioneer self-sufficiency, self-definition, and, ultimately, racial uplift.

MICHEAUX'S FRONTIER REPETITIONS

Micheaux believed in the boundless possibilities of the American West, "the land of raw material, which my dreams had pictured to me as the land of real beginning" (*Conquest* 47). Yet by 1918 Micheaux had given up farming altogether, and some local lore contends that Micheaux left South Dakota with numerous outstanding debts to people around Gregory (Herbert 65). Yet in almost all of his novels, as well as numerous films, Micheaux obsessively returns to his homesteading narrative and a belief that working the land, particularly western land, could provide economic, moral, and corporeal rejuvenation. Though Micheaux left the West a failed homesteader, he maintained an unflagging belief in the opportunities supposedly innate to that vast region.

Micheaux developed three different homesteaders to populate his South Dakota novels, but he also created another autobiographical stand-in for some of his novels set outside the West. Sydney Wyeth, who first appears in Micheaux's second novel, *The Forged Note* (1915; also written in South Dakota), is a South Dakota farmer who sells his autobiographical novel door-to-door in the South (keeping with his impulses for writing thinly veiled autobiography, Micheaux titles Wyeth's book *The Tempest*). Wyeth reappears in Micheaux's sixth and seventh novels, *The Case of Mrs. Wingate* (1945) and *The Story of Dorothy Stanfield* (1946), where he has now become a famous "pioneer Negro Motion Picture producer" living in Harlem (*Case* 73). In these later novels, Wyeth is a celebrated but misunderstood filmmaker who, after a hey-day of activity in the last two decades, has fallen from popularity and makes the bulk of his living writing novels. Distinctive of this later version of Wyeth are narrative references to his earlier life homesteading on the Great Plains, which significantly adds to the respect shown him by others in the novel.

In *The Forged Note*, Micheaux presents his readers with another entrepreneurial adventure. Where *The Conquest* related the story of a black pioneer testing himself against the western wilderness and the politics of the frontier, *The Forged Note* takes up from the failure of that venture and presents Micheaux's success at a new project: novel writing and sales. In *The Forged Note*, Wyeth, fresh from the Dakota plains, travels to Atlanta and Birmingham to sell his novel of frontier life, offering it to bookstores and directly to individuals. Early in *The Forged Note*, Wyeth's wife-to-be, Mildred, recounts to a potential buyer Wyeth's description of South Dakota and its potential for African Americans:

> The story opens up on the banks of the river, near this city. . . . It concerns a young man, restless and discontented, who regarded the world as a great opportunity. So he set forth to seek his fortune. . . . Thus it began, but shortly, it led through a maze of adventures, to a land in the west. It is, perhaps, the land of the future; a land in which opportunity awaits for courageous youths, strong men, and good women. . . . This land is called *The Rosebud Indian Reservation.* It lays in southern South Dakota, and slopes back from the banks of the "Big Muddy," stretching for many miles into the interior beyond. It is a prairie country. No trees, stumps, rocks or stones mar the progress of civilization. So the white men and only a few blacks unloaded at a town on or near the frontier. I think it is called Bonesteel. And then the mighty herd of human beings flocked and settled over all that broad expanse, claiming it by the right of conquest.
>
> Among these many, conspicuous at the front, was the hero of this narrative. He came into a share, a creditable share, and, although far removed from the haunts of his own, and surrounded on all sides by a white race, he was duly inoculated with that spirit which makes men successful.
>
> Time went on, and in a few years there was no more reservation, but it became *The Rosebud Country,* the land of the optimist. (64–65)

Clearly Micheaux saw a need to reconstruct his pioneer narrative to allow for the success of his homesteader; Wyeth's success (albeit displaced into sales rather than agriculture) effectively replaces Devereaux's failure. Starting with

The Forged Note, Micheaux's fiction begins to clash with reality (both his own and that of other western African Americans). Drought remained more powerful than Micheaux's optimism, and, by the time he lauded the golden opportunities of "the land of the optimist" to his southern readers, he had already given up homesteading. By 1915, when Micheaux published *The Forged Note*, he was financially overextended, he had lost his wife's allotment to an unscrupulous banker, and his marriage had failed. By 1917, Micheaux began to keep an apartment in Sioux City, South Dakota, decisively turning his back on "the land of the future," at least outside of his fiction.

Micheaux also retold his homesteading narrative in three films. In *The Homesteader* (1919), Micheaux retells the story of Jean Baptiste's hardships on the South Dakota prairie. Like the novel upon which it was based, the story closes with the revelation that the homesteader's only true love, a white South Dakota neighbor whom he had rejected earlier, actually has black ancestry. In 1931, Micheaux directed *The Exile*, his first talkie, in which a young black man (also named Jean Baptiste) leaves his Chicago fiancée to farm on the plains of South Dakota. He abandons their relationship after becoming distressed over her debauched lifestyle, which he sees as a product of her urban environment. In South Dakota, the hero meets and falls in love with a white woman who eventually discovers that she has black blood. The last retelling of Micheaux's homesteading narrative comes as his last film, *The Betrayal* (1948), a production of his novel *The Wind from Nowhere*. Little is known of this film, as no print survives and it flopped at the box office.[13]

In other films, Micheaux continued to engage the idea that the West provided particular opportunities for African Americans and, if nothing else, rejuvenation for many of his central characters. In *The Symbol of the Unconquered* (1920), a film that condemns the racism of D. W. Griffith's *Birth of a Nation*, Micheaux constructs a hero who homesteads on oil-bearing land and defeats Ku Klux Klan terrorism for his right to this lucrative western property. *Within Our Gates*, Micheaux's second film, opens with a depiction of an upstanding and hardworking black westerner in woolen clothes and a broadbrimmed hat outside a canvas tent. He addresses a letter to his sweetheart from Indian Head, Saskatchewan, the home of Dominion Experimental Farm, an early-twentieth-century experimental dryland farm, thus indicating his connection to agriculture and innovative western farming. In *The Virgin of the Seminole* (1922), a young black man, through pluck and determination, becomes a Canadian Mountie, wins a gunfight with a noted desperado, and buys a large western ranch that earns him great financial success. In *The Dungeon*, also from 1922, a despairing lover heads to an Alaskan mining claim, where he strikes it rich before returning to his lover and righteously winning her over from her crooked husband (by killing him). And in 1927 Micheaux created "Wild Bill of the Pampas" in *The Millionaire*, a black cowboy who finds success and wealth on the plains of South America before returning home for the typical underworld intrigue found in many of Micheaux's films.[14]

But Micheaux's vision of the West in all of these narratives (except *The Conquest*) clashed with western realities, especially for African Americans. About the time that Micheaux extolled the possibilities and prosperousness of the West for African Americans in these films and his early South Dakota novels, the numerous all-black towns scattered throughout the West had begun to crumble both socially and economically. By the 1930s all of the black agricultural settlements on the Great Plains had failed or entered into significant economic downslides. Dewitty, Nebraska, began depopulating in the 1920s after reaching a peak of about one hundred families. The Sully Colony in South Dakota had only eighteen members in it by 1940 (Bernson and Eggers 254). In 1946, Dearfield's total population consisted of its founder, Oliver T. Jackson, now quite elderly, and his niece (Taylor, *In Search of the Racial Frontier* 155). In particular, African American communities in Oklahoma suffered after statehood in 1907 (just one year before Washington visited Boley and about the same time as Micheaux began his homesteading venture further north), when segregation codes and black disenfranchisement measures inaugurated the slow disassociation of the state's all-black towns. As Micheaux extolled the Great Plains as a space of boundless possibilities and success for hardworking African Americans, those very collectives that tried to enact these western ideals had begun to fragment or had disappeared altogether.

Possibly Micheaux was trying to capitalize on the myth of opportunity in the West. But in doing so while creating clearly autobiographical narratives, he effectively denies his own frontier failures and replaces them with autobiographical fantasy. Blake Allmendinger argues that Micheaux's repetitions were driven by a need to revisit trauma, specifically Micheaux's economic failure in South Dakota, his broken marriage, and the death of his son (inferred from the stillbirth of the homesteader's son in both *The Conquest* and *The Homesteader*). Allmendinger calls Micheaux's homesteader narratives "cathartic artistic experiments in which the subject's personal failures come to stand in for the traumatic experiences of African Americans in the United States—

in particular the obstacles they faced on the Western frontier" ("The Pen and the Plow" 562–53). Certainly Micheaux's work points toward an explication of African American difficulties by presenting a need for the uplift offered by the West. But his dedication to narratives of individual success (especially ones that overlay failure) and his lack of attention to projects similar to his own complicate an easy extrapolation from the trauma of an individual to the injustices done to a race. Still, Micheaux's insistence on the validity of the frontier myth acts as a wedge to open official culture to African Americans.

THE WIND FROM NOWHERE AND MICHEAUX'S BLACK UTOPIA

Micheaux's narrative rejection of nearby black communities does not, however, preclude his construction of fictional ones, thus moving his project of western racial uplift even further from real possibilities in that region. Micheaux closes *The Conquest* with a crippling drought and Devereaux's wife's heartbreaking rejection of homesteading; *The Homesteader* concludes on a brighter note with Baptiste's establishment as a writer and his reunion with his true, and now black, love; *The Forged Note* also ends with rejuvenation as Sydney Wyeth and Mildred turn "together . . . to that land in the west" on the very last page (541). But *The Wind from Nowhere* not only establishes Eden's authorial renown and reunites him with his South Dakota neighbor, it concludes heroically with the discovery of an immense manganese deposit on Eden's new wife's property that funds the establishment of a thriving utopian black settlement there.

In many ways, Martin Eden best exemplifies Micheaux's formulation of the Black Turnerian and is Micheaux's last—and most interesting—construction of himself.[15] Unlike his predecessors Devereaux, Baptiste, or even Wyeth, Eden clearly articulates Micheaux's vision of the possibilities of the American West for African Americans, mixing the Turnerian dream with a drive for racial uplift. *The Wind from Nowhere* opens with Eden an already established western farmer. He has completed the acquisition of a full 640-acre section and has turned to other pursuits. While his earlier counterparts scratched unsuccessfully at the South Dakota soil, the beginning of *The Wind from Nowhere* presents Eden preparing to send "a shipment of two car loads of corn fed steers and one of bulging fat hogs to market," thus identifying him as a successful rancher as well as a homesteader (27). In a now familiar tale, Martin Eden transforms the prairie, rejects his white lover, marries an African American minister's daughter from Chicago, and loses her to her father's overbearing ways. Then, as readers of *The Homesteader* would know, *The Wind from Nowhere* concludes with the revelation of Eden's true love's black ancestry and their marriage, though Micheaux then adds the twist of unexpected mineral wealth and town-building to Eden's wellworn narrative.

Micheaux's central character has an obvious parallel with the vaguely autobiographical protagonist of Jack London's *Martin Eden*. Like Micheaux's homesteader, London's Eden is an autodidact, rising from the ranks of his working-class cohorts to become a world-famous novelist. London's Eden battles with the demons of his prose not unlike Micheaux's Eden struggles with the prairie. Undoubtedly, Micheaux saw a bit of London's Martin Eden in himself, the selfmade man fighting to present his vision of the world. From a rough and tumble world, both Micheaux ("tall and rugged" [*Conquest* 69]) and London's Eden ("spilling over with rugged health and strength" [London 356]) persevere through various hardships to meet their self-assigned goals as writers. Even with this ideological affinity, Micheaux insists on the necessity of his Eden's agricultural success, an almost predetermined condition of the frontier myth, while London's Eden commits suicide, a final act of will and determination that caps off his Nietzschean character. The failure of one such as London's Eden is not possible in Micheaux's Turnerian tableaus.

In fact, Micheaux's racial configurations lead him to produce in Martin Eden a kind of Exceptional Negro, a figure exceptional not only in type, but in region as well. Like Devereaux and Baptiste, Eden struggles alone on the prairie. The few other western African Americans Micheaux places in Eden's narrative are unworthy and even problematic for his project of western uplift. Not far from Eden's homestead lives an African American man married to a German woman. He refuses to invite the marriageable Eden to meet his daughters because they desire to pass for white, thus leading Eden to mutter bitterly to himself, *"Dirty old sonofabitch!"* (20). At another point, Eden remembers drinking in a saloon when an African American man passes by on the street. Eager to talk to someone of his own race, Eden moves to speak to this man, until a friend in the bar tells him, "he is one of the Woodsons. . . . He's colored all right, but they don't own to being colored. . . . He'd snub you if you offered to speak to him. . . . [T]hey *hate* colored people" (127). The only African Americans Eden does not vilify are a couple who teach at the nearby Indian day school, but he says little about these people at all. Essentially assailing all other African Americans around Eden, Micheaux ensures his homesteader's exceptional status by presenting him as the only black westerner who understands the value of both hard work and race identification.

Though Eden finds no worthy African Americans near him, he maintains a belief that the West could transform African Americans—if they would only make the effort to get there. Eden criticizes urban African Americans with broad strokes: "As a group, his race had little—almost no conception of what it took to succeed; to acquire, to have, nor to hold. Free and easy going, they did not impress him as ever thinking anything out deeply enough nor far enough to get anywhere" (17–18). Throughout the novel, Eden bitterly proffers his belief that most African Americans desired only to prosper socially by acquiring the trappings of white civilization, the gravest infraction being marriage to a white woman. Since he finds no models among African Americans, he turns to his white neighbors as exemplars of success. He immediately follows the above censure of urban African Americans with accolades for his Great Plains neighbors: "All around him . . . were Germans, Russians, Poles, Bohemians, Moravians, Slovaks—Scandinavians—in short, almost all kinds of Northern Europeans, all struggling to a common end—success! Practical success and security—but Negroes, they didn't even seem to think of it— much less starting to try to make it work" (18). Rejecting African American endeavors again, Eden connects himself to his northern European neighbors and their collective project to subdue the plains. As an Exceptional Negro, Eden provides the model for others' success. If his practical-minded white neighbors could succeed in this vast opportunistic land, so could Eden's black brethren, if they could only see beyond the confines of urban life.

Favoring the rural (and primarily white) West, Micheaux presents Eden as bewildered at the masses of black humanity he sees in cities. Visiting Harlem, Eden watches subway stations swallow and belch out people hurrying to work. "Niggah work, cheap jobs—portering downtown; cooking in Brooklyn; runnin' elevatahs in the Bronx," a policeman tells him (64). Watching these faceless people scurrying to make a living, Eden sighs, "My people, my people" while pondering his own position as "a lone wolf out there in South Dakota" (66). Eden appears alone in this novel as a successful and righteous African American. In fact, even the successful African Americans he believes are intermingled in the Harlem subway crowds—"the doctors, the preachers, some lawyers"—he characterizes as "'hincty' and 'dicty,'" as snobs who remove themselves from the larger black public scraping by in a white-dominated world (61).

While Eden's dedication to uplift is primarily centered in the West, he also presents this project as primarily a masculine enterprise, but one in which women play ancillary but essential roles.[16] Necessary to Eden's success is the acquisition of property, and since he has already received his allotted quarter-section he must find others to assume the title of available government property in his stead. He moves his grandmother and sister to nearby properties (as did Micheaux), because both still had "homestead rights to exhaust" (19), and then looks to a potential wife to complete his full section. (Eden would buy the relinquishments from his grandmother, sister, and wife after they had established title to the land.) He awkwardly, and none too romantically, explains his designs to his wife-to-be, Linda Lee, when he proposes to her: "I've been waiting a long time to be really in love with a girl. But my peculiar position, living off there by myself, alone, has forced me to the conclusion that if I am ever to marry . . . I'll just have to tie it up with business and take a chance if I can find a girl willing to meet me halfway" (146). Eden's earlier love interest, Jessie Binga, proved a disappointment for Eden. Though they loved each other deeply, Jessie suffered from an "inflammation of the ovaries" during Eden's extended absence in the West, which leads Eden to bitterly reject her. When he visits her again, thinking that she might prove to be the wife and business partner he desires, he realizes that "While he had succeeded in lifting himself by his bootstraps, he hadn't expected Jessie, or any other girl, to do likewise. . . . [S]he had to make the most of her limited opportunities" (79). Jessie's infidelity proved that though she might provide Eden the means to complete his landholdings, she might not be able to meet him halfway in love.[17]

Eden's association with Deborah Stewart, the daughter of one of his white neighbors, provides the clearest insight into the intersection of race and gender in Micheaux's narrative project of racial uplift. Women identified as black in *The Wind from Nowhere* (as well as *The Conquest* and *The Homesteader*) tend to be weak, unfaithful, and often helpless; Deborah, the only white female character of consequence, is presented as independent, hardworking, devoted, and legally savvy. But Eden must reject Deborah because he fears that their children would insist on passing as white and reject their black heritage. A marriage with Deborah would end Eden's project of uplift; to marry for love alone would be selfish when the construction of a model African American is at stake. Eden's fictional predecessor, Jean Baptiste, also rejects his white love, Agnes Stewart, and here Micheaux provides a clear presentation of the homesteader's aims for African American uplift: "He had set himself in this new land to succeed; he had worked and slaved to that end. He liked his people; he wanted to help them. Examples they needed, and such he was glad he had become; but if he married now the one he loved, the example would be lost" (*Homesteader* 147). Part of Eden's reluctance to marry Deborah stems from his general criticism of interracial marriages, which he sees as crude attempts at social advancement, especially for African American men. Yet Eden believes his love for Deborah is exceptional and without disguised social desires. His refusal to follow his affections for Deborah, though, stems from a sense of race loyalty and race purity for his progeny, not to mention the illegality of miscegenation in South Dakota at time (initially passed in 1909, the South Dakota miscegenation laws were repealed in 1957). Deborah is willing to cross the color line to marry the man she loves, but Eden will not. He will not forsake his race, even for love. Of course, when Deborah visits Chicago to see her grandfather, whom she has never met but with whom she has corresponded for years, she discovers much to her astonishment that he is black, a narrative move that allows Eden to maintain race loyalty, raise children identified as black, and continue his work to make the Great Plains an African American sanctuary and land of opportunity.

Micheaux's fictional construction of African American pioneer success operates on a careful delineation of worthy and unworthy players. Those not able to work into the project of economic and moral improvement—for reasons of inflamed ovaries, overbearing self-importance, willful paternal devotions, or white blood—Micheaux either drops from the narrative, kills, or rearranges their racial heritage (in *The Conquest*, Devereaux's white love disappears from the narrative immediately after the establishment of the relationship's ultimate failure). Yet even with this narrative sleight of hand, Micheaux still presents Eden as believing in uplift and moral change through a shift in one's environment. Specifically, Eden asserts that if African Americans can transform the West, they can transform themselves. Late in the novel (and foreshadowing its conclusion), Deborah tells Linda of Eden's dream of bringing other African Americans to the South Dakota plains: "What Martin Eden would do for a thousand Negroes families on relief today, would mean almost a new race of the same people, twenty years hence" (371). Eden believes himself a bowsprit of African American change, leading the way for enlightened urban followers. In fact, he tells Linda of his dedication in his initial proposal to her: "My whole life is bound up with the development of the wilderness" (105). Believing that he is part of a historical inevitability, Eden also situates his "development of the wilderness" within a Turnerian mold: "The life of a settler is not an easy lot. . . . Yet *somebody* must make conquest of these undeveloped portions of the West; somebody tore up all the great prairies that once embraced the whole states of Ohio, Indiana, Michigan, Illinois, Iowa and so on down. . . . [W]hat others had done, so could he" (211). By linking himself to pioneer identity, Eden (and Micheaux) asserts his devotion to African American uplift through Turnerian principles, leaving those too selfish to understand hard work or too cowardly to try a new environment awash in the urban backwaters of his frontier configuration.

Clearly Micheaux, through his various homesteading figures, embodies the problematic image of a Black Turnerian. Martin Eden presents the clearest formulation of this apparent impossibility. With *The Wind from Nowhere*, though, Micheaux moved from simple fantasy, which Blake Allmendinger argues is a reconciliation of "regional tensions, racism, and economic constraints that prevented African American men from making their frontier dreams a reality" ("The Pen and the Plow" 548), to a complete disconnection with the African American West. *The Wind from Nowhere* closes with Eden and Deborah's development of the manganese-rich, thousand-foot-tall "Mount Eden" at the center of their newly acquired property. Their mine nets them enough capital to purchase "more than one hundred thousand acres of Rosebud land" where they establish the colony to which Linda alluded in her earlier praise of Eden (422). Micheaux's glowing conclusion is worth quoting in full:

> They manned mighty tractors, equal to compound locomotive power and had the lands deeply plowed. . . . Crop failures were no more. All plant life flourished and crops were ever abundant. Huge yields were harvested from the fields, year after year.
>
> When this had been well established, the farms were divided into ten acre tracts. A modern village was erected in the center of every four square miles, with a school and a church, a small theatre and other needed buildings, including neat little project houses with enough room for all the families who were buying ten acre tracts.
>
> Then Deborah and Martin went East, where unfortunate families of their race had been forced on relief. They selected from them the worthy and industrious ones, brought them hither and permitted each to buy and pay for out of his earnings, ten acres of rich, deep plowed land. And with each purchase, they supplied a cow, a horse, chickens, and pigs. Each family grew its own food. The women were able to make their pin money from eggs and chickens and milk; the men were given work in huge food prod-

uct factories and manganese alloy plants that were built, where they were given a few days work each month.

Twenty five years hence, a great Negro colony will call the Rosebud Country home and be contented, prosperous and happy. (422–23)

At this point, Micheaux's narrative jars harshly with the history of African American settlement in the West. The mix of "black" and "Turnerian" that he establishes in all of his novels—including *The Wind from Nowhere*—collides with both his own history and the histories of other black communities in the West. Micheaux wrote *The Wind from Nowhere* in 1941 and set his home-steading story chronologically later than in either *The Conquest* or *The Home-steader*, probably in the 1930s. Following Micheaux's forecast for a great Negro colony, "twenty-five years hence" places his concluding fantasy in the middle 1950s. But a projection based on the health of the existing black western colonies in 1941 points to their extinction by the 1950s, which effectively was what happened. Micheaux's imagined "great Negro colony" had already come and gone from the plains in the form of Nicodemus, Kansas; Dewitty, Nebraska; Dearfield, Colorado; Sully, South Dakota; and others. In ignoring these utopian settlements in all of his earlier work and then insisting on the fictional construction of just such a communal experiment at the end of *The Wind from Nowhere*, Micheaux manifests his dedication to the work of individual African Americans like himself (as both "lone wolf" homesteader and author) over the collective efforts of others. When viewed through the entirety of his western-focused works, Micheaux's uplift project proves to dissipate into ego and mythology, thus lessening the usefulness of his fictions for providing alternative narratives for African Americans, be they in the East or the West.

As Micheaux moved further from his life on the prairie, he developed a need to reconstruct the narrative of his life there in order to reinforce the beliefs that he originally took to that land. While Devereaux, in *The Conquest*, ends his story with a broken marriage and withered fields (exactly as Micheaux had left his own homesteading venture), Eden becomes the founder of a successful agricultural/manufacturing colony. The Black Turnerian of *The Wind from Nowhere* turns out to be only a historical phantasm that closes this novel of hopeful racial rejuvenation. Like Roosevelt, Micheaux built fantasies that billowed with his geographic and temporal distance from the West. Possibly Micheaux's construction of a Black Turnerian, an African American pioneer dedicated to the ideals of western individualism, self-sufficiency, and the inevitable westward progress of the nation, allowed him to situate both him-self and his narratives within tropes acceptable in the official culture of the early twentieth century. As Jayna Brown argues, "For Micheaux, participa-tion in America's westward expansion embodies a black man's claim to na-tional belonging. By moving West and struggling to tame its soil. . . . he as-serts his right to be considered a founding father of the frontier" (146). Though Micheaux refuses to create raceless homesteaders, he does valorize pioneer mythology over racial realities in the West. If, as Roosevelt and Turner argue, the West becomes the primary signifier of Americanness and its partic-ularity, then Micheaux's novels and films that deal with his homesteading expe-riences propose an avenue for African American social equality, albeit a murky, insecure, and potentially disappointing course when played out in reality.

THE BLACK TURNERIAN FANTASY

In closing, we might ask why Micheaux, a man deeply concerned with the up-lift of African Americans, needs to offer such a fantasy of the rural American West—a region that had recently proven a failure for many African Ameri-cans. Why does Micheaux present both his own history and the history of the region in such a glowing light? Possibly he had become infected with the kind of nostalgia that so influenced figures like Theodore Roosevelt, Frederick Remington, or Owen Wister. In fact, Micheaux's initial vision of the West may have been modeled, at least partially, upon Wister's bestselling novel *The Virginian*. Certainly Micheaux had read Wister's books, since he has Devereaux (as a porter) recognize the Medicine Bow Mountains as the place where "Wister lays the beginning scenes of the 'Virginian'" (*Conquest* 43). As Roosevelt, Remington, and Wister repainted the West in tones they believed existed, Micheaux followed in their steps a full fifty years later to rebuild a sim-ilar mythic West that never was, particularly for African Americans. Though Micheaux failed as a homesteader, he still felt a need to reproduce the myths so entrenched by the Wisters, Remingtons, and Roosevelts of the West in his fiction. Thus each retelling of his personal narrative moves closer to an Afri-can American version of the great opportunistic frontier West. Interestingly, Devereaux's "beginning scenes" of the West may have come from *The Virgin-ian* just as Eden's final success in mineral wealth and town building mirrors the close of Wister's novel. Just as the Virginian marries Molly, who is no longer an Easterner, and settles on a parcel of land rich in coal, Eden reunites with his true love, who is no longer white, and establishes himself through mineral wealth. Wister's hero, with his "strong grip on many various enterprises" (Wister, *The Virginian* 364), however, is a capitalist benefitting from the next form of exploitation of western resources (from cattle to railroads). Alternately, Eden's resources provide the economic backbone for establishing an agricultural venture that guarantee financial and social security for a collective of "worthy and industrious" African Americans. The Virginian mutates from cowboy to capitalist, while Martin Eden develops from homesteader to agricultural philanthropist, developer, and a leader in the forces of racial uplift.

Micheaux rewrites and revises his real-life failures in Baptiste's and Eden's (and Sydney Wyeth's) financial and personal successes. Micheaux believed that if any place could level economic differences based on race, the West, with its mythic drama of human struggle with the land, could give all people the same advantages and the same hardships. The West did not become the mythic place Micheaux originally believed it to be, and he found himself incapable of frontier successes there. But Micheaux did not simply abandon the western myths of inevitable progress and self-definition. Rather, he abandoned his own experiences. Perhaps we remember Micheaux not only because he was America's first successful black filmmaker, but also because we, too, have accepted Micheaux's struggles to redefine himself as a success rather than as a failure, itself the ideal of western drama. Perhaps Micheaux's use of the West in his narratives has taken a back seat to his racial issues simply because we have brushed off his repetitive use of a well-known and stock western trope. But what solace did the West hold for African Americans by 1948? *The Betrayal*, Micheaux's last effort at using the West as a proving ground for race relations, was declared on its release one of Micheaux's worst pictures—the *Chicago Defender*, in a review entitled "'Betrayal', Severely Criticized, A Bore," called it "Flimsy and without purpose. . . . A preposterous, tasteless bore" (28). Possibly the West was not imaginatively important to many eastern African Americans by the midpoint of the century, but it did exist as a mythic place for Micheaux personally. Just as Micheaux moved closer to the myth of the West the further he moved away from his actual experiences there, so did he expand this same myth as he lost popularity and critical acclaim as a filmmaker. Though he sought to establish the West as a space—real or ideological—for racial uplift, thus providing a potential avenue into the cultural resources and power of national belonging, the West became for Micheaux, as it had for thousands of other Americans, black and white, merely a repository for fantasy and a space for the indulgence of idealism.

3

RECASTING THE WEST

FRONTIER IDENTITY AND
AFRICAN AMERICAN SELF-PUBLICATION

UNTIL RECENTLY, THE MYTHIC WEST had appeared definitively—and deliberately—white; the historical presence of western African Americans barely registered.[1] Even today, as more writers and filmmakers celebrate the diversity of the American West, African American westerners tend to remain obscure. Often, contemporary western writers celebrate their regional identity, especially white writers who glorify a connection to the land through labor, pioneer identity, or settlement. Others claim the western landscape as a place of origin, notably Native American and Chicano/a writers who assert ancestral connections to western land. In both cases, the concepts of place and rootedness loom large. In comparison to these claims of authenticity, African Americans' sense of place in the West may seem less tethered, forged more through displacement than any original sense of belonging.

Still, the vast open spaces of the rural Great Plains and the empty American deserts captivated both black and white Americans' imagination as places of freedom, property, democracy, and self-definition throughout the nineteenth and early twentieth centuries. Compared to their white counterparts, few African Americans opted to move westward in search of Turner's "free land" under the terms of the 1862 Homestead Act. Throughout the second half of the nineteenth century, African Americans generally stayed in the South to build communities in familiar territory after the end of slavery or moved northward in search of jobs and relief from entrenched southern racism. African Americans could not trace their origins to the West, nor did most find easy complicity with the narrative of a white-centered Manifest Destiny. Nevertheless, the West seemed a potentially blank canvas for some African Americans who believed they could construct a life free from the intense racism, structural and otherwise, found throughout the East and particularly in urban centers.

Though few African Americans moved westward with the overwhelming march of nineteenth-century pioneers, they certainly represented a significant portion of the western population. In 1879 alone, more than four thousand African Americans—Exodusters—moved to Kansas, exchanging the racism of the South for the hopes of a new and self-determined future on the Great Plains. One in every one hundred miners who rushed to California in 1849 was African American. At the height of the cattle drives in Texas and on the Great Plains during the 1880s, African Americans represented at least 2 percent and possibly up to 15 percent of working cowboys (see Taylor, *In Search of the Racial Frontier* 156–63). Throughout the late nineteenth and early twentieth centuries, African Americans established all-black towns in Iowa, Kansas, Oklahoma, Nebraska, South Dakota, Colorado, New Mexico, Texas, and California, though as noted in the previous chapter almost none of these communities survive today. Western African Americans were cowboys, miners (as well as mine owners), homesteaders, fur traders, financiers, madams, doctors, journalists, lumberjacks, farmers, mayors, military heroes, law officers, teachers, and barbers. Although not large in terms of population percentage, these African Americans nevertheless looked to the West in hopes of a more secure future.[2]

Rarely, though, did African American figures appear within the assortment of western heroes so popular to twentieth-century America. African American singer Herb Jeffries relates a story in the documentary film *Midnight Ramble: Oscar Micheaux and the Story of Race Movies* in which he and his bandmates saw a young black boy in tears running away from a group of white children. When Jeffries and his bandmates stopped the crying boy to see if he was hurt, expecting that the white youths had harassed him, the black boy explained that he and his friends were playing "cowboys" but his friends refused to let him play the part of Western film hero Tom Mix because of his skin color. This incident inspired Jeffries to construct an African American singing cowboy for a series of four all-black Westerns in the 1930s. As the official narrative of the nation had effectively whitewashed the West, Jeffries constructed a fantasy in which African Americans could figure in the mythology.[3] Certainly while the African American presence in the nineteenth- and early-twentieth-century American West generally has been ignored in western scholarship until the last few decades (Walter Prescott Webb's claim that the scarcity of African Americans in the region actually helps to define the West is certainly characteristic), western African American written expression—both fictional and autobiographical—has fallen even further aside in most twentieth-century discussions of the American West. Though this apparent absence of western African American prose may be in part due to the lack of literary notice of the West in general, western African Americans have written novels and memoirs, published local newspapers, and produced collections of essays on various topics.[4] We might include in a list of these often overlooked writers Oscar Micheaux; Jim Beckwourth (fur trader); Mifflin Wistar Gibbs (western financier); Sutton Griggs (author and minister); Thomas Detter (activist, barber, journalist, and minister); and Henry Ossian Flipper (the first black graduate of West Point). All of these writers penned fiction, essays, and memoirs about the American West, generally written from the geographic space of the West itself.[5]

Examining the African American presence in the American West raises the question of how the political rhetoric of national unity and homogeneity produced by the outcome of the Civil War played out within this definitively American and supposedly leveling geographic space. Specifically, we should ask if western African American literary contributions to American culture help to expand the "melting pot" theory of unified difference, or if these literary projects worked to establish a separate black identity forged within the interstices of a more powerful white (and generally male and eastern) cultural matrix. To investigate these questions, this chapter engages the western novels of Oscar Micheaux with reference to his self-publication;[6] the writings of the aforementioned barber and journalist, Thomas Detter; the memoir of Robert Ball Anderson, an ex-slave turned Nebraskan homesteader; and the cowboy autobiography of Nat Love—a.k.a. Deadwood Dick—western rodeo hero, sharpshooter, ladies' man, and railroad porter. I ask here whether their narratives pivot primarily upon racial identification or pioneer experience, or if these narratives lie in some liminal space that forgoes the traditional anchors of essentialist identity, nationalist narrative, or political oppositional stance offered by these two ideological poles. Since identity can be formed through a range of responses, from a simple opposition to some Other to the complicated mediation between self and community, or may be formed beyond the terms of racial or gender similarity and engage relationships to local structures such as region, nation, and citizenship, we might look to a number of different political perspectives to identify where these self-published stories fit into the matrix of American culture. Some of these writers appeal to black identity for ideological mooring, while others use the exceptionalism of the American West to guide their visions. In general, though, most of their narratives lie uneasily between the poles of race identification and American nationalism, forming stories commercially and ideologically marketable to both African American and western audiences.

These western outsiders often embraced the terms of official culture, especially with reference to the American West, to situate themselves within national culture. By embracing the mythologies of the West, they sought to claim that geographic space as devoid of racial injustices and as fundamentally structured through principles of individualism and merit. Like Theodore Roosevelt, Owen Wister, Frederic Remington, and Frederick Jackson Turner, these African American westerners believed that the West held the key to understanding American democracy as well as national character, and that it also provided the promise for the United States's future, a promise they often wove into their narratives. The myth of the West claimed that this region would supply equal opportunities to all who settled there—an American principle embodied in the land—but the narratives by African American westerners often reveal (albeit beneath the boosterism) the fundamental American racism that refused to disappear past the hundredth meridian. The prospects enumerated by many of these western writers often collapsed as the myths of an individualistic western meritocracy collided with racial inequalities.

Though we cannot lump all of these African American memoirs and novels together to form a single cohesive story, we nonetheless can situate them variously with respect to each other and to the apparatus of their circulation to better understand the political and cultural impact of the African American presence in the American West. Micheaux, Detter, Anderson, and Love placed themselves on different coordinates within an ideological matrix of western freedom and self-determination and also in terms of the racial limitations to those ideals within the West and the nation at large. Micheaux, as discussed earlier, recreated a pioneer ideology of self-sufficiency and self-determination in his novels while remaining consistently dedicated to African American uplift. Detter presented his racially complicated western voice by self-publishing domestic fiction with white central characters alongside journalistic essays on western towns and racial injustices in both the West and the East. Anderson combined the genres of slave narrative and pioneer success story while alluding to the blatant racism he experienced in the supposedly "free" and tolerant

West. Nat Love, grandiloquent and heroic, took on the voice of a Manifest Destiny–driven cowboy. Because these writers' stories of self-publication have as much to say about their self-identification as their more literal self-characterizations, I will take a two-pronged analytic approach and simultaneously consider both the content of their narratives and the mechanisms and social realities confronting these authors in terms of their publishing. Discovering exactly how these writers produced and marketed their books sheds light on the social forces that constrained them as they presented their stories to the public; by looking at the content of these narratives we can better understand how these authors saw themselves within the larger framework of U.S. race relations and western American expansion. Taken together, the mechanism and content illuminate these writers' relationship with the narrative of the nation and present the ideological limits and possibilities for their pioneer and western identifications.

THE DOUBLE BIND OF SELF-PUBLICATION

While this chapter focuses specifically on writers who published within the American West, it also concentrates on discrete texts such as novels or memoirs rather than serial forms such as magazine or newspaper articles, primarily because few African American serials existed in the American West during the early twentieth century (not including the scattered and sporadic newspapers printed on the West Coast). In the late nineteenth and early twentieth centuries, many black authors nationwide found avenues for publication in African American magazines such as *The Colored American Magazine, Opportunity, The Competitor, Voice of the Negro, Alexander's Magazine, Horizon, The Crisis, Half-Century Magazine*, and others, yet none of these serials were printed further west than Chicago. While these magazines published short stories and essays by African Americans, they did not necessarily pay any particular attention to the African American presence in the West.[7] In fact, the predominant readership of these publications resided in the urban East and Midwest. Though no African American magazines or serials were published in the West, many newspapers did find readership among western African American communities, especially in San Francisco, Omaha, and cities in Kansas and Oklahoma.[8]

As a literary form, the novel replicates a kind of rugged individualism in supporting unity and cohesiveness of identity (even if that identity appears splintered, as in the modernist works of Faulkner, Woolf, or Joyce). Indeed, we might argue that the cohesion of the novel and the unity of the nation correspond directly. In *Imagined Communities*, Benedict Anderson argues that within the confines of the novel we may "see the 'national imagination' at work in the movement of a solitary hero through a sociological landscape of fixity that fuses the world inside the novel with the world outside" (30). Anderson's approach becomes especially significant when linked to autobiographies, memoirs, or narratives based on place, where the "national imagination" is portrayed through the author's lived experience. In terms of cohesion and unity, novels and memoirs become synchronic texts, reflective of a single cultural moment and its relation to the larger national culture, while serial publishing presents flux in both voice and cultural expression. The clear narrative boundaries of novels and memoirs reflect the imagined clarity of national boundaries, and, in the United States, the supposedly unified culture contained within these boundaries. Through the use of the novel and autobiography as forms, western African American authors attempted to build just such cohesive statements about their place within the American West as well as the nation. By invoking their affiliation with the West within these carefully bounded narratives, these writers sought membership within the official culture of the nation, a culture that ironically disallowed blacks a place in the narrative of the West and its formative ideology for American nationality.

In terms of *self*-publication, African American authors who could not succeed in the white-owned publishing world often turned to the private printing of their works. These writers sought their audiences primarily within the local space of the American West, writing about their communities and often marketing their work directly to those neighbors and friends who might appear in the book. But through self-publication, western African Americans were caught in the double bind of creating their own original stories and replaying available myths of the West. Initially, we might view the act of self-publication as politically progressive for writers who could not get their voices heard in larger mainstream literary circles. However, though self-publication was a tangible progressive outlet for western African Americans' literary expressions, it also retrenched the American ideals of individual merit, self-sufficiency through hard work, and atomistic ideological self-definition—ideas closely associated with the development of the frontier American West. While African American self-publication represented a political statement against institutional cultural gatekeepers, within this act lie precisely those conventions so important to American mythology and frontier ideology. Like Roosevelt's cowboys or Turner's settlers, these self-published African Americans demonstrated self-sufficiency both within their stories and through the production and reproduction of those stories. Both levels of production, then, link their works to American pioneer ideology.

Eastern publishing houses—with white principals—generally limited the range and output of western fiction in the early twentieth century (though certainly horse operas remained popular), but Western African American pioneer success clearly held no market value in the views of these institutions. Black presses also seemed to find these western narratives little more than curiosity pieces, as evidenced by their absence in publishers' booklists. Thus, the dearth of African American stories from the West aided in purveying the notion that this region provided opportunities only to America's white citizens. Therefore, self-publication allowed these writers to be heard when more traditional, and more lucrative, avenues remained closed. The necessity of self-publication, however, placed these writers into a rhetorical dynamic that demanded stories of self-made success, of struggles with the land, and of struggles with the printing presses—struggles that the author necessarily won, just as that author—and the nation—had won the West.

GETTING INTO PRINT

Self-publication allowed African American westerners to present their images of this region without white filters. Yet information on how these authors produced, marketed, and distributed their books remains quite limited. Robert Ball Anderson, for example, printed a relatively short pamphlet that he apparently marketed only locally. Oscar Micheaux, on the other hand, self-published numerous books that he sold as he traveled throughout the country, yet there is no repository for Micheaux's papers that would aid in understanding the details of his books' publication and distribution.[9] Often the only materials that scholars can access to investigate the mechanism of these writers' self-publication are the self-published books themselves and their attendant advertising.

Self-publication was clearly akin to self-creation for these writers. Though not all of the details are readily available, we can make some claims about audience, success, and distribution from the texts themselves, as well as from the authors' own accounts where available. Most of these writers used connections to local papers to promote their books, pressing for announcements of publication and availability in lieu of paid advertising. Writers such as Anderson and Love had no stake in selling themselves as professional writers; they merely wanted to sell their stories. Detter, on the other hand, sought to present himself as a professional author, although his primary income apparently came from his business as a barber who also sold sundry toiletries such as "T. Detter's Cough Tonic" and "hair restorative[s]" (Rusco 156, 161).

Economic necessity, often coupled with an ideological agenda, played a significant role in the production of most autobiographical narratives, a force not wholly unique to western African American writers. Historian Ann Fabian has examined the writings of financially and socially impoverished citizens who felt that their narratives of experience deserved recognition. Fabian investigates slave narratives, as well as autobiographical—and generally self-published—writings from American soldiers, convicts, Civil War prisoners, and mendicants. She argues that these authors primarily traded their narratives for money or ideological attention from their readership: "Every beggar who used a story to ask for relief, every old soldier who used a story in lieu of a pension, every convict who asked support for his innocence or pennies for his orphans, every former slave who told a tale of escape to advance the cause of emancipation, and every maimed and suffering prisoner who asked for support similarly demanded action from audiences and readers" (175). Within the specific context of African American publication, autobiography provided not only a possible, though unlikely, source of regular income, but also a forum for authors to testify to the achievements of African Americans within a segregated nation. Furthermore, autobiography also provided access to African Americans' experiences for a readership otherwise distanced from them.

The construction of autobiography, especially in the American and European worlds, rested on the idea that one lived a life worthy of public interest. As James Olney writes, "The very act of writing a life down constitutes an attempt on the writer's part to justify his tale, and implicit in every act of autobiography is the judgement that his life is worth being written down" (212). For African Americans, autobiography became increasingly important as they fought for recognition as citizens, if not human beings, by using print as a tool. Certainly the political significance of African American autobiography vastly eclipsed that of white narratives of individual success or failures. With reference to the political import of African American autobiography, Robert F. Sayre writes, "A necessary step in anyone's liberation from stereotypes and injustice is the moment when he or she asserts his or her own rights and values against those imposed from without" ("The Proper Study" 251). For many African Americans, this moment was the production of a life story; indeed, Sayre calls autobiography "an important ideological weapon" (251).

For African American westerners, the act of autobiographical production established not only that their lives were worth living (and reading about) but that they also could participate in the progress of the nation through their establishment in Turner's untamed wilderness. In the introduction to *African American Autobiography*, William L. Andrews asserts that "African American autobiography has testified to the ceaseless commitment of people of color to realize the promise of their American birthright and to articulate their achievements as individuals and as persons of African descent" (1). As westerners, African Americans such as Micheaux, Anderson, and Love (Detter less so) expressed their commitment to this birthright through western tropes of pioneer accomplishment and conquest. Their success stories (such as they are) sought to celebrate their achievements, not just as individuals or merely as African Americans, but rather as American citizens operating within a culture that demanded westward movement, agricultural establishment, and individual self-sufficiency. Self-construction, then, especially as African Americans, pulled these writers toward the official culture of the nation.

Part of the autobiographical act of self-construction in an environment generally unfriendly to African American expression (if not African American identity) was the acquisition of the means to make the story public. The African American westerners discussed in this chapter all resorted to self-publication of their works, funding the books themselves and marketing them directly. To build a readership, these authors looked initially to local communities (which were generally white) where they were known and their story might be recognized. For example, Robert Ball Anderson marketed his *From Slavery to Affluence: Memoirs of Robert Anderson, Ex-Slave* (1927) to his neighbors with the help of a local paper, *The Hemingford Ledger*. The announcement of the publication of his book, printed on the *Ledger*'s presses, declared, "Robert Anderson, well-known colored man, an old homesteader, has prepared a little book, his Memories, telling something of his life and conditions in slavery, and his efforts to get on top." The blurb reminded the readers, "Anyone desiring a copy can get it from Uncle Bob [Anderson] or his wife, or at the Ledger Office. The supply is limited. Get yours now before they are all gone" (Wax, "Robert Ball Anderson" 185). No evidence presently exists that Anderson tried to sell his book outside of western Nebraska. Anderson's wife, Daisy, brought his text back to life in 1967 when she composed a nineteen-page addition to *From Slavery to Affluence* entitled "Have You No Shame?" that was addressed to white Americans who have historically ignored racial inequalities. In this addendum she writes a memoir of her own life, but her chronology is often so jumbled it is difficult to tell if she is relating incidents from her life in Nebraska or her present home in Steamboat Springs, Colorado. Regardless, she consistently addresses her narrative and her criticisms to "you," indicating that the intended readership of *From Slavery to Affluence* was undoubtedly white. She rather pointedly opens her addition to her husband's autobiography with what amounts to a damnation of white America: "I wipe the tears from my eyes in sorrow for you and your teachings" (61). She also admonishes her readers a number of times with "SHAME ON YOU" when discussing racial inequalities that have not come undone in her lifetime (see 61, 71, for example). Daisy Anderson likely solicited sales locally through friends and her Colorado community, though the *Denver Post* also pitched *From Slavery to Affluence* in a 1997 article about her trip to Gettysburg, as one of three surviving Civil War widows, as well as in her 1998 obituary.[10]

Of the four writers discussed in this chapter, only Micheaux continued his publishing career past the first book. Micheaux was a master of self-promotion, and the Micheaux-doubles he created aided in constructing an ever-unfolding and impressive multitext pseudo-autobiography. Little evidence exists for authenticating Micheaux's history and his business tactics, but the repetition of numerous narratives, the obvious stand-ins for himself, and the thinly veiled accounts of verifiable history found in *The Conquest* allow us to read many of Micheaux's constructions as retellings of his life. In *The Homesteader* (1917), Micheaux's pioneer double, Jean Baptiste, turns to writing his "life of hell" (401) after three successive years of crop failure and a failed marriage. When a Chicago publisher rejects his manuscript, Baptiste self-publishes his book by securing prepaid orders from his neighbors. He obtains 142 orders on the first day of his solicitation; by the end of two weeks he has sold 1,500 orders. Two months into his bookselling venture, Baptiste deposits $2,500 in profits into his bank account (410). Baptiste's story is apparently Micheaux's as well, since Micheaux had sold copies of *The Conquest* through subscriptions to his neighbors after the end of his first marriage and the loss of his crops in the crippling drought of 1910–11. (Micheaux used the same door-to-door technique in 1918 to sell interest in his first film [see Bowser and Spence 11].)

Micheaux presents Baptiste simply as a hardworking pioneer who happens to pen an alluring story, but Micheaux himself was more a salesman and a showman than a farmer. He worked doggedly and deliberately to convince people to buy his books. In December 1912 the *Dallas News*, a local South Dakota paper, reported that Micheaux's first book was in preparation for serialization in the *Saturday Evening Post* and that the complete book would soon appear from the McClury Publishing Company, neither of which occurred (VannEpps-Taylor 74).[11] Micheaux stretched the truth in both instances in order to generate excitement about his work. In the next six months, local papers helped to promote Micheaux's now self-published book and to laud both its narrative and its sales by announcing his presence in town to take orders. Other papers, such as the local *Colome Times*, promoted Micheaux's following titles with similar announcements over the next few years (VannEpps-Taylor 83–84).

Though Micheaux sold his first book, *The Conquest*, to primarily a rural midwestern white audience, he marketed all of his subsequent productions, both novels and films, more directly to African Americans. In fact, his second book, *The Forged Note*, provides a fictional retelling of his marketing and sales process. In *The Forged Note*, Micheaux's proxy, Sydney Wyeth, travels to the South selling his self-published story of pioneer homesteading entitled *The Tempest*. Wyeth's story picks up where Micheaux's narrative ended in *The Conquest* and illustrates—albeit through a melodrama—Micheaux's attempts at distribution of his first self-published book outside of the Midwest. Micheaux, as seen through Wyeth, engaged agents to further the sales of his book. In an ad for *The Forged Note*, Micheaux advises his readers to "step to the telephone and ask your leading bookseller if he has it," while in an adjoining column he advertises for solicitors of his book. In this informal distribution system, which Micheaux claims is "almost perfect," agents request circulars or prospectuses from the Western Book Supply Company (Micheaux's company) that they then use to sell prepaid copies of the book, which the seller had subsequently acquired COD from Micheaux. The advertisement claims that the seller needs no bond and "All you fail to deliver are returned to us without cost to you." Thus Micheaux could sell his books in bulk to what amounts to distributors with less likelihood of loss through failed payment on subscriptions. Micheaux presents this system as already in place by telling the readers of the ad, "Out in South Dakota and Nebraska 2500 white people have purchased THE FORGED NOTE through solicitors" (ad reprinted in Sampson 148). Also implied here is the sense that purchasing Micheaux's book would make readers part of a collective racial uplift effort. If we are to believe Micheaux's descriptions of this operation in *The Forged Note*, he sold his book via agents throughout the North, South, and Midwest (*Forged Note* 70, 127, 491). While Micheaux promoted *The Conquest* amongst his neighbors—other farmers, settlers, and pioneers in the West—Wyeth sells *The Tempest* door-to-door in black communities and to black service workers through kitchen doors in white middle- and upper-class homes. By the time Micheaux wrote his second book, or more precisely, with his sales attempts of *The Conquest* outside of the Great Plains, he had turned his attention strictly to an African American audience. In fact, for *The Homesteader*, Micheaux's third foray into self-publication, he prepared a promotional booklet directed at African American readers that suggested, "Why not as a change from the usual run of Magazine stories and novels by white authors . . . try this book?" (Bowser and Spence 12). Micheaux also wove pitches for his books into advertisements for his films. The advertisement for the premier of Micheaux's first film, *The Homesteader*, declared it "A powerful drama of the great American Northwest, adapted to the screen by the author from his popular novel of the same name" (*The Homesteader*). Lobby posters for both *The Exile* and *The Betrayal* noted that the films were adapted from *The Conquest* and *The Wind from Nowhere*, respectively (see Kisch and Mapp 12, 25).

Micheaux self-published all seven of his books. *The Conquest* and *The Forged Note* were both printed by Woodruff Press in Lincoln, Nebraska, a press that focused on local materials, but after 1916 Micheaux distributed all of his books through his own imprint, the Western Book Supply Company.[12] In various permutations, Micheaux kept this publishing enterprise alive as the Micheaux Book and Film Company (through which he produced the film of *The Homesteader* in 1919) and, later, the Book Supply Company after his move to New York in the 1920s. His publishing venture produced only Micheaux's own novels; he never undertook to publish or distribute other writers' work.[13]

Primarily, though, African American westerners looked to local printers who might produce their works inexpensively and then leave the distribution and sales to the author. Robert Ball Anderson, in a far less assuming fashion than Micheaux, published his brief autobiography on the presses of the *Hemingford Ledger*, though we do not know the specifics of the financial or business arrangements for this production. Anderson marketed his book to his Nebraska neighbors in the same way Micheaux did, and, like Micheaux in *The Conquest*, he does not dwell on any racism he encountered homesteading on the Great Plains, likely because he saw no need for alienating any of his white neighbors within the tight-knit community of northwestern Nebraska.

Other writers such as Thomas Detter already had connections with presses. By 1871, when Thomas Detter published his only book, *Nellie Brown or, The Jealous Wife, with other sketches,* he was already well known as a correspondent for a number of African American Pacific Coast newspapers. Detter printed *Nellie Brown* with Cuddy & Hughes Printers of San Francisco, a firm that produced various materials including the rather mundane prospectus for the California Ice Manufacturing Company (1871) and the Picacho Mill and Mining Company. Cuddy & Hughes also printed the scrip ("Bonds of Empire") issued in lieu of cash by the noted San Francisco eccentric Joshua Norton, self-proclaimed Emperor of the United States (1869). But the printer clearly worked with the African American population of the West, as is evidenced not only by Detter's book but also by their printing of the racially charged *Orations Delivered on the Proclamation of Emancipation and the Fifteenth Amendment* (1873), by James H. Hubbard, pastor of the Grass Valley, California, A.M.E. Church, and the *By-Laws of the California Cocoanut Pulverizing Company* (1874), an African American business venture.

Further south and thirty-five years later, Nat Love printed his autobiography with another small printing house, the Wayside Press, in Los Angeles. Most scholars believe that Love's *Life and Adventures of Nat Love* (1907) was distributed and marketed privately, possibly by Love himself. The Wayside Press, though, did not have any particular leaning toward African American narratives or even stories particular to cowboys and the Old West. In fact, many of the titles printed by Wayside in the early twentieth century were local poetry, such as Edward O'Leary's *Lyrics of California* (1919), Arthur Franklin Miller's *California and Other Selected Poems* (1921), and William Hathorn Mills's *Californica* (1923) (Wayside published a number of books for this minor California poet). Wayside also printed histories such as Jorge Vera Estañol's *Carraza and His Bolshevik Regime* (1920) and Warren F. Lewis's much later *History of the 413th Regiment* (1943).

WESTERN STORIES, BLACK LIVES

Despite these unorthodox publishing methods, these texts still managed to reach their target audiences, even if they generally disappeared from public view relatively quickly when compared to texts published through more mainstream channels. Some of them, particularly Micheaux's novels and Love's autobiography, continue to circulate widely today.[14] While an understanding of the mechanism of self-publication can shed light on the political and social obstacles facing these western authors, examining the content of their narratives provides a window on the African American experience in the American West. The narrative and textual content of these books suggests how the ideologies of western expansion and race intersect in the American West. Often these narratives promote the ideals of self-sufficiency and self-determination, conventions important within the mythic West, but underneath the plots and the memories, as well as in the amalgamation of different narratives published together (particularly in Detter's book), the uneasiness of black lives in a predominately white region emerges. Within these apparent narratives of success, or at least of proud posturing amidst failure in the case of Micheaux, we can see that the myth of opportunity for all within the American West did not necessarily apply fully to African American westerners.

Detter's *Nellie Brown or, The Jealous Wife, with other sketches* was the first book published by an African American in the American West. Within this book, Detter publishes his novella, "Nellie Brown or, The Jealous Wife," a short story, "The Octoroon Slave of Cuba," and a number of short essays that read like newspaper articles, journalistic correspondences, local boosterisms, and sketches. Detter writes here within two distinct literary traditions: American domestic fiction, focusing on the sanctity and occasional instability of marriage, and an African American rhetorical tradition urging African American unity and political progressiveness (in Detter's case, specifically in the American West). Detter chose to put these two voices together—evidenced on the one hand by "Nellie Brown" and on the other by a number of the collected essays and sketches—for reasons unknown, though we might speculate that the printing of two separate titles proved too dear for this barber *cum* author.

Unlike the writings of most other African Americans who self-published in the West, "Nellie Brown," the centerpiece of his book, has nothing to do with the geographic (or ideological) space of the American West. Instead, "Nellie Brown" is set in the rolling hills of northern Virginia and concerns the potential divorce of a locally respected white couple, Ben and Nellie Brown. Mr. Brown's visits to a nearby widow provide fodder for a conniving group of busybodies who want to tear Mrs. Brown from her husband for sport and financial gain. This group of women provides false evidence to Mrs. Brown of her husband's infidelity in exchange for fifty dollars, which an old flame of

Mrs. Brown's pays them in the hopes that the divorce will bring her back to him. Eventually, the machinations of these "malignant characters" (Detter 1) comes out in the course of the Browns' divorce trial. Nellie loses her suit and tearfully falls back into her husband's arms while the presiding judge admonishes the meddlers, commanding them to "Leave the Court, you vile wretches" (84). Fundamentally a moralizing tale extolling the virtues of marriage, "Nellie Brown" has more in common with the domestic fiction of Fanny Fern, Maria Cummins, or Mary J. Holmes than the rollicking contemporary expositions on the American West made popular by Mark Twain or Bret Harte. Detter also makes no overtures to racial politics in that the plot of "Nellie Brown" revolves around a white slave-owning family whose slaves are caricatured as docile, servile, single-mindedly religious, and dull. In fact, without the inclusion of other material in Detter's book, a reader might reasonably assume that Detter was white, given the racial depictions in "Nellie Brown."

"Nellie Brown" by itself might be read not so much as a novel about passing, but as an example of a *novelist* passing. However, Detter prohibits this possible reading immediately on the title page, which reads, "Nellie Brown—or—The Jealous Wife—with—Other Sketches, Written and Published by Thomas Detter, (Colored,) of Elko, Nevada" (from the original; the title page is not reprinted in the University of Nebraska Press reissue). Within the book itself, Detter clearly presents his racial concerns through the *Other Sketches* of the title, which comprise a mix of fiction and essays that distinctly identify him as African American. Here Detter generally turns to the first person and relates stories such as "My Trip to Baltimore," in which a friend who could pass for white gets invited into white homes for breakfast while the darker-skinned Detter is consistently forced to eat in kitchens and sleep in barns. He also drafts a plea to white America entitled "Give the Negro a Chance," demanding "Give him the same wages you give the white man. We are natives of the soil. . . . Close not against us the door of industry. Help us to rise from the pit of degradation" (117–18). Thus any question concerning Detter's racial politics that might linger in a reader's mind after reading the problematic racial depictions in "Nellie Brown" are answered by these essays and sketches. Some of Detter's essays display flagrant boosterism, such as "Idaho City, Its Customs and Future Prospects," in which Detter declares, "The mines are inexhaustible. The future prospects of the city are flattering. We expect [Idaho City] to become . . . the emporium of the North. Why the Territorial Fathers don't introduce gaslights to the city is really astonishing"

(111). He also cheers all of America in "Progress of America," where he declares, like Nat Love (as we shall see), "This government is advancing, step by step, to the grandeur and glory of greatness. . . . May this Republic forever be 'the land of the free and the home of the brave'" (113). Yet the West, for all of Detter's praises, remains racist. At no point in these essays does Detter claim a special providence to be found for African Americans in the West; he never lauds it as a salvational territory, as Micheaux does almost half a century later. In fact, in a sketch of Boise City, Detter describes an incident in which a bartender calls him by name before asking him to leave: "The polite and accommodating Mr. Old bent over the counter and said, in a low tone of voice: 'Detter, I cannot accommodate you" (115). Retaliating, Detter names the establishment in his essay and laments that "many of [Boise City's] citizens are afflicted with the terrible disease of Negrophobia. The very air seems to be pregnated with this disease" (115).

Detter also includes in *Nellie Brown* a short story, "The Octoroon Slave of Cuba." In this tale, a young octoroon woman, Jane, who is ignorant of her parentage, marries a wealthy Cuban planter, only to discover her long-lost sister among her husband's slaves. Jane leaves her husband and forces him to marry the sister, with whom the planter has fathered three children. In this critique of the now deposed planter class, Detter presents a picture of African Americans, both slaves and passing octoroons, full of passion and devotion—quite a different picture from his unflattering depictions of the Browns' slaves in "Nellie Brown." The multiple voices found in *Nellie Brown* make Detter difficult to pin down. Also, Detter provides no information as to whether any of these discrete essays and stories had appeared elsewhere, which would give the reader a clearer sense of his audience. Undoubtedly, though, Detter advocated for the rights of African Americans in the West (he wrote in the *Pacific Appeal* [October 24, 1874], "Let us vote for no candidate who believes a white American citizen is entitled to more privileges and consideration than a colored citizen" [quoted in Foster xii]), but he did not see the West as a panacea for America's racialized social ills. Instead, he presented the West as a land of general opportunity, albeit no less racist or necessarily more democratic than other regions of the country.

Unlike Detter, Micheaux's great faith in the ideas of individual uplift and vocational success advocated by Booker T. Washington allowed him to assert that the rural American West provided exactly the opportunities that urban African Americans needed to succeed. During the period that Micheaux lived in South Dakota, he remained ideologically hostile toward urban environments, believing that land itself was colorblind and urban environments produced sloth and ideological shallowness. Thus, as demonstrated in the preceding chapter, we can read in Micheaux's western novels an embracing of the ideals of western mythology such as free will, self-definition, and ideological freedom.

But the realities of western racism seep through Micheaux's narratives, and we can find lurking within his South Dakota novels an anger at racial segregation that can be traced through the ever-appearing neighbor whom Micheaux cannot love because she is white. Even after publicly admitting his prohibited and unlawful love in *The Conquest*, Micheaux showed his white readership that he knew his place: "I would have given half my life to have her possess just one drop of black blood in her veins, but since she did not and could not help it any more than I could help being a negro, I tried to forget it, straightened out my business and took a trip east, bent on finding a wife among my own" (168).[15] *The Conquest* is a narrative of failure. Micheaux's attempt at farming literally dries up, and he faces foreclosure; his marriage fails, his child is stillborn, and he must disavow his true love. But his later narratives suggest that through the pluck of self-determination represented by self-publication and farming, his character can overcome drought, financial hard times, and meddling fathers-in-law. True love, however, can only be accessed through the structural manipulation of ancestry. The "one drop of black blood in her veins" for which the homesteader yearns cements the racism evident in Micheaux's West of freedom and self-definition; only by constructing a lover whom the homesteader can honorably (and legally) marry can Micheaux produce the colorblind—and fictional—West that he desires. Like Washington, Micheaux determines his future through self-promotion and practical sustainability. But the cracks in the western mythology appear when free will and self-determination stumble up against local miscegenation laws.[16] Micheaux's antidote for this apparent betrayal of ideals, then, is to create a racial fantasy out of the scraps and pain of his failed farming career and his lost love.

Robert Ball Anderson's *From Slavery to Affluence* reads much like Micheaux's *The Conquest*, except that Anderson began his life in slavery. Not unlike many other ex-slaves' autobiographical narratives, Anderson's story relates his early life as a slave, his escape from the plantation, and his establishment as a landowner and self-sufficient American citizen. Though Anderson spent the majority of his life as a westerner, fully 70 percent of Anderson's memoirs relates his experiences as a slave. After his master's wife arbitrarily beat him one time too many, Anderson turned the whip on her. Soon thereafter, Anderson slipped from the plantation to sign up with the Union army. He joined the 125th Colored Infantry in Kentucky in the fall of 1864 but saw no action during the Civil War due to the surrender by the South six months later. He was then transferred to Missouri and after that Kansas, where he belonged to one of the troops of Buffalo Soldiers that "correlled [sic] the Indians on their reservation" (Anderson 44). He was mustered out in the late summer of 1867 in Missouri and then discharged with his company soon thereafter in Louisville, Kentucky.

The title of Anderson's memoirs, *From Slavery to Affluence*, denotes a story of success, an economic movement and progressive vitality. By the end of the 1920s, Anderson was the largest black landowner in Nebraska, working 2,080 acres valued at $75,000 (as well as owning two tractors, a truck, and various machinery). While Micheaux's *The Conquest* reveals a kind of western failure that he shores up as a triumph of spirit in his later productions, Anderson's autobiography paints a picture of African American accomplishment. He writes near the end of *From Slavery to Affluence*, "A slave at the age of twenty, penniless at the age of forty-five, I am a rich man today" (58). But by the time of his death in 1930, Anderson's affluence had become fleeting and unstable. His property had remained mortgaged throughout his life, and just eight months before he died he deeded his property, mortgage and all, to his wife Daisy (Wax, "Robert Ball Anderson" 185–86).

Anderson's memoir, while following the structure of many slave narratives, presents the West as a land of opportunity. He offers his life not only as an inspirational story for African Americans but as a vision of success for western homesteaders more generally. Anderson became familiar with the West during his tenure with the military in Kansas, Missouri, Texas, and New Mexico. Later, finding himself dissatisfied with working for wages, Anderson embraced the ideal that farming provided a more authentic work experience and an ideal alternative to wage labor. He writes, "The idea of owning my land and being independent had been given me while I was in the army, and I was never able to get rid of it" (51). Thus Anderson took a homestead in Nebraska, where he improved his land (according to the rather ludicrous provisions of the Timber Culture Act[17]) and became a member of the burgeoning community of northwestern Nebraska, particularly in the towns of Nonpareil and Hemingford.

Anderson closes his narrative by celebrating his friendships: "[I] cannot help but feel that every one in Box Butte County, and western Nebraska, regardless of color, is my friend and I am proud of it" (58–59). While evidence points to Anderson's general popularity, he remained demarcated as a unique or unconventional Nebraskan. In a study of Anderson's life, Darold Wax writes that local papers, when noting the activities of local farmers, employed not only the patronizing moniker "Uncle Bob" when referring to Anderson but also "Zip Coon," the nineteenth-century minstrel construction that mocked urban blacks with middle-class pretenses ("Robert Ball Anderson" 180). Anderson was generally well liked, but, as Wax points out, for some of his neighbors his affability meant that he "was a first class nigger" (quoted in Wax, "Robert Ball Anderson" 178).[18]

Twenty years before Anderson cranked out his brief memoir of Nebraskan success on the *Hemingford Ledger*'s press, Nat Love, also an ex-slave, self-published his life story, effusively entitled *The Life and Adventures of Nat Love, Better Known in the Cattle Country as "Deadwood Dick," By Himself, A True History of Slavery Days, Life on the Great Cattle Ranges and on the Plains of the "Wild and Wooly" West, Based on the Facts, and Personal Experiences of the Author*. Love's narrative begins with his childhood memories of a plantation in Tennessee. Much younger than Anderson, Love focuses his pre–Civil War recollections on boyhood games and tricks, though he reserves enough space to discuss the beatings, whippings, and sale of slaves around him by "the perfect devils in human form, men who delighted in torturing the black human beings, over whom chance and accident of birth had placed them" (11–13).

Love does not know his birthdate, echoing the beginning of numerous other slave narratives, but his story soon mutates from a slave narrative to a blueprint for *The Virginian*. Free after the Civil War, Love wandered west through Kansas, Texas, and into New Mexico Territory as a cowhand, landing his first job after proving his abilities at breaking horses. Love's West, like Micheaux's, is colorblind. His narrative holds itself together with references to "the boys," his range-riding companions who bond through a kind of masculine loyalty based on gender and labor identity. *The Life and Adventures* abounds with Love's references to "duty": to move cattle, to hunt down rustlers, or even to obey his bosses. Indeed, literary critic Blake Allmendinger writes, "*The Life and Adventures* reads less like an ex-slave narrative and more like a cowboy autobiography" (*Ten Most Wanted* 21). With the demise of the great cattle ranges and trails after the 1880s, many cowboys, Love included, cashed in on their experiences by writing autobiographies, giving to the (generally eastern) public the mythic stories of a great and free land where one slept under the stars and truly owned one's own labor.[19] In fact, Love closes his autobiography with a list of distinctly—if stereotypically—western pleasures:

> The wild and free life. The boundless plains. The countless thousands of longhorn steers, the wild fleet footed mustangs. The buffalo and other game, the Indians, the delight of living, the fights against death that caused our every nerve to tingle, and the every day communion with men, whose minds were as broad as the plains they roamed, and whose creed was every man for himself and every friend for each other, and with each other till the end. (161–62)

The Life and Adventures takes Love from the plantation and instills him into a mythology that refuses the structural conditions of most African Americans in the United States at the turn of the century. Love becomes much like Roosevelt's cowboy statesmen, prevailing through common sense, antipathy toward danger, and masculine camaraderie (figure 10).

Love writes his narrative so as to highlight his experience not as an African American man in the West but as a raceless cowboy on the colorblind frontier. He glosses over any injustices done to African Americans and, rather than critique his white trail bosses, he turns his animosity toward Native Americans and Mexicans, invoking racist epithets such as "demons" (42), "bucks" (42, 58, 65), "red devils" (65), and "greasers" (57, 75, 150). After a seemingly random and unprovoked attack on Love and his compatriots by an unspecified group of Indians, Love crows, "Holley was the only man killed on our side though a few of the Indians were made better as the result of it" (65). Unlike Micheaux's presentation of racial isolation in the West, Love does not cast himself as a lone black cowboy; in fact, upon approaching an outfit in Dodge City when initially looking for work, Love tells the reader quite specifically, "There were several colored cow boys [sic] among them, and good ones too" (41). Regardless, his references to black cowboys come few and far between in *The Life and Adventure*, while his racial epithets for other non-whites flow quite easily.

Although Love generally ignores his own racial significance in the region, he provides distinctly racial narratives as bookends to his western adventures: he opens his autobiography as a slave on a Tennessee plantation and closes with a discussion of his life as a Pullman porter, a distinctly African American

FIGURE 10 Nat Love as
Deadwood Dick. The caption
to this photo in *The Life and
Adventures* reads "In My
Fighting Clothes." Denver
Public Library, Western His-
tory Collection, Z-147.

profession at the turn of the twentieth century (figure 11). Love's West may
have been relatively colorblind, a space concerned more with labor than color,
but once out of this environment Love's career choices became clearly limited
by his skin color. With the end of the open range by the 1890s, many cowboys
turned to the railroads for new work, and thus Love's career transition mirrors the career changes of many of his cowhand companions. Love paints his
new work as a porter as once again instrumental to the opening, expansion,
and subjugation of the western landscape to human progress; he ultimately
swells so immensely with pride over the landscapes he has traversed by rail
that he concludes his penultimate chapter, *fortissimo*, with "America, I love
thee, Sweet land of Liberty, home of the brave and the free" (147). Yet the
home of the brave and the free provided limited career opportunities for
Love, who remained in his position as many white associates from his cowhand days moved easily into higher positions as railroad managers, conduc-

FIGURE 11 Nat Love as Pull-
man Porter. The caption to
this photo in *The Life and Ad-
ventures* reads "This is Where I
Shine. Now I am Out for the
Money." From Nat Love, *The
Life and Adventures of Nat Love*,
(New York: Arno Press, 1968).

tors, supervisors, and passenger agents (Love 149). Nowhere in his autobiography does Love comment on this inequality.

The style of Love's narrative and his adeptness at creating a larger-than-
life image of himself as a western character ultimately made him famous as
Deadwood Dick, a nickname supposedly given to him in 1876 after he won a
roping contest at a rodeo in Deadwood, South Dakota. But a fictional Deadwood Dick also appeared in thirty-three Beadle and Adams dime novels, the
first fittingly entitled *Deadwood Dick, The Prince of the Road: or, The Black Rider
of the Black Hills* (1877). This fictitious Deadwood Dick roamed the West ad-
venturing, wooing, and doing good deeds in *Deadwood Dick's Doom; or,
Calamity Jane's Last Adventure, a Tale of Death Notch* (1881), *Deadwood Dick's
Dream; or, The Rivals of the Road* (1881), and *Deadwood Dick's Protégée: or, Baby
Hess, The Girl Gold Miner* (1887), among others. Ninety-seven more Beadle
and Adams novels related the adventures of his son, Deadwood Dick Jr., in

such adventures as *Deadwood Dick, Jr. in Chicago: or, The Anarchist's Daughter* (1888). Whether Nat Love inspired the Deadwood Dick character or was merely knighted with the dime novels' moniker remains unclear, as only Love's narrative verifies the christening of his nickname.[20] By 1907, when Love published his autobiography, he had obviously internalized the fictional Deadwood Dick as an image of himself, professing, "I was not the blood thirsty savage and all around bad man many writers have pictured me in their romances, yet I was wild, reckless and free, afraid of nothing . . . with a wide knowledge of the cattle country and the cattle business and of my guns with which I was getting better acquainted with every day, and not above taking my whiskey straight or returning bullet for bullet in a scrimmage" (70).

Though Love left his cowboy life in 1889 to work for the railroad, he did not publish his narrative until 1907. Given the popularity of the other cowboy narratives, especially Owen Wister's stories, Love likely attempted to ride the wave of popularity for remembering a West of cowboys and gunfights now beyond the western horizon. Love's *Life and Adventures* disappeared early in the twentieth century but has reappeared in numerous forms from various publishers over the last thirty-five years, celebrated as a story of black self-made success. Beginning in 1968, Arno Press republished Love's autobiography for a number of years, seemingly in concert with a sudden surge of interest in black cowboys, particularly in the juvenile market. In 1965, Philip Durham and Everett L. Jones published *The Negro Cowboys*, a relatively uncomplicated history with a chapter devoted to Love, as well as a children's book entitled *The Adventures of the Negro Cowboys*. A year after the Arno edition, Harold W. Felton published *Nat Love, Negro Cowboy*, also aimed at children.

On this sudden interest in black cowboys, Blake Allmendinger writes, "low culture's minions have hog-tied [Love's autobiography], confining the retelling of Love's story to the pages of coloring books and short stories," which, he argues, could be in response to the aggressive activist prose of African Americans during the Civil Rights era ("Deadwood Dick" 87). Following Allmendinger's argument, we might also argue that the reappearance of Love's autobiography and its celebration in the late 1960s sought to quell charged racial sentiments of black separatism and social redress through its conciliatory narrative of one individual's success in a land where color mattered little compared to the role of labor: "It was our duty to save the cattle, and every thing else was of secondary importance" (Love 54).[21] In 1995, the University of Nebraska Press republished Love's *Life and Adventures* with an introduction by Brackette F. Williams that vacillates between criticism of Love's racism and a celebration of his ability to tell the "quintessential American tale. . . . [The kind of] tales we hear as we sit around family gatherings wondering what ever happened to ole So-and-So" (Williams xviii). Williams understands the importance of hearing this voice of an African American cowboy, though he simultaneously apologizes for Love's racism and presents him as an all-American—and racially transparent—Western hero. The publication—and republication—of *The Life and Adventures* sheds light not only on Love's life and the African American experience in the West, but on the cultural milieu of each publishing moment as well.

ALPENGLOW OR DUST:
AFRICAN AMERICAN AUTOBIOGRAPHY IN CONTEXT

Fundamentally, each of these writers presents different relationships to the issue of race in the American West. For example, both Anderson and Love produce autobiographies that begin with their lives as slaves. Following the examples of Benjamin Franklin in his *Autobiography of Benjamin Franklin* and Frederick Douglass in *The Narrative of the Life of Frederick Douglass*, Anderson and Love tell the stories of their self-made lives and their successes at overcoming the hardships of their youth. Anderson shows a clear awareness of the peculiarity of his race in the Nebraska farmland, even closing his narrative with the sage advice of a stranger in a strange land: "I always try to attend to my own business and never interfere with any one else" (59). But Love consistently refuses race as a category, and once past his descriptions of plantation injustices he actively ignores the potential differences between himself and the other cowboys, many of whom went on to positions in other industries that Love could never attain due to race.

Primarily, the more thoroughly these African American westerners embraced the myths of western self-sufficiency and social advancement through hard work and merit, the less likely race was to play a critical part in their narratives. Detter focuses quite closely on the injustices African Americans have endured in the West and in the United States more generally, and in doing so he never once portrays the West as holding special opportunities for African Americans. Contrastingly, Micheaux, who advocated in many of his works (both novels and films) that African Americans look westward for prosperity and justice, quite clearly painted the West and its tillable land as potentially colorblind.

Through these self-published and mainly autobiographical works, these African American westerners could create idealized identities that straddled the lines between racial identification and western mythologies. By melding together the issues of racism and African American equality with a western ideology of freedom, progress, and democratic principles, these writers collectively produce a cultural narrative that lies between nationalist unity and essentialist separation. Undoubtedly, Love's cowboy autobiography most uncritically accepts the precepts of western progress such as Manifest Destiny, while Anderson's story—also the autobiography of an ex-slave—tends toward an exposition of racial injustices, especially when coupled with his wife's narrative. Micheaux, like Love in his descriptions of slavery, reserves much of his criticism of racism for eastern environs, thus leaving the West open as a potential space for race equality. Micheaux also internalizes the western ideal of freedom through land ownership (an ideal implicit in Anderson's book) and claims that agricultural improvement may prove to be the race leveler in this country. Detter is more clearly implicated in race politics than these other authors, given his role as a journalist for African American publications on the Pacific Coast. But Detter's foray into fiction with "Nellie Brown" complicates an easy reading of his vision by recreating a narrative of paternalist slave owners and their obedient and obsequious slaves. Within Detter's writings from Idaho and his reminiscences of eastern racism, though, his sense of western intolerance and racist segregation reveals a western America very different from Love's cowboys or even Micheaux's helpful neighbors.

Numerous other self-published books and pamphlets from western African Americans exist beyond the ones discussed here. Some resemble Anderson's narrative (or his theirs), such as William Robinson's 1913 *From Log Cabin to Pulpit; or Fifteen Years in Slavery* (published in Wisconsin). Others demand that the author's voice, the voice of the ordinary black citizen, be heard, such as Garland Anderson's San Francisco success story from 1925, *From Newsboy to Bellhop to Playwright*, or George Washington Jackson's *A Brief History of the Life and Works of G. W. Jackson; Forty-Five Years Principal of the G. W. Jackson High School, Corsicana, Texas* (Corsicana, 1938), or a book whose title tells all, Ide D. Nash's *Bootlegging a Failure and a Lecture to Young Men: My Prison Experience in Oklahoma* (Hugo, Oklahoma, 1918). Certainly the autobiographical mode was a popular form of written expression among African American westerners, though not necessarily any more so than among their white counterparts. Throughout the West in the beginning of the twentieth century, and continuing today, westerners have felt that autobiography tells the truth of their hardships in subduing and domesticating the harsh western soil. A brief perusal of any western bibliography will turn up autobiographical tales of pioneering and place, such as Millie Jones Porter's *Memory cups of Panhandle pioneers: A belated attempt at Panhandle history, with special emphasis on Wheeler county and her relations to the other counties in the long ago as told by the few remaining old times and the records* (Clarendon, Texas: Clarendon Press, 1945) or Solomon Alexander Wright's *My rambles as east Texas cowboy, hunter, fisherman, tie-cutter* (Austin, Texas: Texas Folklore Society, 1942). In fact, the popularity of this motif in the West has not yet faded, as is evidenced by recent publications such as John W. Kolness and Bryan Jacobson's *Hard Times and Strange Tales: True Adventures of Life in Eastern North Dakota and Western Minnesota* (Hendrum, Minnesota: Heritage Publications, 1999). Besides the hardship of pioneering and breaking the supposedly "free land" of the American West, these writers, black and white alike, insist that their memories represented a kind of epitaph to the West; they had seen the western sun set on a distinctly American era of homesteading, cowboying, individual freedom, and development. Complicit with this myth of western progress, these autobiographies rarely mention western genocide, ecological devastation, poverty, or labor unrest, all significant elements of the history of the development of the American West. These autobiographies, including those of Micheaux, Anderson, and Love, work in concert with the American myth of westward progress to paint a picture of the West as a land of endless possibilities now gone.

But for western African Americans, the autobiographical form provided a forum for voices that might get lost in the sea of pioneering white noise. The West was not colorblind, as we can see from these autobiographies—the successful Anderson remained known as "Uncle Bob." Without these self-published black voices, the history of the African American presence in the West would literally fade. Self-publication sometimes provided the only outlet for these voices as eastern publishers found little interest in western stories, especially those that might complicate racially unified notions about both the geographic space of the West as well as the process of U.S. expansion. While the voices of white pioneers—the memoirs of grandmothers and ranchers and cousins to Billy the Kid's saddlemaker—tend to recreate the dominant political ideology of the Old West, these voices of western African American homesteaders, cowboys, high school principals, lawbreakers, and—like most self-published autobiographers—generally ordinary citizens, complicate our narrative of this ideologically significant region. Though Detter, Micheaux, Anderson, and Love produced divergent accounts of the African American experience in the West, they collectively form a spectrum of perspectives that helps us to understand the limits and possibilities of the mythic West.

4

THE MAKING OF AMERICANS

ASSIMILATION AND MORMON LITERATURE
OF THE MID-TWENTIETH CENTURY

IN 1858, A YOUNG U.S. Army assistant surgeon named Roberts Bartholow found himself stationed forty miles south of Salt Lake City at dusty Camp Floyd, the hastily erected garrison for roughly three thousand U.S. Army troops sent to quell a rumored Mormon insurrection. From this position Bartholow was able to observe Mormon culture—and of particular interest to him, Mormon physiology—and send along these observations to the surgeon general with his otherwise rather bland "sanitary reports" concerning the health of his division of the army (see Bush Jr. 61–62). In 1860, Bartholow's assessment of Utah Mormons appeared in a Senate Executive Document from the Surgeon General of the Army's office, where he claimed that "The yellow, sunken, cadaverous visage; the greenish colored eyes; the thick, protuberant lips; the low forehead; the light yellowish hair; and the lank, angular person— constitute an appearance so characteristic of the new race, the production of polygamy, as to distinguish them at a glance." For Bartholow, Mormon polygamy, a practice that Mormon leaders had publically advocated only eight years earlier, had produced a new race of people, the mark of their peculiarity carried in their physiognomy. Separating Mormons from other Americans, Bartholow continued, "The women of this territory, how fanatical and ignorant soever, recognize their wide departure from the normal standard in all Christian countries, and from the degradation of the mother follows that of the child" (quoted in Bancroft 587 n. 39). Following from his observations, Bartholow concluded that "if Mormonism received no addition from outside sources, these influences continuing, it is not difficult to see that it would eventually die out" (quoted in Bancroft 777 n. 13). Clearly Mormonism posed no threat to "Christian countries" like the United States, since Mormons' enervating nature would soon extinguish the problem itself. Certainly Bartholow was mistaken in both his Lamarckian observations and his discounting of the perceived threat Mormons posed to American identity over the course of the next one hundred years. Indeed, as late as 1911 journalist Alfred Henry Lewis wrote in a *Cosmopolitan Magazine* series entitled "The Viper on the Hearth," "[Mormonism] lies coiled on the country's hearthstone, and asks only time to grow and collect a poison and a strength to strike" (439).

Yet, as literary critic Terryl L. Givens notes, present-day Mormon Americans are almost caricatures of ideal U.S. citizens: "[Today] 'Mormon' can occasionally serve as shorthand for a certain vision of mainstream American values typified by healthy, patriotic, family-centered living" (7). Indeed, in 2004 there were five U.S. senators and twenty-one representatives who identified themselves as Mormon. One of them, Orrin Hatch, a longstanding conservative senator from Utah, even made a presidential bid in 1999. Mormons have become important figures not only in U.S. politics, but also in American sports (Steve Young of the 49ers, Olympic wrestler Rulon Gardner) and entertainment (Gladys Knight, the Osmonds, Randy Turner, Sharlene Wells Hawkes [Miss America 1985]). Over the course of the twentieth century, American Mormons clearly shifted their identity from reviled outsiders to model American citizens.

This chapter will explore this transformation within the establishment of Mormon literature. Speculative Mormon literature did not appear until near the turn of the century (barring a few fictional didactic departures such as early Mormon convent Parley P. Pratt's "A Dialogue Between Joseph Smith and the Devil" [1844]). This new addition to the Mormon artistic canon, therefore, was created almost wholly within the period in which Mormons sought cultural alliance with the nation. We can thus use this literature, some of which Mormon leaders actively rejected as unrepresentative, to follow the development of Mormon historical narratives as Mormon authors constructed stories to fit American standards and to track the strain of Mormon assimilation into a larger—and more secular—American society. Mormon literature of this early period tends to meditate primarily on the function of polygamy in collective Mormon identity as well as its role in complicating Mormons' cultural acceptance into the nation. To this end, certain novels— almost all written by women—explore polygamous relations by expounding on the hardships of Mormon women in polygamous families. These novels often present Mormon men as rising above familial tensions, leaving Mormon women to suffer from polygamy's collective consequences. Other novels—

generally written by men—rewrite Mormons' westward movement as a masculine Mormon epic, highlighting Mormons' pioneer qualities. Echoing Turner's proclamation that "the frontier has gone, and with its going has closed the first period of American history ("Significance" 60), these authors conclude their narratives with the Mormon disavowal of polygamy at the end of nineteenth century, thus participating in a molting of Mormon peculiarity and assimilation into U.S. national culture.

Mormonism began as a distinctly American religion, rising from the Burned-Over District of New York State in the late 1820s. Formally established in 1830 by Joseph Smith, the Church of Jesus Christ of Latter-day Saints boasted a membership of over two hundred and fifty thousand in 1896, the year of Utah's statehood.[1] Mormons played an immensely important role in the development of the American West and today are generally hailed by both gentiles (in the Mormon lexicon, "gentile" denotes all non-Mormons) and American Mormons themselves as exemplars of an American pioneer spirit. From Joseph Smith's hardscrabble roots in rural New England to the establishment of blooming desert cities, the Mormon narrative appears as one of success through hard work, self-sufficiency, and a dedication to ideals. Indeed, throughout the latter half of the nineteenth century, Mormons traveled overland to Utah in wagons and on foot—sometimes even pushing handcarts full of their belongings—symbolizing to many people the pioneer gumption seemingly inherent in the United States's westward expansion.

But in truth Mormons were chased across the continent by bigoted citizens who found the Mormon brand of Christianity and communitarianism troubling. In 1838, Missouri governor Lilburn Boggs issued an executive order declaring that "The Mormons must be treated as enemies and *must be exterminated* or driven from the state" (quoted in Givens 26, emphasis in original). Three days later, Missouri vigilantes killed seventeen Mormons at Haun's Mill, including a ten-year-old boy they found hiding behind a stove. After establishing a thriving city at Nauvoo, Illinois, almost ten thousand Mormons were forced across the frozen Mississippi after the state withdrew the city's charter and nearby settlements suffered from renewed and regular vigilante violence. Only eighteen months earlier, a mob killed Joseph Smith and his brother while they were supposedly being held safely in a jail in Carthage, Illinois, twenty miles from Nauvoo. Following this chain of violence, Brigham Young and his followers chose to settle at the edge of a massive salt lake in an inhospitable desert valley only because they thought the United States government and its citizens might simply overlook them once outside national boundaries. But even in this dry, alkali valley, which became U.S. soil only a year after the first Mormon companies arrived there, legislative assaults and military threats against Mormons increased. One-half of the nation's standing army marched against Utah Mormons in 1857 in the fizzled, embarrassing, and bloodless Utah War. In 1887 the Edmunds-Tucker Act stripped Mormon women of their voting rights, which they had held since 1870, and disenfranchised male Mormons who refused to denounce the church's polygamous practices.[2] This same legislation divested the LDS Church of all but $50,000 of its assets, including many of its buildings and properties.

These relentless physical, legal, and cultural assaults eventually led the LDS Church to capitulate to the demands of the nation at the end of the nineteenth century. Though this capitulation allowed for the reinstatement of Mormon suffrage (legally for Utah's women and effectively for Mormon men), the release of many imprisoned polygamous LDS leaders, and eventual statehood for Utah, Mormons as a people—the vipers on the hearth—remained reviled in American culture. Throughout the latter half of the nineteenth century, Mormons shared the stage in nineteenth-century political cartoons with caricatures of African Americans, Native Americans, and Chinese Americans, minority groups seen as troublesome to U.S. national identity (figure 12). In the twentieth century, these association were hard to shake. In response, the LDS Church began an aggressive policy of assimilation into a secular and pluralistic American society, shaping their imagery and history in order to secure acceptance.[3] Primarily, Mormons sought to embrace and highlight their historical self-sufficiency and self-determination such that these things might mark them as western citizens and thus model Americans. By dropping their earmarks of difference, at least publicly, they could join the nation by proving their adherence to the tropes of the American West that helped to define U.S. national culture in the early twentieth century. Through a careful restructuring of identity, American Mormons narrated a shift from persecuted outsiders to a people who most embody an American pioneer sensibility.

DEVALUING MORMON HISTORY

We cannot extract Mormon history from American history, nor can we write American history of the nineteenth and early twentieth centuries without considering the impact of Mormon culture, society, and religion on the forma-

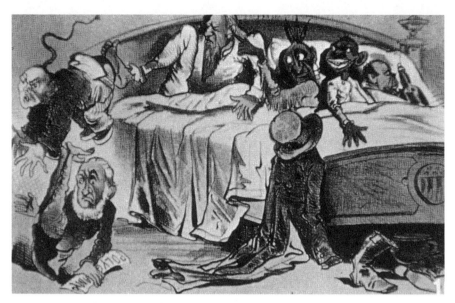

FIGURE 12 "Uncle Sam's Troublesome Bedfellows." Originally published in *The Wasp*, February 8, 1879.

tion of the United States as a cohesive nation. More so, we cannot consider the place of the American West in the process of nation formation without considering the Mormon presence there. Yet discussions of the Mormons' role in American cultural history rarely appear outside of scholarly circles dominated by Mormon intellectuals and academics. This paucity of broad-based discussions of Mormons' influence on the formation of national consciousness may say more about the nature and depth of religious and cultural prejudice in the (non-Mormon) American academy than about the importance—or seeming irrelevance—of the Mormon presence in American culture.

Mormons, even during their most intense period of estrangement from the United States, appeared outwardly akin to the rest of white middle-class America. They fervently followed the pioneer ethics that so defined American exceptionalism throughout the twentieth century. They were ardent churchgoers as well as prudent and successful capitalists. They engaged in Victorian morality in terms of sexual relations (save for the existence of polygamy itself) and day-to-day social etiquette. Unlike the other minorities struggling for recognition, one could not identify a Mormon walking by on the sidewalk in any large nineteenth-century American city (Bartholow's observations notwithstanding). Mormons of the nineteenth and early twentieth centuries looked, acted, dressed, spoke, and shopped much like the rest of middle-class America, and as farmers, businessmen, religious leaders, shopkeepers, wives, or mothers could pass for their non-Mormon counterparts anywhere in the United States. Mormons' general cultural sensibilities made them quite familiar by American middle-class standards, yet their polygamous history framed them as alien and their tendency toward theocracy marked them as distinctly undemocratic. With the effective undoing of both of these problematic markers of identity, Mormons began to fit cleanly into models of white, middle-class, American nationalism. Without a clear sense of any racial, ethnic, or cultural difference, the Mormons' influence on American national consciousness seemed negligible within contemporary models of American nationalism. Thus gentile scholars easily ignored the Mormon presence and their complicated contribution to American national character.

However, the impulse to remove Mormon history from the story of national cultural formation stems not only from gentile Americanist scholars, but also from the Mormon community itself. By the end of the nineteenth century, with the Mormon Church officially denouncing polygamy and the acceptance of Utah as the forty-fifth state of the Union, Mormon leaders were poised to present themselves as upstanding U.S. citizens fully immersed within the national culture. By attempting to shed their status as a "peculiar people," a label given to them in the nineteenth century, Mormons themselves contributed to the downplaying of their own history. Likely in reaction to its overexposure during the second half of the nineteenth century, the Mormon Church proceeded to step back from the public eye in the early twentieth century, advocating that its members look inward for identification through church-sanctioned activities and channels while quietly presenting itself to the rest of the nation as patriotic, entrepreneurial, and morally conservative—all positions endearing to U.S. national culture of the time. By keeping out of the limelight, Mormons believed that they could begin to rid themselves of the baggage that so burdened them during the nineteenth century, thus allowing for a greater— and more expedient—acceptance into the broader fabric of American culture.

THE GREAT ACCOMMODATION

A period in Mormon history termed the Great Accommodation began in 1890 with LDS Church president Wilford Woodruff's proclamation that the Mormon Church would not sanction polygamous marriages (see Gottlieb and Wiley 13–19). This pronouncement, known as the Woodruff Manifesto, arrived only after three decades of federal persecution of Utah Mormons, including military action by the U.S. Army and legislative attacks by the U.S. Congress.[4] The issuance of the Woodruff Manifesto constituted a turning point in terms of the LDS Church's relationship with not only the federal government but the U.S. gentile public. In a succinct, five-paragraph document, Woodruff effectively rearranged Mormon society internally as well as with respect to the nation as a whole. Defensively, Woodruff opened the manifesto with an allegation of false reports of church-sanctioned polygamous marriages, indicating that the LDS Church in fact had abided by federal law in disallowing such ceremonies:

> Press dispatches having been sent for political purposes, from Salt Lake City, which have been widely published, to the effect that the Utah Commission, in their recent report to the Secretary of the Interior, allege that plural marriages are still being solemnized and that forty or more such marriages have been contracted in Utah since last June or during the past year, also that in public discourses the leaders of the Church have taught, encouraged and urged the continuance of the practice of polygamy.

In careful words, Woodruff refutes these reports and then establishes the future adherence by the LDS Church and its members to both federal legislation and the more mainstream American sentiment with regard to matrimony:

> I, therefore, as President of the Church of Jesus Christ of Latter-day Saints, do hereby, in the most solemn manner, declare that these charges are false. We are not teaching polygamy or plural marriage, nor permitting any person to enter into its practice. . . . Inasmuch as laws have been enacted by Congress forbidding plural marriages, which laws have been pronounced constitutional by the court of last resort, I hereby declare my intention to submit to those laws, and to use my influence with the members of the Church over which I preside to have them do likewise. There is nothing in my teachings to the Church or in those of my associates, during the time specified, which can be reasonably construed to inculcate or encourage polygamy. . . . And I now publicly declare that my advice to the Latter-day Saints is to refrain from contracting any marriage forbidden by the law of the land. (*Doctrine and Covenants* 291–92)

The Woodruff Manifesto not only became representative of new church doctrine for Utah Mormons, but it also served as an extremely successful public relations device that allowed Utah to finally win its bid for statehood in 1896, a petition that had begun in 1849, just two years after the arrival of the first Mormon settlers. Through the manifesto, Utah and the LDS Church moved toward unification with the nation and curbed their identification as a rebel territory that continually abnegated federal laws as well as generally accepted American social (and religious) principles.

To prove Utah's adherence to national moral standards, the Utah state constitution quite specifically disallows polygamous marriages. In an "Address to the People of Utah" found at the beginning of the state constitution, the framers declare, "We have inhibited for all time polygamous or plural marriages" (Vexler 30). Within the constitution itself, article 24, section 2, states quite specifically that "The act of the Governor and Legislative Assembly of the Territory of Utah, entitled, 'An act to punish polygamy and other kindred offenses,' approved February 4th, A.D. 1892 . . . is hereby declared to be in force in the State of Utah," while article 3, section 1 (on religious tolerance) explicitly states that "polygamous or plural marriages are forever prohibited."[5] Such specificity in a state constitution on the contentious issue of polygamy and its attendant religious overtones presents a political advance (as opposed to a religious concession) toward denying the presence of divine authority in Utah's government, thus allowing Mormon Utah a place in the secular American Union.[6]

Over the first few decades of the twentieth century, Mormon society looked inward for inspiration against an expanding and pluralist American society while simultaneously extending its religious administration into parts of the country outside of Utah and eventually outside of the United States.[7] Besides these essentially spiritual endeavors, the LDS Church also involved itself heavily in local business ventures, allying itself with numerous industries. During the first few decades after the Woodruff Manifesto, the LDS Church owned or held major shares in Zion's Cooperative Mercantile Institution, Utah Light and Power (which eventually merged with Consolidated Railway and Power to form Utah Light and Railway, a virtual monopoly on electricity generation and street railways in the area), Utah-Idaho Sugar Company, Amalgamated Sugar Company, Beneficial Life Insurance Company, Hotel Utah, and Zion's First National (bank). High-level Mormons (often the president of the church) headed almost all of these business ventures. Clearly, by the early twentieth century the LDS Church had become much more than just a religious institution. Now a formidable business force, it maintained a built-in local clientele and fostered corporate boards tied together commercially as well as civically and spiritually (see Alexander 74–92).

By the 1940s, when self-identified (as opposed to church-sanctioned) Mormon authors began to appear, Mormon life in Utah was in a great state of flux. During the 1920s and 1930s, many Mormons left Utah for (quite literally) greener pastures in the East and California. Not unlike other rural parts of the country, young people in the Great Basin turned to cities for better opportunities and left rural and agricultural vocations behind. By the 1940s, the Mormon Church seemed potentially a kind of American oddity left out in the arid desert. Mormon culture changed as the grandchildren of (often polygamous) Mormon pioneers cast their identities within the context of American nationalism rather than apart from it. After almost a century of community building based on exclusiveness and separation (combined with their forced exoduses), Utah Mormons began to expand their world outside of a religious nationalism. They no longer could—or needed to—separate themselves from the rest of the nation. In response to secular pressures, however, the LDS Church asked its members to grasp more tightly the social world prescribed by church authorities and to join only LDS Church–ordained institutions, even as it sought more general ideological absorption into the nation (Alexander 135). While the Mormon community in nineteenth-century Utah strove for a cohesive and monocultural articulation of their society, Utah Mormons during the first half of the twentieth century found themselves simultaneously pulled outward by an expanding secular society and inward by church forces demanding adherence to doctrine and custom.

ORIGINS OF MORMON FICTION

Overall, the tradition of Mormon writing stemmed from the construction of the Mormon community experience throughout the nineteenth century. Most Mormon prose from the nineteenth century focused on prescriptive or edifying tropes that sought to strengthen church members' attachment to the ideals and guidelines of the Mormon Church. Poetry and hymns, in particular, could be consumed and internalized by entire communities and then shared at moments of communal and collective stress, of which there was no lack for nineteenth-century Mormons. Autobiography, as a condensation of lived experiences into a narrative form, helped solidify Mormon communities by providing narratives of personal history that reaffirmed the collective psychological bonds established against late-nineteenth-century federal assaults. Essays were often tools for instruction and maintenance of Mormon religious and social ideals; discourses and addresses, including sermons and didactic speeches given at tabernacles or stake houses,[8] often instructed church members on the finer points of cosmology and everyday religious living. (Many of these early addresses are cataloged in the *Journal of Discourses*, a twenty-six-volume collection of stenographically recorded Mormon oratory spanning 1851 to 1877.)

Yet throughout the nineteenth and early twentieth centuries Mormons produced very little imaginative prose. In fact, no discussion of Mormon literature appears until 1888, in Apostle Orson F. Whitney's essay "Home Literature," published in the official LDS periodical *The Contributor*. In this essay, Whitney argues in a well-known phrase among Mormon literary critics that "We will yet have Miltons and Shakespeares of our own. . . . [God's] brightest spirits are held in reserve for the latter times" (Whitney 206). For Whitney, Mormon literary culture had not yet hit its zenith, but rather sat in preparation for such a time. Rationalizing this apparent quiet literary reserve, Whitney also argues that Mormon literature, "like all else with which we have to do, must be made subservient to the building up of Zion" (205), a seemingly sensible call for a people barely holding on to their church property at this time.

The Home Literature movement became the model by which church officials chose literature for publication within their serials, a model that continued for the church throughout the twentieth century (Geary, "Poetics" 15). The names of most of the authors of Home Literature have faded from bibliographic memory, as the purpose of this literature was not to extol individual authorship, but to build dogmatic narrative. Growing from Whitney's proposal, Home Literature mandated the creation of narratives that affirmed Mormon ideology and cosmology and celebrated Mormon habits and perspectives. In 1917, in the official church magazine *The Improvement Era*, Osborne J. P. Widtsoe (brother of *The Improvement Era* editor John A. Widtsoe) advised Mormon readers, "Read with the view and purpose of finding the message. . . . Read then, I repeat again, to discover the author's message; find that above all things; and though I may perhaps get myself into trouble by saying this, I will venture it, that if you find a book on the reading course which does not have a message . . . report it to the chairman of the reading course committee, and let him correct the evil" (quoted in Rees 22). Nephi Anderson, an early and widely read author of Home Literature, laid out the moralizing impulse to his fiction in his 1898 essay "Purposes in Fiction": "He who reaches the people, and the story writer does that, should not lose the opportunity of 'preaching.' . . . A good story is artistic preaching" (quoted in Esplin 17). Anderson's first novel, *Added Upon*, a wandering narrative of Mormon pre- and post-Earthly existence, has remained in print for over one hundred years, rivaling Wister's *The Virginian* for publishing longevity.

Today, even Mormon scholars see Home Literature as thematically narrow and ideologically limited. Mormon literary critic Edward Geary, for example, wrote in 1978, "[Home Literature] is not a powerful literature artistically, nor is it pure" ("Poetics" 15), capsizing Whitney's 1888 demand for "a literature of power and purity . . . proceed[ing] from a pure and powerful people" (Whitney 206). Another Mormon critic, Richard Cracroft, writes that Home Literature may represent "the Mormon penchant for the didactic," evidenced by the "sententious and vapid didacticism . . . [of] a plethora of predictable Mormon stories and poems" ("Didactic Heresy" 117, 131). Home Literature was almost always published in official church organs such as the *Contributor*, the *Young Women's Journal*, and *The Improvement Era* around the turn of the century.[9]

But the high point of Home Literature passed by the 1930s, when Mormon authors began to explore narratives outside the Mormon prescription; Mormon literature outside of didactic essays and Home Literature only emerged in the years between the world wars. Some scholars argue that during the late nineteenth century the Mormons' preoccupation with establishing the State of Deseret (which would reach to Oregon, Mexico, and the Sierra mountains) and defending themselves against legislative, military, and literary attacks on their culture and property prohibited the production of substantial fiction. Through the same logic, Mormons at the turn of the century were again too busy to produce literature as they busily rebuilt those same cultural and material institutions destroyed during the previous two decades. Then, as some scholars argue, Mormon culture was too caught up in World War I to produce any significant literature due to external political concerns; with the onset of the Great Depression, Mormon literature again foundered as would-be authors concentrated on producing the necessities of life rather than prose. But I would caution against this oft-cited logic.[10] First, such reasoning appears specious because the same scarcity of literary production did not occur in the rest of American culture. Second, an argument that prioritizes a primacy of materialist processes assumes that literature is social excess, a kind of lavish or exorbitant cultural product. Certainly within Mormon circles, and particularly ecclesiastical ones, this logic of "art as excess" held true. Church president George Q. Cannon wrote in 1884, "Novel reading has the same effect on the mind . . . as dram drinking or tea drinking has upon the body. It is a species of dissipation" (quoted in Cracroft, "Didactic Heresy" 119). But literature—though clearly not novels—in Mormon society performed a greater social task, namely the maintenance and propagation of religion. Literature per se was not frowned upon, only the sort of literature that did not speak directly to the importance of LDS religion and culture. Thus as LDS culture expanded into a pluralistic United States, a kind of expressive paralysis might have gripped potential authors, who could not yet articulate the bridge between Mormon and American identity.[11]

Social, economic, and political changes in Mormon culture during the first four decades of the twentieth century allowed for the appearance of a new Mormon literature that did not merely rehash Mormon faith or cosmology. Mormon writers during the late 1930s and 1940s sought to establish narratives that remained simultaneously Mormon and secular. They understood the importance of their Mormon culture but rejected the earlier necessity to reproduce doctrine in their imaginative prose. In fact, many Mormon novels of the late 1930s and 1940s display a sense that the peculiar nature of Mormon culture was dwindling. Sociologist Armand Mauss argues that in the latter half of the twentieth century the Mormon Church had "deliberately turned partially away from Americanization toward a policy of retrenchment in an apparent effort to stop (or slow down) the erosion of the unique Mormon identity" (131–32). Thus these authors sought to embrace secular American ideals while holding fast to their Mormon identify; to do so, their literature redefines Mormonism as a less peculiar Americanism by confronting the heritages of a threatening and problematic Mormon past.

With the pronouncement of Turner's closed frontier behind them and the historical import of polygamy dwindling, these authors sought to embrace parts of American identity that could prove their commitment to the nation. By looking closely at a number of Mormon novels whose narratives deal with both nineteenth- and early-twentieth-century Mormon issues, we can unravel the pull toward assimilation within an ostracized American religious group and can better understand both the forces of Americanization in the early part of the twentieth century and the cultural boundaries for the absorption of outsiders and minorities in the United States at this time.

The list of American Mormon writers from the mid-twentieth century is quite extensive—not necessarily so compared to numbers of other white American authors, but significant nonetheless for a religious group totaling only around one million members by the end of World War I. All of these authors had varying relationships with the LDS Church. Some were devout Mormons, while others were official apostates or remained clearly distant from the church. Certain writers, such as historian Fawn Brodie, were even excommunicated from the church for their prose. A rudimentary list of these midcentury authors includes Paul Bailey, Blanche Cannon, Vardis Fisher, Ardyth Kennelly, Lorene Pearson, Elinor Pryor, Richard Scowcroft, George Dixon Snell, Virginia Sorensen, Samuel Taylor, and Maurine Whipple. We can divide the works of these writers—whom Edward Geary calls the "lost generation," echoing the name bestowed upon American expatriate writers of the 1920s and 1930s ("Mormondom's" 26)—into three distinct categories by theme: those dealing directly with the thorny issue of polygamy; those composing historical epics; and those writing novels focusing on contemporary issues of Mormon culture and assimilation.

Almost all Mormon novels of this period center on Mormon history, incorporating important Mormon settings (Salt Lake City or Nauvoo, Illinois, for example) or significant Mormon events (the expulsion from Nauvoo or the Woodruff Manifesto). Certainly the most problematic aspect of Mormon history is the past practice of polygamy (also termed plural marriage), and most novelists of this period incorporate polygamy within their narratives in some form. Novels such as Maurine Whipple's *The Giant Joshua* (1941), Virginia Sorensen's *A Little Lower than the Angels* (1942), or Ardyth Kennelly's *The Peaceable Kingdom* (1949) place polygamy at the center of their narratives and explore the personal nature of these marriages beyond muckraking anti-Mormonism or church-sanctioned historical silence. Other novels, such as Sorensen's *The Evening and the Morning* (1949), allow polygamy to hover within family backgrounds of the narrative—informing but not sullying the contemporary Mormon identities they explore. A number of novels of this period strive to forge Mormon historical pageants, tracing Mormon history from the founding of the church to the issuance of the Woodruff Manifesto or Utah's statehood in 1896. Vardis Fisher's *Children of God: An American Epic* (1939) and George Dixon Snell's *Root, Hog, and Die* (1936) are essentially historical romances of the Mormon trek westward from Palmyra, New York, to the Salt Lake Valley, though Snell's conclusion, as we shall see, presents a rather strange twist to the standard conclusion of the Mormon narrative with the 1890 manifesto. These novels fictionalize Mormon history, placing fictive characters within a framework of easily recognizable Mormon leaders and events. A third group of novels focuses on concurrent social issues in Mormon culture of the 1940s. These novels, such as Virginia Sorensen's *On This Star* (1946) and the aforementioned *The Evening and the Morning* or Richard Scowcroft's *Children of the Covenant* (1945), directly interrogate the problem of Mormon culture as it fits into the mid-twentieth-century United States. I will not discuss this last collection of novels in detail here, as this study focuses primarily on the reshaping of Mormon history by midcentury Mormon authors. A single unifying characteristic of all Mormon novels of the mid-twentieth century is that they share and illuminate a common history through references to Joseph Smith, Smith's murder, polygamy, geographic deportation, Brigham Young, Wilford Woodruff, the LDS Church hierarchy and health code, and recognizable Intermountain West place names. These fictional enterprises meditate on the connections between Mormon culture and American culture more generally, assuming familiarity with Mormon references for both Mormon and non-Mormon readers alike. While the United States of the nineteenth century endeavored to expunge cultural differences through exclusion, twentieth-century Mormons sought to reintegrate themselves into this now supposedly unified national culture through an erasure of their peculiarity. Primarily, Mormon authors undertook this erasure with an exorcism through unveiling, particularly as that peculiarity appeared condensed in polygamy, or by conferring an *ur*-pioneer status upon Utah's founders and its early citizens.

EXORCIZING POLYGAMY

Maurine Whipple's *The Giant Joshua*, Virginia Sorensen's *A Little Lower than the Angels*, and Ardyth Kennelly's *The Peaceable Kingdom* provide examples of the ways in which Mormon novelists unveiled the peculiar past of Mormon polygamy. These novels exorcize an unwanted and shameful history by sketching narratives of nineteenth-century Mormon culture swept under the rug of assimilation during the fifty years following the Woodruff Manifesto. These novelists endeavored to speak a repressed history, engaging polygamous peculiarity so as to relegate it to the past. Combined with the social and material forces that pulled Mormons away from Utah and the Intermountain West, this Mormon literature aided in assimilation and gestured toward the withering away of Mormon cultural and social peculiarity near the middle of the twentieth century. These novels present fictionalized histories, calling forth and expelling the demons of polygamy so that Mormons could push on into the second half of the century as proud and untainted Americans.

All three of these novels build from historical bases, using archival as well as personal material for frameworks. Whipple's *The Giant Joshua* explores the fictional MacIntyre family within the historical setting of the development of Utah's Dixie (the southwest corner of present-day Utah); Sorensen's *A Little Lower than the Angels* centers around the life of the author's husband's great-grandmother in the nineteenth-century Mormon city of Nauvoo, Illinois; Kennelly's *The Peaceable Kingdom* retells the story of the second wife of Kennelly's grandfather. By providing authentic place names (St. George/Nauvoo/Salt Lake City), recognizable historical church figures (Erastmus Snow, John D. Lee, Brigham Young/Joseph Smith, Eliza Snow/Wilford Woodruff), and verifiable historical events (the Virgin River floods/expulsion from Nauvoo/the Woodruff Manifesto), these novelists effectively write historical fiction. Though these historical settings allow Mormon readers easy identification, non-Mormon readers can negotiate the historical terrain with little difficulty since the overarching narrative of westward U.S. expansion, within which Mormons played a primary role, rings familiar and even experientially accessible for many midcentury readers. The specifics of these narratives aim at painting Mormon history and Mormon characters for American audiences, not just Mormon audiences. The Mormon story here is told as a distinctly American tale—a pioneer tale—with the foible of polygamy exposed as a historical and cultural blip, not to be ignored, but to be contextualized and understood as no longer necessarily informing the future.

The Giant Joshua

Maurine Whipple wrote only one novel, *The Giant Joshua*, which was published by Houghton Mifflin in 1941.[12] *The Giant Joshua* is a sweeping epic of a single generation of the MacIntyre family, called by Brigham Young to settle St. George in southwestern Utah; the narrative centers around Clorinda Agatha, the third wife of Abijah MacIntyre, one of the men called by the church to lead the Dixie Mission, as the settlement was known. *The Giant Joshua* opens in 1861 with seventeen-year-old Clory married to Abijah MacIntyre and on her way to settle St. George under the charge of the Mormon Church. Sixteen years earlier, Clory's father had converted to the LDS Church in Philadelphia, baptized by Abijah himself. After Clory's mother rejects her husband's newfound religion, Clory's father leaves Philadelphia with his infant daughter and six-year-old son for the settlement of Winter Quarters, the Mormons' frigid and diseased home in Nebraska set up after hostile gentiles expelled them from Nauvoo in the dead of winter. In Winter Quarters Clory's father agrees to join the Mormon Battalion (the Mormon military contribution to the U.S. war with Mexico). He never returns, the victim of an Indian ambush on the Carson River, which leaves Clory and her brother under the guidance of Abijah MacIntyre and his first wife, Bathsheba. Later, en route to Utah, Clory's brother, Will, dies after eating a poisonous weed. By the time the young Clory reaches the Salt Lake Valley, she had become the MacIntyres' charge, if not ostensibly their daughter.

At the opening of the novel, Abijah has three wives: Bathsheba; Willie, who was originally a domestic for the MacIntyres; and, of recent marriage, Clory. The family also has six children, all from Bathsheba; the oldest child, Freeborn, is only a year younger than Clory. Abijah's three wives differ profoundly from each other. Bathsheba, the matriarch of the family, runs the household, attends to the children, and consistently reins in the power of the other two wives. Her physical stature and tenacity match her matriarchal role: "She was nearly six feet tall, broad of bosom and hip, strong and tireless as a good horse," (99) as well as "aggressive and efficient as a good sheep dog" (111). Willie, thirty-six years old as the MacIntyres enter St. George, is thin and diffident. She is "drab and unbelievably homely," her "pale eyes rimmed with stubby, colorless lashes" (6). Urged by Brigham Young to take a second wife, Abijah married Willie "because she had no home of her own and she was right there in the house" (6). Clory is young and free-spirited, frequently opposing Bathsheba's irritable and authoritative control. She is also clearly the most sexually appealing to Abijah.

Each of these three women acts as a particular sexual and maternal signifier within the narrative. Bathsheba is fertile and sensible, bearing six children and treating their upbringing with the kind of regular attention and devotion she bestows upon the weekly laundry. Willie, on the other hand, with a "scrawny neck, her bosom flat as a squaw track" (154), embodies physical barrenness and desolation—she has had "nothing but miscarriages all her life" (488) and dies from complications of the birth of her only child. Clory, the third point in this triad, is highly sexual—"fresh . . . glowing" and "ripe" (92, 492)—as well as emotionally irresponsible. Clory's sexuality, in fact, often drives Abijah into fits of rage as he finds that he cannot control Clory's spiritedness or his own sexual desires for her.

Though *The Giant Joshua* primarily outlines the settling of St. George, the establishment of this town and the advancement of the Mormon frontier merely provide a familiar pioneer setting upon which Whipple can sketch the troubled cultural history of nineteenth-century Mormonism. Clory remains at the center of the novel's drama, raising children, fighting for power with Bathsheba, and building her home in the southern desert. As the town grows and the Mormon toehold in southern Utah finds stability, Clory moves from her rough quarters of mud and canvas to a house of lumber and rock. The material changes in Clory's world match the transformation in the social and physical landscape of southern Utah as well as the unfolding of Mormon life in the United States more broadly.

But beneath this surface narrative of pioneer establishment, *The Giant Joshua* engages in an exposure and exorcism of the ghosts of polygamy and undertakes a clear critique of Mormon patriarchy. By bringing polygamous relations to the forefront of a novel about settling the West, Whipple undoes the narrative of darkness and peculiarity that shrouds Mormon history. Her characters speak to both Mormon and gentile audiences, thus attempting to literarily weave together disparate sensibilities. But Whipple does not write *The Giant Joshua* to defend her religion, much less Mormon history. *The Giant Joshua* does not answer the numerable anti-Mormon novels, plays, melodramas, and tracts from the late nineteenth and even early twentieth centuries.[13] She instead questions the principles of polygamy and particularly its effects on the wives of polygamous marriages. Whipple does not argue for the imminence of Mormon assimilation, but rather she constructs a distinctly Mormon narrative with reverent attention to the principles of the religion while deflating polygamy of its cultural charge as either blissful and untroubled or merely pathetic and unjust. The novel maintains the distinctiveness of Mormon identity (through its history) while claiming Mormons' place in the modern American nation.

We can divide Whipple's narrative into three separate stories: Clory's marriage, testimony, and eventual death; the establishment of the Dixie Mission at St. George, Utah; and the success of Zion, both in the United States and more generally in the terrestrial world itself. Clory's narrative centers around her conflicted feelings toward polygamy, her role as a third wife to a man many times her own age, her absence of a testimony, and her charge as a Mormon pioneer settling in an alien land. Clory marries Abijah because Brigham Young convinces her that as third wife to Abijah she will become "a handmaiden of the one true God" (73). Over the years she comes to love her husband, though she remains emotionally distant, eventually pushing away his sexual advances altogether. In fact, after holding the envied and problematic position of the youngest wife for twenty-six years, Clory angrily yearns for her vision of monogamy. She wants to "declare before all the world: 'This is my husband. Not just a third my husband, but all of him'" (600). At the end of the novel Clory is alone, only one of her four children still alive, desperately in fear of "the nameless horrors of widowhood" (617). Though Clory internalizes the principle of plural marriage, her lack of power in the relationship leaves her with the feeling that monogamous love, and especially love for a man closer to her own age, could have given her more emotional richness and stability.

Throughout Clory's time in southern Utah, she searches for a testimony, a public affirmation of one's belief in the truth of the Gospel. She seeks the inner spark that will spiritually justify her life, not only as a faithful Mormon, but as a polygamous wife living a divine principle. She regularly attends church meetings in which members of the congregation testify to their belief in Joseph Smith and his message, but she finds the words of others trite and uninspired. Frustrated that she does not see this glint of affirmation spontaneously within her, Clory thinks to herself, "The old phrases glib on the tongue: *I know Joseph Smith to be a prophet of God!* But how, *how* did one know it? . . . Clory wondered again if this dreadful lack in her soul would some day fester upon the surface for all men to see; she was like a person born with a hand missing, or an eye" (283). Clory enters polygamy somewhat naively, which is not surprising given her young age, only to discover that "polygamy is simply a means whereby a man might inherit a higher degree of glory in the next life . . . Its purpose is not earth-happiness but earth-life discipline . . . To give succeeding generations a superior fatherhood and motherhood" (101, ellipses in original). Yet she knows that a testimony would cement her spirituality to an inner foundation, one not partial to the whims of male power within terrestrial marriage.

Clory searches for some representation of grace she calls the "Great Smile," a kind of inner eminence of God that might seal her faith. Perhaps taking the idea of testimony too literally, Clory does not allow it to be a ritual, the content of which may be precisely the act itself. She consistently finds emptiness in her heart where she believes God should be. Polygamy, even as sanctified by God, has not satisfied her, and the end of the novel finds Clory's terrestrial life empty. Her husband replaces her with an even younger fourth wife. Her first three children die, including her beloved first daughter, Kissy. Bathsheba has never liked her, and Clory has even become estranged from her closest friend, Palmyra. Clory has nothing left to seek but the "Great Smile," and now, on her deathbed following the stillbirth of her last child with Abijah, "the Great Smile beckons" (633). Clory discovers in her last moments a spiritual truth that she could not find in her world: "That which she had searched for all her life had been right there in her heart all the time. She, Clorinda MacIntyre, had a testimony!" (633). But Clory's death, as well as her distinctly private testimony, enacts a criticism of Mormon patriarchy as portrayed through Abijah. A testimony is meant to be a public affirmation of a fact, an expression made before peers. A testimony binds one to a group through the articulation of similar beliefs. But Clory finds her testimony only in the private moments immediately before death. Her testimony, thoroughly personal and private, maintains her difference from the Mormon group. The only outward manifestation of Clory's revelation are her rather mundane last words to her son: "'Jimmie,' she said very clearly and distinctly, 'will you see that my fingernails look nice? Sometimes the women neglect the fingernails'" (633).

Perhaps Whipple desires Clory's salvation, despite her apparent failure as a wife in a plural marriage. Clory's testimony is, in fact, bittersweet, in that she finally reaches the spiritual calm she sought all of her life, but she can only attain this salvation through death. Through Clory, Whipple criticizes the structures of Mormon politics while celebrating particular parts of Mormon spirituality. Within the framework of the nation and nineteenth-century anti-polygamy debates, Whipple reproves Mormon social ideology—not the spiritual realm that Clory has entered.

While Whipple portrays most polygamous relations as detrimental to women's spirits and women's lives (while providing greater glory to men in both their terrestrial and heavenly lives), she does not paint all polygamous relations with the same brush. Clory's best friend, Palmyra, is the first wife of another St. George settler, David Wight. Pal and David are roughly the same age and marry more out of attraction and love than duty. Even so, after a few years in St. George, David takes a second wife. But, while in marriages such as Abijah and Bathsheba's, the second or third wife represents a threat to the stability of an earlier arrangement, Pal and David enter into polygamy on equal terms. Pal, in fact, undertakes the search for David's second wife, announcing, "if I've got to live with her, I might as well pick out someone I like" (283). Pal's marriage is happy; she bears healthy children, grows buxom and stout, and loves her husband deeply. Whipple writes, "When a woman was the mother of six children and still managed to come first with her husband and yet be adored by his pretty second wife, she had no fear of middle age" (535). Palmyra, David, and the second wife, Lucy, appear as a model of polygamous domestic bliss, a life that runs distinctly counter to Clory's experiences with her husband as well as his first wife. Regardless, the impulse to enter into plural marriage is supposed to emanate from the Mormon spiritual realm, not an earthly, much less a carnal, one (polygamy's Abrahamic roots were ordained by God). Palmyra justifies polygamy by saying, "A lot of women would have been old maids without it, and it's building up the kingdom" (550). But Clory becomes frustrated with Palmyra over the years and finds her friend's life, though secure, quite empty of intellectual and emotional breadth: "How very simple was Pal's life . . . with its values nicely pigeonholed, its two passions, family and religion. . . . [W]hite was white and black was black with none of Clory's troubled grays between" (310). Clory's search for happiness in the terrestrial world of "grays between" leads her to question the value of polygamy within the Mormon quotidian. Setting herself against Palmyra, as well as the other church members who dispense their testimonies effortlessly and regularly, Clory remains outside the promises of Mormon St. George and, as a plural wife, outside of the United States as a whole.

Though Clory remains the central character within *The Giant Joshua*, her narrative moves within a larger story of the establishment of St. George in southern Utah. Primarily constructing a pioneer narrative, Whipple tells a familiar story of Anglo settlement in a harsh and unknown western land. Following the rhetoric of Turner's Frontier Thesis, the settlers, all of whom have been called by Brigham Young for this mission, shed the relative civilization in the Salt Lake Valley for the wilds of Utah's Dixie. A central motif within this pioneer narrative is the repeated damming of the Virgin River, a symbol of the level of establishment the Mormons have reached in St. George. Immediately upon their arrival in St. George, the settlers work to dam the river for irrigation. Indicative of their industriousness, the settlers build not only a dam but a nine-hundred-foot-long tunnel leading to a six-mile irrigation canal. But they do not count on the fury of the Virgin's cyclical flooding. Midsummer the following year the river floods, breaks through the dam, and completely destroys the summer crop of wheat, corn, and sugarcane. Every year thereafter the river floods, sometimes fortuitously late in the summer, sometimes disastrously early. One summer, the settlers rebuild the dam nine times (326). Eventually they devote a great deal of money and labor to a pile dam, its moorings driven deep into the riverbed, which, just like the earlier dams, eventually washes away in a summer flood. While fighting for control of the Virgin River, the settlers of St. George also manage to erect a stone tabernacle building (for church affairs) and as well as a massive temple (for religious rituals and rites). But even as these imposing testaments to the subjugation of the region rise from the town, the Virgin River continues its blind inundation. The regulation of the Virgin River becomes a sign of Mormon industry; until the river can be fully controlled, the Dixie Mission cannot claim success as a Mormon colony.

Other developments in the narrative also grow from the classic pioneer story. As Abijah becomes more successful, he manages to build houses for his wives—they move from tents to homes of stone and wood. Tracking St. George's development along a true Turnerian trajectory, Clory thinks to herself, "Civilization was after all just a matter of sounds: first the coyote and the tom-tom, then the cowbell and the bass drum, the bands, and now this last triumphant token, the Tabernacle bell that Abijah said you could hear clear down in the fields" (505–6). In Clory's thoughts, the establishment of religious buildings, then, brings St. George almost to the end of its pioneering story. Indeed, the chapter in which Brigham Young dedicates the St. George Temple concludes with Whipple's declaration "An epoch had passed" (534), echoing the closing words of Turner's famous essay.

Whipple's story of the success and failure of Zion within the context of U.S. history and culture underlies the entire narrative of *The Giant Joshua*. While Whipple paints a balanced portrait of Mormon life in the nineteenth century, complete with healthy as well as harmful polygamous marriages, virtuous leaders and repulsive leches, and pioneer triumphs as well as spiritual failures, Whipple alludes to the deteriorating of Mormon peculiarity within a larger American culture. Traditionally, literature about Mormons appearing before the publication of *The Giant Joshua* tended toward bifurcated and shallow narratives with either lascivious bishops who prey on young gentile women or simplistic and pedantic narratives with spotless Saints. Thus Whipple's novel represents a change in the tradition of Mormon literature. Embedded within this move away from simplistic narratives lies a sense that Zion, if not Mormonism altogether, may have by 1941 lost its political force as well as its distinctiveness in American culture. *The Giant Joshua* pivots on important western conventions such as frontier hardiness, self-determination, and individuality and points readers toward an identification with broader American cultural values instead of the cultural specifics of the Mormon world.

By the end of *The Giant Joshua*, Clory, mirroring the status of the post-1890 Mormon Church in the United States, has become disciplined in Abijah's eyes. After three years abroad, Abijah returns to St. George and upon seeing Clory for the first time remarks on the change in her demeanor: "Even the rebellious hair was netted. Abijah was pleased. Here was a wife who had done considerable retrenchment, a wife more to his liking" (464). Yet even with this newfound satisfaction, Abijah abandons his first three wives when he moves with his young fourth wife to become the president of the new temple in Logan, 250 miles to the north. Though *The Giant Joshua* ends with Clory's testimony, thus allowing for Clory's personal salvation, the question of the health of Zion remains, particularly with sexually/maritally fickle men such as Abijah MacIntyre at the helm. As the novel closes, we must wonder as to the future success of Mormon marriage relations, the settlement of Dixie, and the LDS Church as a whole.

The health of St. George, as evidenced by the settlers' inability to deal with a cycle of destruction by the Virgin River, also becomes questioned near the end of the novel. In the years before Clory's death, silver had been discovered near St. George, thus providing a financial boom for the town. But the income from silver remained fleeting as it literally disappeared from the ground. Just before Clory's death, Palmyra's husband concocts an elaborate plan to dam the Virgin River permanently, but the town does not have the backing for this project until a group of Irish workers, momentarily idle, offers to work for land and water scrip. With this providential boon of inexpensive labor, the town wins its battle with the river; the pioneer narrative appears complete with this final control of nature. Thus, coincident with Clory's death, Zion as a material pioneer enterprise has triumphed, but the more problematic elements of polygamy and spiritual progress remain.

The Giant Joshua, filled with childhood deaths, stillbirths, and miscarriages, represents a disheartening and unhopeful image for the continuance of Mormondom through birth. Possibly as a final statement on the future of

Mormonism, Whipple has Clory's death come at the heels of her birthing a stillborn child. Whipple presents the lot of Mormon women as physically demanding and spiritually unrewarding as they watch their children, potential and otherwise, die on the rough Utah frontier. Within this patriarchal world, Whipple's story argues that the disruption of the Mormon order is imminent. Though a number of Abijah's children from Bathsheba survive and become successful members of the church and the nation, Willie provides Abijah with only a single daughter, likely destined for the polygamous life of her mother; Clory's only surviving child, Jimmie, deeply fears his father, sensing that "Papa was on Aunt 'Sheba's side and was not really his friend" (547). Primarily, though not completely, Whipple disrupts the patriarchal lineage necessary for the continuance of both Mormon polygamy and its attendant world view. As Abijah leaves Clory for Logan, he thinks to himself, "the past, the past, we've had a good time, my lass, but what will be, will be, and we maun think of us all as meeting on the Other Side" (611). Abijah can move on "to build up his dynasty with another woman" (629) and still foresee salvation, yet Clory—as well as Bathsheba and all Abijah's children—are left behind to fend for themselves in the temporal world of Mormon St. George.

Whipple's novel argues that Mormonism's future must afford the possibilities of women's power and spiritual doubt, not just a terrestrial masculine drive toward subjugation of both the physical earth as well as non-Mormons, which for Abijah includes women, since he claims early in the novel, "Women couldn't quite belong to the Kingdom. He felt that Brother Brigham and he saw eye to eye in that" (102). Though by the end of the novel St. George is firmly established as a Mormon town, evidenced by its tabernacle and temple, Whipple paints a grim picture of the future of Mormon social relations. The establishment of St. George evidences the permanence of Mormons in the fabric of the nation, but the instability illustrated by the unjust internal patriarchal relations of the church point to the eventual dissolution of its separation from the nation at large.

Though Whipple's novel was originally published by the distinctly non-Mormon Houghton Mifflin Company, from whom she also won the $2,500 Houghton Mifflin Literary Prize to help her complete the manuscript, Whipple assuredly directs *The Giant Joshua* to a Mormon audience. Given that the close of the novel rests on Clory's final personal testimony, *The Giant Joshua* demands an intimate understanding of the religious principles and theology of Mormonism, more so than the more culturally Mormon novels of a writer like Virginia Sorensen. Thus, even though *The Giant Joshua* appeared through the auspices of a large, gentile, East Coast–centered publishing house, Whipple seems to speak directly to a Great Basin Mormon public.

But Whipple's reception by Utah Mormons and by the officials of the church remained cool at best until well into the 1970s. Whipple writes that church officials "condemned" her book ("Maurine Whipple's Story" 60). While working on the manuscript, Whipple claims that "one of the teachers at Dixie College [a predominantly Mormon college in St. George, Utah] saw me on the street and he threw a quarter at me and said, 'You might as well pick it up; this is all you'll ever be worth'" ("Maurine Whipple's Story" 61). Even Whipple's father labeled *The Giant Joshua* "vulgar" (Geary, "Women Regionalists" 150). *The Giant Joshua* sold well through Houghton Mifflin, remaining in print for eleven years, but its sales remained flat in Utah, likely due to its censure by the Mormon Church. John A. Widtsoe, an apostle in the LDS Church as well as the editor of the church serial *The Improvement Era*, criticized Whipple's depiction of polygamy, claiming that her narrative of "a life defeated because of polygamy, leaves a bitter, angry distaste for the system" (Widtsoe 1941, 93). In his decidedly lackluster review, Widtsoe asserts, "The evident straining for the lurid obscures the true spirit of Mormonism, and misleads the reader" (Widtsoe 1941, 93). Since *The Improvement Era* acted as an authority on officially sanctioned culture for its Mormon readership, anything but an enthusiastic review would effectively ruin sales of Whipple's novel within the Mormon community. This clear geographic/cultural split in the book's sales figures illustrates the tension between the nation's hope for bringing Mormons into the fabric of U.S. national culture and Mormons' possible reluctance for such familiarity with gentile America (or their deeper desire to repudiate such candid accounts of polygamy, especially from an insider's perspective).

Nonetheless, most non-Mormon reviews of *The Giant Joshua* were favorable. A review in the *Southwest Review* claimed her novel to be an "honest picture" full of "vivid descriptions and gripping incidents" (Wilson 263, 265), while Ray B. West (a fellow Mormon author) wrote in the *Saturday Review of Literature*, "the book as a whole . . . makes excellent reading and catches . . . the tenderness and sympathy which existed among a people dogged by persecution and hardship" (5). Most reviews of *The Giant Joshua* in publications such as the *Nation*, the *New Yorker*, the *New York Times Book Review*, and the *Saturday Review of Literature* found Whipple's novel vibrant and intimate with reference to Mormon life, claiming that Whipple had spun a more personable tale compared to Vardis Fisher's historical Mormon epic *Children of God*, published two years earlier. Also, most reviewers found that Whipple's novel provided an insight into the world of this "peculiar people" without an obvious pro- or anti-Mormon spin. One reviewer for the *New York Times Book Review* wrote:

> *The Giant Joshua* is a rich, robust and oddly exciting novel which brings the Mormons as close home to the reader as they have ever been brought before. Not only in this book are they likeable, but they have a certain magnificence which fully explains their history. Watching them struggle against the elements, improvising homes and food and a whole social system, one is compelled not only to respect but to marvel at them. (Walton 6)

Clearly an outsider to the hearth of American literature, Whipple acts as a kind of cultural operative from an alien world, bringing her world—western, rural, and vulgarly polygamous—to a mainstream—eastern, urban, decorously monogamous—reading public. Evident from by reviews such as the above, *The Giant Joshua* was clearly successful in establishing Mormons' pioneer heritage while simultaneously personalizing, contextualizing, and then exorcizing polygamy from Mormon identity. By excusing polygamy through "a certain magnificence that explains [Mormon] history," non-Mormon readers could understand and empathize with the Mormon narrative. Thus *The Giant Joshua*—for gentile readers—paints Mormon history as U.S. history, bringing Mormons "close home" and into the national culture of the United States.

A Little Lower than the Angels

Virginia Sorensen has been called Utah's First Lady of Letters (Bradford xvii), an honor bestowed at her induction into Phi Beta Kappa at the University of Utah in 1989, only two years before her death. Though she is likely the most famous Mormon author in scholarly circles today, the Utah Mormon public did not receive her novels well when they were originally published. Only after decades and within a radically different social context were her novels accepted as genuine and legitimate expressions of Mormon sensibility or vision. In the last few years, the Mormon press Signature Books reprinted two of her novels and a collection of her short stories, thus situating Sorensen in a distinctly Mormon frame for their consumption by a new readership. Neither Signature Books nor any other Mormon publishing concern has reissued novels by any of the other authors considered in this chapter.[14]

Although a handful of Mormon novels appeared before Virginia Sorensen's first book in 1942, *A Little Lower than the Angels* is often considered the first Mormon novel because of Sorensen's continued connection to the church. Besides Whipple's *The Giant Joshua*, published just a year earlier, George Dixon Snell published *Root, Hog, and Die* in 1936, though without much of a splash, and Vardis Fisher, often considered an apostate or, at best, simply hostile to church organizations, issued his Harper Book Prize–winning epic, *Children of God*, in 1939. Sorensen, while not a devout Mormon in her adult life (Howe vi), wrote eight novels dealing with Mormon issues and Mormon country, all of them composed outside the borders of her home state of Utah.[15] Though widely published through eastern publishers (primarily Alfred A. Knopf, Harcourt, Brace and Company, Reynal & Hitchcock, and Charles Scribner), she saw little or no support from the Mormon Church, or any Mormon public. In fact, her early books were rarely sold in Utah; the Deseret Book Company, a bookselling venture of the LDS Church, canceled its order for Sorensen's first book, claiming that there was nothing of the "base character" in Mormon culture that the Deseret Book Company found in Sorensen's portrayal of Mormon life in Nauvoo (quoted in Bradford x).

A Little Lower than the Angels closely resembles Whipple's story in that Sorensen sets the struggles of a polygamous family against the backdrop of the settling of a Mormon town. Sorensen's narrative centers around the fictionalized life of Mercy French Baker, Sorensen's husband's great-grandmother. While Sorensen does not attend to the historical specificity of her relative's life, she uses Mercy Baker as a platform on which to build a narrative of personal struggle within a growing—and often perplexing—Mormon community. Sorensen does not write a memoir of this historically verifiable woman, but rather uses her presence in Nauvoo as a pretext for dramatizing this new religion and its struggle with the distinctly antagonistic practice of polygamy.

Like *The Giant Joshua*, town-building, the development of agriculture, and burgeoning commerce abound in this novel. In fact, barring the distinctly Mormon components—polygamy, the presence of Joseph Smith, and temple building—*A Little Lower than the Angels* could read like many wellworn narratives of frontier development. The introduction of polygamy into the Bakers' lives, however, dismantles *A Little Lower than the Angels* as a pioneer story because this new marital relation destroys the Baker family through internal jealousies, disagreements, and Mercy's eventual death. The parallel destruction of Nauvoo and the winter Mormon exodus across the frozen Mississippi River mirror the Baker family's internal disintegration.

Mercy and Simon Baker move from New York State with the first wave of Mormons forced westward through Ohio and Missouri, eventually establishing themselves in Iowa just across the river from Nauvoo. At the opening of the novel, Mercy and Simon have five children, with a sixth on the way. Within the next two years, Mercy bears another daughter and then twins, one of whom dies soon after birth. Mercy falls ill, apparently from the toil of excessive childbirth, though possibly from an invasive disease such as cancer: "Within there, something. Gnawing and sucking at strength itself" (327). Given Mercy's infirmity, Brigham Young, now the leader of the Mormons after Joseph Smith's murder, advises Simon to take a second wife, not only to aid him in the domestic tasks now left unattended, but also as an act of faith in the new tenet recently revealed to church leaders by Joseph Smith. Brigham Young tells Simon, "I'd say it was a mighty foolish thing for a man like you to pay the right sort of woman to keep his house. Too many women who'd like to do it for nothing" (281). Brigham Young then introduces Simon to Charlot Leavitt, who becomes Simon's second wife that same afternoon on board the ferry back to Iowa. Simon presents Charlot to Mercy as domestic help, replacing the young girl who fled after Simon discovered her and his eldest son, Jarvie, indelicately engaged one night. Mercy is relieved and overjoyed for the help. Soon, however, Mercy discovers Simon's secret when she arises early one morning and finds her husband sleeping in "Aunt Charlot's" bed; she concludes that the rumors concerning Joseph Smith's revelation on plural marriages are true and have now bodily infiltrated her home, taking from her what she believed was her sacred role as the singular wife to Simon Baker. This revelation sends Mercy deeper into her illness, now fueled by a sense of betrayal, by not only her husband, but the leaders of the faith on which she has staked her life. Mercy eventually acquiesces to this new marriage arrangement, but with bitterness and a degree of scorn toward Charlot, who takes over Mercy's domestic affairs and installs herself as the center of Simon's sexual and emotional stability.

As the Mormons continue to build and politically strengthen Nauvoo, the tensions between Illinois Mormons and gentiles mount. Vigilantes torch Mormon houses and fields. Simon is tied to his fence and beaten one afternoon while working in his fields. Inevitably, the Baker home on the bluff across the river from Nauvoo also goes up in flames one night, and the entire family is forced to move into the city of Nauvoo, where Charlot still owns a small house. Soon thereafter, Brigham Young agrees to abandon Nauvoo in the coming spring, though gentile pressure—both vigilante and political—forces them across the frozen Mississippi River in the middle of winter. Simon bundles Mercy, who is still deeply ill in both body and spirit, into their wagon for the long trek west. They leave Nauvoo by the light of the vigilantes' fires: "Something familiar and terrible, a sudden flaring, a red glow that spread almost instantly and then began leaping toward the sky" (426). Mercy, so sick she can barely speak, sits proudly in Simon's first wagon—"First wife, first wagon" (423)—but as they climb the bluff above the river and pass the turnoff to the Baker's incinerated home, she "slip[s] quietly from the high seat" and dies (427).

Mercy, like Clory in *The Giant Joshua*, suffers from an ambivalent faith. Though Mercy has followed her husband to Nauvoo, she has not yet been baptized into the Mormon Church when the novel opens. When her son Jarvic becomes sick with "swamp fever" from draining the land upon which Nauvoo will be built, Joseph Smith and a bishop arrive to lay hands upon the boy. Smith tells Mercy, "There's a remedy we've found effective . . . and we're not among those who won't advise remedies when faith is lacking" (21–22), thus revealing his frustration at Mercy's spiritual ambivalence. Mercy disregards Simon and runs off into the forest. Now in a panic and at the very end of her sixth pregnancy, Mercy ends up giving birth among "the leaves and the squirrels and the brittle bark" (28) and stumbles home bloody and exhausted. Not unlike Abijah MacIntyre, who hastened his second wife's death by refusing medical help in favor of faith in his leader's recommendations (including anointings and the laying on of hands), Simon pushes his wife into infirmity and exhaustion by insisting on his own stalwart faith as curative. Throughout the period of the novel, Mercy is haunted by a neighbor's assessment of her character back in New York: "Mercy Baker, she was always one to wonder" (22), a verdict that connects her character to Clory and her "troubled grays between." Just before leaving Nauvoo, Eliza Snow, a Mormon poet and Joseph Smith's undisclosed second wife, who is quite close to Mercy, admonishes Mercy to reject her melancholy and "Just think of ordinary little things, anything" (415) to help her with the impending difficult westward trek. Eliza advises her that "It's a matter of faith, really" (415), to which Mercy can only silently respond, "And a matter of will" (425). But childbearing, disease, polygamy, and patriarchy have broken Mercy, and neither faith nor will can keep her alive. Like Clory, she finds respite only in death, though here without the potential salvation of the "Great Smile." Rather, she only seeks home, away from Charlot, Simon, Mormons, and gentiles: as the Baker wagons pass "the little road to the bluff . . . [with] new snow . . . doing its best to hide it entirely," Simon realizes with her death "that she had not forgotten the place where the road turned, after all; she had simply turned with it, and gone home" (427).

In many ways, *A Little Lower than the Angels* and *The Giant Joshua* present similar readings of Mormon polygamy and its role in ending Mormon distinctiveness. In both novels, the wives (whether first or third) suffer from their relationships with polygamy. Mercy and Clory find these relationships troubling, not simply in the domestic sense, but in the suffering caused by a marital structure ordained and controlled by men in the name of a higher law in which these women placed their trust. Like the conclusion of *The Giant Joshua*, what remains at stake at the end of *A Little Lower than the Angels* is the future of Mormondom, not so much as an ideal or a religion but as a separate and distinct culture and ideology. Mercy's death, like Clory's, demands a questioning of the principles that have brought such sorrow to these women's lives. Both novels engage polygamy by exposing and critiquing the institution and simultaneously bringing it, with all of its problems, to the forefront of consciousness, thus paving the way for its eventual erasure from Mormon life and, more importantly, from Mormon identity.

Sorensen's novel condemns polygamy more harshly than does Whipple's *The Giant Joshua*, but her impulse seems more to evoke the human side of polygamy. Mercy's multidimensional character leads the reader toward an understanding of this troubled relationship rather than toward moralizing overtones. Mercy's death and the Mormon expulsion from Nauvoo, as well as the actual publication of Sorensen's novel, represent a pivotal moment for Mormon culture. Mercy's death signifies the passing of a peculiar practice; Sorensen's book evinces a moment in which the stories of this peculiarity can now be embraced. Defeat and isolation have now become signifiers of difference adopted by Mormons for their historical specificity, replacing the necessary peculiarity of their earlier identity. Mercy's death begins a new era of Mormon cultural consciousness, an era in which Mormons become full-fledged members of the nation rather than antagonistic outsiders.

Sorensen's first novel received distinctly positive reviews from serials as wide ranging as the *New York Times Book Review* and *Rural Sociology*. Wallace Stegner, the gentile Utah-born author who published his sympathetic narrative history of Mormondom, *Mormon Country*, in the same year, wrote, "every member of [Sorensen's novel] is real enough to make the average historical-novel character look like Grandfather's stuffed Sunday suit" (11). He praises "the sophistication and polish of her prose," claiming *A Little Lower than the Angels* "the best fictional record of a polygamous household that I know" (11, 12). Mormon Church officials, though, reacted to Sorensen's book otherwise. Apostle Widtsoe claimed in a review in *The Improvement Era*, "As a Mormon novel it is ineffective. . . . Joseph Smith and his associates become, in the telling, ordinary, rather insipid milk and water figures. That does not comport with the historical achievements of the Mormon pioneers" (Widtsoe 1942, 380). Widtsoe also finds "trivial and repulsive" certain moments in the narrative, such as the continuous bedwetting by Mercy's adolescent son, Bert, and Jarvie's "sex temptation" with Vic, the Baker's domestic help (Widtsoe 1942, 380). For Widtsoe, ostensibly a mouthpiece for the LDS Church's cultural values, Sorensen's novel does not tell an appropriate Mormon story—of the past or for the future—at all.

The Peaceable Kingdom

Ardyth Kennelly's *The Peaceable Kingdom* (1949) relates the story of the second wife of an established tailor in Salt Lake City in the 1880s. Like Whipple and Sorensen, Kennelly unmoors Mormon polygamy from its troubled past, but her central character, Linnea Ecklund, neither dies nor becomes sick or physically overburdened with childbearing in the process of this exposition. Instead, she demands her independence from her husband and his first wife (though not through divorce), thus both troubling the patriarchal order of the polygamous system and complicating gentile critics' simplified moral division between polygamous and monogamous marriages.

Linnea has a distinctly cold relationship with her husband's first wife, Sigrid; the wives live in separate homes, attend different church houses, and rarely attend social gatherings simultaneously. Sigrid has no children, so the designation of "family" rests with Linnea and her children. Linnea eventually leaves her husband, Olaf, due to her bitter resentment toward Sigrid as well as the mounting tensions from the presence of federal agents hunting "co-habs," as Mormon polygamists were called. Linnea, now making a living as a midwife, raises her children with the help of her female neighbors, eschewing Olaf even when he comes to make amends. Linnea's anger at Olaf increases when she discovers that he has built Sigrid a house, expending his savings and leaving none for Linnea's half of his family. At the conclusion of the novel, Olaf and Linnea tearfully reunite, partially contingent upon his guarantee of a house for her and the children. Polygamy continues in the Ecklund family, though now with Linnea asserting her day-to-day independence along with reestablishing her love for her husband.

Like many Mormon novels that close the era of Mormon peculiarity at the end of the nineteenth century, the last third of *The Peaceable Kingdom* centers around the announcement of the Woodruff Manifesto and Mormons' reaction to this disruption of principles. After Woodruff's declaration, the estranged Olaf visits Linnea, mistakenly believing he can now reunite with her, since the U.S. marshals sent to arrest "co-habs" will now be leaving Utah, allowing its Mormon citizens to quietly return to their earlier lives. Somewhat naively Olaf declares to Linnea, "the [LDS Church] President ain't so dumb. He's got something up his sleeve all right. There won't be no new plural marriages, like he says, but he'll fix it up so all the old marriages can go right on without no more trouble and persecution" (251). Olaf believes that the manifesto will end "all this sneaking around. Going against the government and everything" (251). But Linnea, unlike Olaf, was born into the LDS Church and believes more strongly in the eternity of the Gospel given to Joseph Smith. She finds no such relief with the issuance of the manifesto. In fact, she sees Woodruff's declaration as a submission to the demands of outsiders, and even more so as a tacit overlooking of the women involved in polygamous marriages. Linnea declares that God, who gives revelations, including the one to Joseph Smith directing the reconstitution of Abrahamic polygamy as well as the insight to Woodruff to end this Biblical restoration, is "like a doggone spoiled young one that hollers for something and his idiot of a mother gives it to him and when he gets it, he throws it right away" (255). Particularly as a second wife, Linnea recognizes that the Mormon leaders' disavowal of polygamy restores the rights of Mormon men in Utah, men who had been harassed, arrested, and even imprisoned for their beliefs, without providing any support for the women in the polygamous marriages that will soon be nullified. Linnea turns her anger from an apparently fickle God to the lineage of men who interpret and manifest God's will, often on the backs of Mormon women. Deeply angry at Olaf's joy for his newfound sexual and marital freedom, Linnea angrily rebukes her husband:

I'm mad enough to chew nails. It makes perfect fools out of all us women that trotted right along doing the doggoned men's bidding like we didn't have sense enough to come in out of the rain. Sometimes I'd like to tell the whole kit and kaboodle of you to go and jump in the river! That includes the Almighty, too[,] the Lord God Himself, if you want to know! (254)

Linnea asks Olaf to divorce Sigrid, demanding that he take Linnea and their children out of the state. Olaf refuses on the grounds that he now owns property in Utah—Sigrid's house. Linnea realizes that Olaf has placed the welfare and prosperity of his first wife ahead of Linnea and their children and bitterly asks herself, "Who am I? Nothing, nobody, the mother of five children that the Lord and President Woodruff get their heads together and decide they should never have been born" (256). She bitingly terminates Olaf's visit by telling him, "I'm so sick of you, so finished with you, I can't even see you no more, like I was stone-blind" (256). Understanding Olaf's opportunism, Linnea loses all faith in the possibilities of the Mormon Church with reference to temporal and earthly ideals. She maintains her faith but rejects the lineage of male law, stretching from Olaf—through Smith, Young, and Woodruff—to God.

Though Linnea holds the Gospel as timeless, and particularly Joseph Smith's revelation on polygamy, Kennelly paints the civil world of 1890s Utah as deeply immersed in the social and cultural sensibilities of the United States at large, and not of some other, peculiar, nation. Immediately after Olaf's mistakenly optimistic visit, Linnea must attend the birth of a neighbor's third child. Young Mrs. Monteith's birth is notably belabored because as a second wife she signed an unusual agreement with the childless Old Mrs. Monteith that designated that the first female child should go to her. Young Mrs. Monteith, the mother of two boys, desperately fears the potential loss of this child to the sixty-four-year-old first wife of her husband. Acting as midwife, Linnea assures Young Mrs. Monteith that she will not lose her child, no matter its sex. Referring to the agreement, Linnea upbraids Mr. Monteith, exclaiming, "Tell her it was crazy tomfoolishness and that she had better tear up that paper! Where do you think we're living at? Some foreign country or something?" (277). Yet Young Mrs. Monteith delivers a girl and Old Mrs. Monteith lays her claim, saying, "it's nothing so out of the ordinary. It ain't nothing that couldn't of been done in Bible days" (279). Linnea, responding to Old Mrs. Monteith's logic by saying "Ain't we took any steps forward since Bible days? Why, them was ignorant people" (279), represents a sensibility that holds deeply onto religious convictions and duties while remaining centered in the civil world of the United States. Linnea claims that this transaction of corporeal tender will only aid in the present vilification of Mormons by showing the outside world that they remain backward and peculiar. By recanting their agreement, the Monteith wives can prove that Mormons have moved beyond their various religious and social eccentricities and can function in the civil society of the United States. Old Mrs. Monteith is convinced to withdraw from the agreement by President Woodruff, and when a reporter for the gentile *Salt Lake Tribune* arrives after hearing about "something funny going on up here in regard to a baby" (282), he gets no story. The women's silence on this affair thus aids in the further Americanization of Utah Mormons in 1890—as well as in 1949.

Young Mrs. Monteith and Old Mrs. Monteith together represent a Mormon world in transition. Old Mrs. Monteith holds claim to the logic of "Bible days," an authority grown from the Abrahamic defense of polygamy, which includes a first wife's absolute power over a household (including its other wives). But this world in which social logic develops from singular religious texts and revelations without regard to the social conventions of the nation in which these people reside is no longer tenable. Linnea represents the new Mormon world of the twentieth century. She can hold on to her deep religious convictions while living in the world of civil American society. Linnea can maintain her belief in the divinely sanctioned practice of plural marriage, yet she can distance herself from it in the terrestrial world. Linnea believes that Mormons have a place within the framework of the United States, though they need not become completely assimilated. She disagrees, therefore, with the acquiescence by the patriarchal church leaders to federal demands as well as with the complete cultural separation evidenced by Old Mrs. Monteith's world view. Through the character of Linnea, Kennelly unearths polygamy to engage in placing Mormon culture within American culture. Her vision, though, appears more hopeful than Whipple's or Sorensen's in that though all three of the central characters from these novels hold deep spiritual convictions, ones that conflict with the patriarchal reality of Mormon life, only Linnea survives the tribulations of polygamy to continue with her life on earth. While Clory and Mercy find salvation in death, Linnea finds that Mormon spirituality may be progressive, leading her forward to a union with both other Mormons and the nation as a whole.[16]

1890: THE END OF MORMON HISTORY

While Whipple, Sorensen, and Kennelly effect the containment of polygamy through the critique of its consequences in the domestic realm, the grand historical epics of Vardis Fisher and George Dixon Snell clearly strive to end Mormon history in 1890 with the issuance of the Woodruff Manifesto and the subsequent dissolution of plural marriages. Implicit in these novels is the assumption that after 1890 Mormon and U.S. histories become coincident, no longer proceeding along separate trajectories. These novels also embrace Mormon history as primarily pioneer history. Even as these narratives unfold with evictions, ostracization, and violence against Mormons, the consequent westward migration emanates from Mormons' pioneer grit and ability to deal with rough and inhospitable conditions—both geographic and social. Fisher and Snell present polygamy as part of the fabric of Mormon life, but the structures of their novels emphasize the collision of Mormon and U.S. history when Mormons enter the American narrative at the end of the nineteenth century. Mormons become quintessential pioneers in these narratives as they establish their Americanization by shedding polygamy and embracing the larger values of the nation. As the pioneer narrative becomes the distinctive and definitive story of the United States, Mormons in these novels take center stage.

Children of God

In 1939, Vardis Fisher won the distinguished Harper Book Prize for his fictional chronicle of nineteenth-century Mormonism, *Children of God: An American Epic*. Fisher's novel, which follows three generations of the fictional McBride family as they join the LDS Church in the East and subsequently move westward to build up Zion, covers the carefully bounded territory of nineteenth-century Mormon history that begins with Joseph Smith's visions and his founding of the LDS Church in 1830 and ends with the pronouncement of the Woodruff Manifesto in 1890. In fact, one reviewer of *Children of God* had internalized these historical limits so deeply that he wrote, "Vardis Fisher's novel has done the whole thing, from beginning to end" (Marsh 1), evidencing a belief that Mormon history, if not attendant Mormon identity, had ended with the dissolution of polygamy. Fisher supports this particular view of Mormon history by dividing his narrative into three sections, titled "Morning," "Noon," and "Evening." The first two sections end respectively with the deaths of the first two presidents of the LDS Church, Joseph Smith and Brigham Young; the final section concludes with the determined departure of Nephi McBride and his family from the Salt Lake Valley after the issuance of the Woodruff Manifesto. Fisher weaves the lives of the McBride family amongst the well-documented history of the growth and persecution of Mormonism in the nineteenth century. His Joseph Smith and Brigham Young are not merely fleeting historical apparitions but prominent figures in this narrative. Fisher's novel sweeps across sixty years and three generations in an attempt to both illuminate and encapsulate Mormon history. By providing a fictional central family, Fisher transforms a clearly understood historical narrative into a fictional story in which the boundaries between historical reality and fantasy shift and blur.

Children of God opens in Palmyra, New York, with Joseph Smith's first visions and his subsequent formation of the LDS Church. Tim McBride, the eldest McBride in the story, first appears in Missouri, where Mormons were often beaten, tarred and feathered, raped, and fatally whipped by enraged locals, all vividly described by Fisher (132–42, for example). The reader can track the movement of the LDS Church and its adherents by following the McBrides as they, with the rest of the embryonic Mormon flock, are violently pressed from Missouri, and then Nauvoo, to the inhospitable deserts of Utah. Fisher traces in great detail the persecutions of Mormons on their westward trek, their establishment in the Salt Lake Valley, the federal military and legislative attacks on Mormon society, and the final stability of Mormon Utah within the United States at the end of the nineteenth century.

Children of God implicitly insists that the 1890 Woodruff Manifesto marks the end of the Mormon era. As the McBrides depart from Utah, the grandson, Nephi, says "They'll excommunicate us," to which his elderly father sarcastically replies, "Oh, no. We'll excommunicate them. We're taking the principles" (766). Thus as the McBrides leave they effectively abandon the organization of the church as well. Nephi and Moroni, the grandson and son of Tim McBride, turn their backs on the Mormon Church because Wilford Woodruff has "sold us out" (758) by issuing the manifesto in exchange for the cessation of federal harassment. Nephi exclaims to Woodruff, "You made a political horse trade and told your conscience that God would bless you for it" (762). Nephi and Moroni represent a conservative and devout strain of Mormonism that holds to religious principles rather than civil law. Both Nephi and Moroni believe that the social order of the church provided for the welfare of all of its members and that the renunciation of any principles under pressure from a secular government meant death to the church as an institution and as a creed. Nephi continues his harangue after discovering that Woodruff did not actually have a revelation concerning the manifesto, but rather he merely "felt inspired" after significant time spent in prayer (759). He surmises that Brigham Young would have had the "courage" to stand against the federal government at this juncture and that Woodruff's decision evidences the weakness of the church leadership and its present material goals:

> "What have we done, what can we do, without him? Why, go on and yield principle by principle until our church is only a wealthy corporation of special privilege and power! The covenant of plural marriage is gone. The Orders [social units of communal ownership] are destroyed. These two were the blood and life of our religion. . . . The time is coming, President Woodruff . . . when the saints and gentiles will mix and marry, dance and love together, trade votes, perjure themselves, and worship the same god— and that god will be money. This church that was to establish a new gospel of brotherhood on earth will have bigger banks and factories, its millionaires and beggars." (763–64)

Certainly Fisher places his own harsh criticisms of the LDS Church into the mouth of an angry 1890 character, but within these words we can read the assumption that the utopian experiment has ended. Seventeen days after Woodruff issued the manifesto, Nephi, his extended family, and a collection of followers, forty-seven wagons in all, steered south for Mexico, where they believed, not unlike their brethren in Nauvoo, that they could live the principles of the only true church in peace.

Fisher, like Whipple, Sorensen, and Kennelly, argues that Mormon peculiarity is vanishing. The McBrides represent a Mormon ideology out of step with mainstream America; they, in fact, must leave the boundaries of the nation to follow their principles, not unlike Mormons of two generations previous who had settled outside the United States in the Salt Lake Valley. The post-manifesto Mormon world has agreed to abide by the terms of the American nation (for which Utah was awarded statehood six years later). Those members who chose to adhere to all of Joseph Smith's doctrines, no matter how alienating they might have been to the rest of America, had to remove themselves, not only from the United States, but also from the Mormon community itself. Peculiarity, for Fisher, had literally gone south.

Fisher's novel sold exceedingly well and garnered various reactions from both Mormon and gentile critics. His narrative apparently inspired a number of conversions, though Fisher also received irate letters from Mormons who felt that his history was misleading and damaging (Arrington and Haupt 42, 44). According to Leonard Arrington, the LDS Church never took an official stance on Fisher's novel; accordingly, none of the official publications of the LDS Church reviewed *Children of God*. A reviewer for *The Nauvoo Independent*, an organ of the Reorganized Church of Jesus Christ of Latter-day Saints (which split from the LDS Church after Joseph Smith's death), however, declared that Fisher's novel "ought to be dynamited" because "[t]he noble generation of our fathers is pictured with gutter ideals and grog shop habits" (quoted in Arrington and Haupt 45). The LDS Church may have kept mum with regard to Fisher's book because they felt no need to alienate a novel that garnered a national fiction award, or perhaps the leadership simply found no fault in Fisher's narrative, despite his scathing attack on the growing corporate mentality of church planning.

Most reviewers found the size of the novel daunting (769 pages), claiming, "It is repetitious, wordy, and freighted with interminable dialogue," and that Fisher's prose was "often careless, often tumid" ("Mormons, Armenians" 53). Yet almost all reviewers found the narrative to be genuinely captivating and absorbing. A reviewer for the *New York Times* gushed his approval in a lead review, claiming "You can't spoil the Mormon story. But Vardis Fisher has brought something approaching genius to it" (Marsh 1). The prizewinning *Children of God* was the best known and most widely read of Fisher's novels during his life. It was also the source for the screenplay of Henry Hathaway's 1940 film *Brigham Young—Frontiersman*. Presently, though, *Children of God* remains out of print in favor of many of Fisher's rough-and-tumble western novels. Likely his Mormon epic served its purpose at midcentury in offering to a wider audience an easily digestible narrative of nineteenth-century Mormon history.

Root, Hog, and Die

George Dixon Snell published his Mormon historical romance *Root, Hog, and Die* (1936) three years before Fisher's *Children of God* with little fanfare. *Root, Hog, and Die* appeared through Caxton Printers of Caldwell, Idaho, a small publisher best known for producing western fiction, especially manuscripts of the type eastern publishing houses eschewed. *Root, Hog, and Die* is a dreadfully boring novel, particularly for any reader familiar with the Mormon saga, until its final pages when Snell presents a scathing assessment of the church's relationship to labor within its own factories and mines. Like *Children of God*, Snell's novel retells the story of the founding of the LDS Church and its movement westward. Many key players of nineteenth-century Mormon and

Utah history appear: Joseph Smith, Brigham Young, Erastmus Snow, Wilford Woodruff, Grover Cleveland, Chief Justice Zane (who saw that anti-polygamy legislation was enforced in Utah), Salt Lake City Mayor Abraham Owen Smoot (father of Mormon Senator Reed Smoot), and even labor activist Big Bill Hayward. Snell interweaves their stories with the narrative of the fictional Jim Brent, a young convert to Mormonism in the 1830s who becomes a church leader as well as a Utah mining magnate by the end of the nineteenth century. Echoing Fisher's condemnation of the LDS Church's increasing attention to commercial rather than spiritual affairs, *Root, Hog, and Die* critiques the loss of communalism and social equality within the Mormon Church that begins concurrently—though not causally—with the church's capitulation to federal demands.

Snell's novel, like *Children of God*, follows the patriarchal narrative of Jim Brent's offspring. But where Nephi McBride (as well as his father and grandfather) is primarily a pioneer figure fighting for the maintenance of religious principles in the barren Utah desert, Jim Brent gradually improves his lot within the Mormon Church and becomes a formidable economic force in the mining industry. In many ways, Nephi McBride's diatribe against Woodruff at the end of *Children of God* ought be directed squarely at Jim Brent. Five years after the Woodruff Manifesto, Mark Brent, grandson to Jim Brent, attends Deseret University in Salt Lake City. Dedicated to his Mormon heritage and the pioneer history of his father and grandfather, Mark dreams of writing a history of the Mormon Church and then becoming an editor of the *Deseret News*, a Salt Lake City newspaper owned by the LDS Church. But at school Mark meets Melvin Katz, a Jewish student from New York City who introduces him to new ideas that prompt him to examine the church's late-nineteenth-century drive toward capitalist expansion as well as the unbalanced increases in the wealth of individual church leaders. Reading Charles Darwin, Edward Bellamy, Henry George, Karl Marx, Ernest Renan, Arthur Schopenhauer, and T. H. Huxley, Mark questions the religious principles instilled in him as a youth and concludes that the Mormon Church and its leaders have forsaken their egalitarian origins. Inspired by these readings and his friendship with Katz, Mark decides to involve himself with his father's business in order to eventually offer profit-sharing to the miners. But before he can enact his plan, the miners strike. Mark visits them in Bingham City to offer up his plan, but before he can do so, angry strikers kill him as he talks with deputies sent to protect strikebreakers.

Mark's radicalization takes up only the final forty-eight pages of an otherwise 419-page narration of predictable nineteenth-century Mormon history. His death, which occurs with the coincident passing of his grandfather from unspecified afflictions of age, points to the end of Mormon power—here bitterly associated with business ventures encouraged and often owned by the church. Mark is his father's only son, who himself is the only son of his father's first wife, who had died though complications from his birth. Mark's death thus closes the patrilineal force that opens with Jim's first marriage, a force important to the development and progress of any Mormon narrative of the nineteenth century, if not to Mormon society in general.

Root, Hog, and Die is more of a lament than a reflection in that the novel presents an essential failure of Mormonism. According to Snell, the brand of assimilation advocated by late-nineteenth-century Mormon leaders had been of the worst kind; from its roots in early communism, Snell presents a Mormonism mutated so as to internalize Darwinian principles of industrial capitalism. Indeed, Mark's father says, "You ain't interpreted events right, my boy. The Lord planned for us to progress, and He gave His wealth into the hands of a few so it would be taken care of" (398–99). *Root, Hog, and Die* criticizes the trajectory along which late-nineteenth-century Mormonism developed, though Snell does not necessarily equate this trajectory with a drive toward social or political assimilation with the rest of late-nineteenth-century America. Snell's conclusion, however, lacks any sense of fixed causality for this mutation of religious principles into those of industrial capitalism. While Fisher's novel claims that the drive toward cultural assimilation prompted the rejection of religious principles, particularly evidenced by Woodruff's disavowal of doctrine through a mere feeling, *Root, Hog, and Die* points to the LDS Church's investment in industry as problematic in itself, not merely in relation to the disjuncture between worldly enterprise and religious principle. Yet Snell clearly remains critical of a Mormon world that embraces capitalism and industrialism as God's will, damning through Mark's death the capitalist-Mormon rationalization of God leaving "His wealth into the hands of a few."

The combination of Mark's death at the hands of striking miners and the withering away of the Brent patriarch, a leading member of the LDS Church, represents a critique of the future direction of the LDS Church, both culturally and as an institution. Snell's novel presented to its 1930s readers a vision of Mormonism deeply invested in the capitalist objectives of the twentieth century while simultaneously retreating from its religious ideals (problematic and otherwise). Indeed, the church was at that time still relatively silent on its desire to fit in with the rest of American culture, ruminating quietly on assimilation while carefully establishing itself in large-scale business ventures such as beet-sugar manufacturing, electrical production, and local service industries. Snell's novel sits awkwardly in a lineage of Mormon literature. No critics have undertaken an analysis of this novel, barring a few passing bibliographic references by some Mormon writers. While this lack of attention seems reasonable given Snell's tedious prose, Mormon critics in particular may have been hesitant to consider works (including Fisher's as well) that so clearly criticize Mormon social ideology and entrepreneurial impulse, especially those that could not simply be written off as simply anti-Mormon.

From the perspective of the 1930s, Snell finds Mormon peculiarity tragically dissolved. His novel does not present a hopeful Mormon future; he reserves his critique mainly for industrial capitalism, not Mormonism per se. If the Mormon Church continues down Snell's literary trajectory, assimilation will become complete along the axis of capitalist production, devoid of religious integrity or any attention to religious identity. Assimilation happens, not through the withdrawing of Mormon religious beliefs or social practices, but through the active embracing of foundational American economic principles.

MORMON AMERICANS

The novels of this first generation of Mormon authors proclaim an end to their peculiarity, often by situating the molt of Mormon difference within the tumult of late-nineteenth-century Utah. Novels such as those by Whipple, Sorensen, Kennelly, Fisher, and Snell relegate Mormon distinctiveness to the past. Whipple and Sorensen rather deliberately exterminate Mormon oddity, evidenced though the deaths of their central characters. Fisher, who like Snell condemns the loss of community through church-based entrepreneurial greed, drives the heterodox principles to Mexico (where LDS splinter sects continue to practice polygamy even today), and Kennelly removes Mormon polygamous wives from their supposedly grotesque roles to establish an early Mormon feminism. According to these writers, the American future now lay open to Mormons; they could embrace their distinctive history with no threat to American national principles (or federal law, for that matter) and carry on as exemplary members of American society. Gentile society clearly accepted these novelists, as is evidenced by the predominance of non-Mormon publishing houses for these books as well as the tenor of their reviews. At the time of publication, these novelists were widely read, particularly by non-Mormon readers, thus effecting a reduction in the apparent cultural differences between Mormons and other white Americans by both Mormon writers and gentile readers and reviewers.

The American West has been a battleground for constituting U.S. national identity, and Mormons played a role in establishing that mythic place. But unlike western African Americans, Native Americans, Asian Americans, and other visible minorities, Mormons did not literally embody their difference, especially once the social markers of polygamy had been removed. Much of the success of Mormon assimilation rests on their coincident racial similarity with the dominant peoples in the United States. While polygamy, theocracy, and early communitarianism made Mormons alien to most of America in the nineteenth century, their collective whiteness eased their ability to drop those peculiarities and become leading—or at least representative—members of American society. Following pressures in the 1960s and 1970s to incorporate minorities within the church, LDS leadership allowed men of color into the lay-church priesthood in 1978. (Although minorities, particularly African Americans, were welcomed into the church before this time, like Mormon women of all races, they could not ascend within the church hierarchy, thus designating them as inferior to other male members of a patriarchal organization.) With the church appearing more multicultural near the end of the nineteenth century, Mormons seemed to increasingly represent the nation.

Ironically, the trend in Mormon writing today is to embrace peculiarity; with the loss of outsider identity, Mormons today welcome their particular history into their identity. Now, however, they situate their peculiarity as contributing to a multicultural nation rather than menacing national cohesiveness. Many contemporary Mormon novels celebrate Mormon cultural distinctiveness, often employing the same techniques used by midcentury novelists, particularly through references to shared history and cultural practices. But rather than working to expunge a problematic past, end Mormon history, or justify Mormon distinctiveness to a more powerful gentile world, these novels often use Mormon life as a backdrop to other narratives (often set in the Intermountain West). In these novels, a character's Mormonism is usually uncontested but elicits distinct practices and beliefs that often complicate interactions with a non-Mormon world. Mormons have become, at least narratively, peculiar again but now woven firmly into the fabric of American pluralist culture.[17]

No longer a renegade territory, cultural backwater, or den of polygamous iniquity, Mormon Utah clearly saw itself as part of the nation by the late twentieth century. On January 3, 1976, historian Richard D. Poll gave the annual Statehood Day address to an audience at the Salt Lake Tabernacle. By delivering a secular speech in a religious building, Poll—and the state of Utah—unmistakably blurs the distinction between the LDS Church and the state of Utah and merges together their histories and futures. In his concluding remarks, Poll brings together Utahans and Americans, implicitly situating Mormons within this mix:

> I shall not speak tonight of what has happened in Utah since the Second World War—of Fort Douglas or Hill Field, of Canyonlands or Snowbird, of Geneva Steel or Thiokol, of the Utah Symphony or Ballet West, of the Brigham City Indian School or the NAACP, of urban sprawl or energy shortages, of soaring divorce rates or whether Johnny can read. They are all parts of Utah today, and they collectively testify—both activities and problems—that the integration of Utah and the United States is complete. (Poll 92)

By the nation's bicentennial, eighty years after Utah had joined the Union and only eighty-six years after the LDS Church caved to the nation's moral demands, Mormon Utah mirrored the United States's highs and lows as well its boons and scourges.

5

BUFFALO BILL'S
OBJECT LESSONS

❖

NATIVE AMERICAN SURVIVANCE IN THE ARENA

My first caller was old Blue Horse. . . . Blue Horse had been, as he
claimed, a friend to the white man, for he was one of the first Sioux
army scouts, and one of the first to cross the ocean with Buffalo Bill.
The old man wanted nothing so much as an audience, and the tale
of his exploits served to pass the evening. Some one had brought in
a cot and an armful of blankets, and I was soon asleep.

—CHARLES EASTMAN, *From the Deep Woods to Civilization* (1916)

IN JAMES WELCH'S 2000 NOVEL, *The Heartsong of Charging Elk*, the title character is accidentally left behind in Marseille by Buffalo Bill's Wild West after
he contracts the flu and subsequently injures himself during a performance,
sending him to the hospital. Charging Elk speaks almost no English and even
less French. In an attempt to identify himself to the American vice-consul
there, he speaks from his hospital bed the only words he thinks can connect
him to the United States and his home.

> Charging Elk gestured toward himself with his hand. "American. Lakota."
> As he thought of something else to say, he remembered how he had gotten
> there. "Pahuska [Long Hair]. Buffalo Bill." Then he remembered the
> Lakota who had been appointed the chief of the show Indians. . . . "Rocky
> Bear," he said. "Big Medicine. Oglala. Wild West." (13)

Haltingly, in single and seemingly unlinked words, Charging Elk describes
himself to the vice-consul. Collectively, these words present him as a composite of his American nationality, his Lakota (Oglala) ethnicity, his job, and
his bosses. Trying to make himself recognizable to whites, he identifies him-

self as both American and Indian, linked together momentarily through the medium of Buffalo Bill's Wild West, an American institution with international flair and appeal. Though Charging Elk identifies himself as American, his Americanness is established through his attachment to the Wild West, which does not necessarily prohibit his self-identification as Lakota (in fact, Buffalo Bill's Wild West highlights this identity). But outside of the United States, Charging Elk must establish his ethnic identity within the geographic borders of America, embracing both labels through the Wild West to produce an identity sensible to others.

But Charging Elk's already problematic identity does not stay stable for long. He soon escapes from the hospital and is quickly arrested for vagrancy. He is then temporarily released to a guardian family while he finds work to fund his return to Buffalo Bill's Wild West, now elsewhere in Europe, or home to the United States. But through a bureaucratic error, the French government mistakes Charging Elk for another Indian from Buffalo Bill's Wild West, Featherman, who died from influenza at the same hospital from which Charging Elk escaped (an Indian with the Wild West named Featherman did die in Marseilles, but of smallpox). Through a simple bureaucratic slip, Charging Elk officially ceases to exist, in France or in any country, for that matter. Charging Elk in fact cannot prove his personhood, for as the vice-consul tells Charging Elk's guardian, "There is the matter of proving he exists, getting him papers—he has no birth certificate, no passport. I just don't know" (181). Charging Elk's existence in body is not contested; the American ambassador frets, "Unfortunately, we still have a very real *indien* on our hands" (179). But his identity and uniqueness cannot be proven. Lakota, Oglala, actor, Wild West employee, American—all become empty without papers and documentation.

Charging Elk rests in a world between U.S. nationality and Lakota identity. His corporeal existence is later accepted by France when he is convicted of murder and sentenced to life in prison. He is released years later, however, when the French government realizes that he had been tried as a U.S. citizen rather than as a member of a sovereign nation "not subject to the legal agreements between the United States and France" (Welch 361). Within the novel, Charging Elk's identity shifts from a Native American specter in Buffalo Bill's arena to a non-person—with no proof of existence—and then to an individual defined by his *non*-Americanness. In his last permutation, at the close of the novel, Charging Elk finally acquires an official nationality; he has become a French citizen through marriage. Despite the fluidity of his public identity,

Charging Elk's general sense of self-identification rests on his Lakota identity. Throughout his time in France, he dreams of Paha Sapa (the Black Hills) and his family; he turns to Wakan Tanka (the Great Mystery) for support and prepares his *nagi* (spirit), which ought not depart his body in a strange land. But he must live in two worlds. In the United States, Charging Elk rejected reservation living by choosing employment with Buffalo Bill's Wild West and so moved between two worlds even amongst his own people. Within the Wild West, he played himself and Other simultaneously—he was Lakota and he was a savage specter. Now, in France, he must construct a new identity consisting of American and, as the French generically call him, Peau-Rouge, or redskin.

Charging Elk is a fictional character, but his story might well have come directly from one of the Native Americans who participated in Buffalo Bill's Wild West over the almost thirty years of its existence. Native Americans working for Buffalo Bill, as well as other shows, did in fact get stranded in England and other European countries. Nicholas Black Elk, who related his autobiographical narrative to the poet John G. Neihardt to produce *Black Elk Speaks*, was stranded along with three other Native Americans in Manchester, England, in 1888. He eventually reunited with Buffalo Bill's Wild West over a full year later in Paris where, rather than rejoin the show, he requested that Buffalo Bill send him home. Connecting Charging Elk's story to the actual stories of Show Indians (the term used by the Bureau of Indian Affairs in referring to Native Americans hired in Wild West shows), Welch stitches Black Elk's remarkable return into *The Heartsong of Charging Elk*, where a wide-eyed Charging Elk watches the "Indian man, dressed in a rough suit, [smile] sheepishly" and relate his adventurous story to a nodding and attentive Buffalo Bill (57). At the end of the novel, Charging Elk reconnects with the Wild West when it stops in Marseille during the 1905 season, sixteen years after it had left him behind, forgotten in a hospital bed. But unlike Black Elk, Charging Elk does not desire a return to the United States or even to the Black Hills for that matter. He does not approach Buffalo Bill, nor does his return cause a commotion in the encampment, as did Black Elk's reappearance. When a young Lakota show employee urges Charging Elk to return to Paha Sapa, or at least to the reservation, Charging Elk tells him, "This is my home, now, Joseph. I have a wife. Soon I will have a child. . . . [H]ere I am a man of thirty-seven winters. I load and unload ships. I speak the language of these people. My wife is one of them and my heart is her heart" (437). But even given his dedication to his new life and nationality, Charging Elk remains Lakota, part of him pining for life back on the plains: looking at the young Lakota man's aunt, Charging Elk thinks, "Her face was round and smooth and the color of pecans. He looked at her and realized how much he had missed his own people" (431). But the pull of Lakota identity is not enough for him to break his new French constitution. His father dead, many of his people slaughtered at Wounded Knee (Charging Elk saw the massacre in a dream), and his Lakota identity shuffled and undercut by reservation life, Indian schools, and U.S. federal Indian policy, Charging Elk feels no pull to return to the America of his birth. No mythology, no sense of American identity, can detach him from his new life. He is Lakota, but he is no longer of the Lakota world; a return to the Great Plains gives him no hope. In fact, all that is left for him in America is a narrative of loss and destruction.

PERFORMING THE WILD WEST

Unlike African American pioneers or Mormons who adopted the roles of western pioneers, Native Americans such as Charging Elk or Black Elk saw no foundational part of their identity constituted through the dominant pioneer narratives of the American West, except in terms of their marginalization and being labeled as suspect. Still, while those Native Americans participating in Buffalo Bill's Wild West had no relationship to those pioneer myths that drove the self-representations of African American westerners or Mormons, their lives played a distinct role in the creation of western mythologies. Within the standard narrative of western conflict, Native Americans represented primarily a barrier to white civilization and westward development. Certainly Indian violence toward whites posed a genuine threat in certain areas, especially when settlers and the U.S. military insisted that Native Americans be removed from the land that gave them sustenance. But they were also distinctly imagined threats, appearing daily in the anxiously scribbled fears of Conestoga wagon travelers' diaries and in dime novels and magazine serials as bloodthirsty savages seeking scalps and young women. Thus William F. Cody's spectacle played on these suppositions and created an image of primitive, but noble, Indians as the vanquished as well as vanishing antagonists of U.S. westward expansion. While other westerners, particularly those who resided outside of the structural boundaries that defined exactly who a westerner could be, sought to locate their Americanness through their attachment to pioneer ideals and history, Native Americans by definition could not seek these ideals;

their roles were already scripted. Native Americans were not pioneers, and never could be; they were the aboriginal inhabitants of this continent and had to play the role of savage resistance in the stories of westward expansion and settlement. In fact, their own stories of western settlement arose in opposition to those very pioneer identities that promised Americanness to writers such as Micheaux, Love, Sorensen, or Whipple.

Native Americans who participated in Buffalo Bill's Wild West performed their identity within the artistry of Cody's spectacle. No imaginable space existed for Native Americans to aspire to the adoption of identities as cowboy, settler, miner, or stagecoach driver. If Micheaux's depiction of an African American homesteader seemed to jar America's definition of a western pioneer, Black Elk depicting George Armstrong Custer, or one of his soldiers for that matter, seemed downright ridiculous. But these Native Americans present a truly ironic appropriation of American identity in which a subjugated people play hyperstylized images of themselves while actually participating in their Americanization through employment as actors in the show. While some westerners embraced the mythology of the West to prove their national attachment, Native Americans with the Wild West embraced the economic and social opportunities provided by Cody, thus cementing themselves within the spectacle of that very same western mythology. Marginalized westerners such as African Americans and Mormons sought to relieve their marginalization through the production of narratives matching those of official culture, but Show Indians necessarily remained marginalized through the narratives of Cody's show; their art, unlike that of other western outsiders, demanded their subjugation. But from this subjugated position, Native Americans in Buffalo Bill's Wild West worked to restructure their identity through the terms of the show to empower themselves as potential Americans—specifically of the qualified type, that is, *Indian*-Americans.

Both Cody and the Native Americans he employed worked to produce myths about the West and its aboriginal people. In this chapter, I will look at Cody's construction of Indian identity as well as the production of Indianness by the Native American actors themselves. Cody created western history in his arena, including a particular image of Native Americans as simultaneously threatening and noble. But rather than merely being victims of Cody's concepts, many of the Native Americans who participated in the Wild West embraced some of the underlying terms of Cody's vision of Indian identity for practical and political purposes. Native Americans such as Sitting Bull,

Luther Standing Bear, and Black Elk, all of whom participated in Cody's Wild West, used their attachment to the show to forward a recognition of Indian lives. Sitting Bull rejected all attempts at assimilation, while Luther Standing Bear actively built institutions (such as an Indian employment agency) to furnish Native Americans with the tools through which to fully join American society. Black Elk's position becomes complicated, as we shall see, through the editorial manipulations of his scribe. As marginalized people in the United States, Native Americans could not seek cultural citizenship through the myths of Roosevelt, Remington, Wister, or Turner. But they could turn their depictions—both within the show as well as afterward in print—to their advantage by proving an ability to move within Anglo society in order both to achieve alliance with U.S. national culture and to demand acknowledgment of their identity and history.

BUFFALO BILL'S WILD WEST: AMERICA'S NATIONAL ENTERTAINMENT

Buffalo Bill's Wild West had extraordinary public appeal in its day, declaring itself "America's National Entertainment." Indeed, today most scholars acknowledge the widespread influence of Cody's show and interpret its influence as formative of American cultural norms, if not of U.S. history itself.[1] Cody's fame began when Edward Zane Carroll Judson, publically known as Ned Buntline, used Cody's nickname and a composite of him and Wild Bill Hickok for a serial novel published in 1869 entitled *Buffalo Bill, the King of the Border Men*. Though Cody was relatively famous as a U.S. Army scout at the time, his entry into popular culture was essentially a fluke. As Buffalo Bill became a household name, thanks to Buntline, Cody turned to the stage for work during his off-season from scouting, appearing with the Buffalo Bill Combination, a show that included fellow scouts Wild Bill Hickok and Texas Jack Omohundro in hackneyed dramas of border life.[2] Cody founded the Wild West in 1883 when, inspired by the success of the "Old Glory Blowout," a Fourth of July celebration he had planned for the town of North Platte, Nebraska, the year before, he decided to produce his own traveling show built on a combination of circus and ethnographic themes. Buffalo Bill's Wild West ran for almost thirty years, though management and ownership changed hands numerous times. From 1883 to 1916, literally millions of people saw Buffalo Bill and his Wild West in cities as diverse as Omaha, Barcelona, and Birmingham. The total income for the show is impossible to estimate, but during flush times, such as the performances in conjunction with the 1893 Columbian Exposition in Chicago, the Wild West produced profits close to $1,000,000 in only a few short months (Russell 375).[3] In Cody's first season, during which the show traveled as the Wild West, Rocky Mountain, and Prairie Exhibition, he included trick shooting, "Cowboy Fun" (with bucking horses and fancy riding), a race between a mounted Indian and another on foot, a Pony Express sprint, the Deadwood Mail Coach, and an exhibition of buffalo, elk, deer, and other western animals (Russell 298; Kramer 91).

By the turn of the century, Buffalo Bill's Wild West included exhibitions of U.S. artillery units, performances by a Congress of Rough Riders of the World (including Hungarian, Arab, and Mexican horsemen, among others), fully staged attacks on cabins and mail coaches, military musical drills, ethnographic exhibitions by Native Americans, and elaborate reenactments of Custer's Last Stand, the Battle of San Juan Hill, or other often unspecified military skirmishes. Cody's first show traveled without lighting or tents and very little material support, but by 1895 Cody claimed to have fifty-two railcars for moving the show, more than either Barnum or Ringling. In 1898, Cody had 467 employees, moved over four hundred horses (and mules) for each show, and carried two electrical generators for lighting the show (Schwartz 659; see also Blackstone 46, 49–52). By the 1890s his show drew thousands of people for each performance. In 1908, though, Cody merged his Wild West with Pawnee Bill's Great Far East, due to financial difficulties arising primarily from Cody's mismanagement. By 1909, Cody no longer held a financial interest in the show, and by 1913 he was bankrupt. For the next four years Cody appeared in the Sells-Floto Circus and the Miller Brothers 101 Ranch Wild West Show, but here he remained only a figurehead and name with a salary. By this point, Buffalo Bill's Wild West was no longer attached to its originary performer (and owner), as the owner of Sells-Floto Circus now controlled the name. After almost three decades of continuous performances, the largest and most popular Wild West show in the world effectively closed when Cody died in 1917.[4]

But Buffalo Bill's "National Entertainment," advertised complete with "Object Lessons" and "Educational Exhibitions," sought to create a myth of the American West (and also the United States's burgeoning global powers) through presentations of carefully staged tricks, reenactments, and the presence of special performers. Cody was in the business of presenting history as spectacle, and part of the allure of this spectacle was the appearance of "real" historical figures. Audience members already knew Cody as a successful army scout, and his presence thus evoked an authenticity of frontier experience. But Cody also hired a slew of sheriffs, outlaws, and other vaguely known (or created) westerners to bolster the image that the Wild West was truly only one step removed from the actual geographic and historic space itself. His arena provided a forum for Native American performers, demanding, of course, that they play their vanquished roles in history, though he also incorporated ethnographic exhibitions of Plains Indians traditional culture. Even the much maligned Hunkpapa Sioux chief Sitting Bull traveled with him in the 1885 season, though he did not perform in any fights or reenactments; Cody did not sensationalize him but rather simply presented Sitting Bull as a surviving leader from the still smoldering Indian Wars. Cody hired surviving members of Custer's Seventh Cavalry for his recreation of the Battle of Little Bighorn and, later, as discussed in chapter 1, he hired sixteen members of Roosevelt's Rough Riders as part of his reenactment of the Battle of San Juan Hill, the presence of these soldiers again giving a touch of authenticity to his arena shows. Cody's spectacles also highlighted authentic historical artifacts such as the Deadwood Mail Coach, which was attacked in almost every performance, and other miscellaneous paraphernalia that supposedly saw service in the West.[5] Within the arena, Cody creatively mixed these historical figures and artifacts with skilled equestrians, fancy shooting, and live animals to create, without deceit or trickery, a historical exhibition that fed directly into the audiences' ideological expectations and thus helped to solidify Cody's myth of the West as an authentic history.

Cody's very narrow version of history, which claimed to be nationally expansive and all-inclusive, created clear identities for his audience's easy consumption. Cody's West consisted of cowboys, Indians, stagecoach drivers, sharpshooters, scouts, and occasional miners and U.S. soldiers. Nowhere did he present bankers, railroadmen, farmers, shopkeepers, land speculators, day laborers, or even ranchers. In fact, according to Jonathan Martin, Cody's West boiled down to little more than "racial warfare and the glorification of individualistic scouts and cowboys," plainly ignoring the massive economic expansion and subsequent inequalities within the region (106). Indeed, Paul Reddin notes that reporters (as well as Cody's publicity agents) proclaimed Cody's Wild West "the gladiatorial contest revived" (62). For the 1886 season, Cody prepared *The Drama of Civilization*, a series of tableaux depicting first contact and then the subsequent conquest of the continent through various "epochs," as he called them. In that year *The Drama of Civilization* opened with "The Primeval Forest" and continued with "The Prairie," "The Cattle Ranch," and "The Mining Camp." In 1887 and in the following years, Cody's vision of American victory still began in "The Primeval Forest" (which depicted only wild animals and Native Americans, thus linking them as evolutionary equals), but he closed *The Drama of Civilization* with "Custer's Last Stand." The official depiction of U.S. history through the Wild West began with a primitive Eden and its peaceful aborigines and concluded with the establishment of Native Americans as ruthless savages incapable of living with whites, thus narratively necessitating their subjugation (if not extinction). The struggles of history transformed into battles between individual men in Cody's arena, justifying U.S. expansion, genocidal violence, and the conquest of the American continent.

In 1893, Cody introduced his Congress of Rough Riders of the World. While the term Rough Riders has become mythically attached to Theodore Roosevelt and the First Volunteer Cavalry in Cuba, the Rough Riders of Buffalo Bill's Wild West were an international collection of skilled horsemen and cavalry soldiers. While highlighting the American cowboy, Cody featured Mexican vaqueros, South American gauchos, and German, French, and English cavalrymen, as well as Native American, Cossack, Arab, and even Japanese horsemen. Pushing the boundaries of horsemanship, and possibly undercutting the stature of these Rough Riders, Cody even included Carter the Cowboy Cyclist, with "His Aerial Leap Through Space" (Reddin 148; Rosa and May 276). Later, Cody added to his entourage Cuban "insurgents," to help bolster America's position against an imperial Spain, as well as Hawaiian and Filipino riders. Though Cody often presented the various members of the Congress of Rough Riders under headings such as "savage" and "civilized" (he sometimes advertised Rough Rider horse races as "Wild Rivalries of Savage, Barbarous, and Civilized Races" [poster in Rennert 66]), he featured the collective group as ultimately cohesive and united by horsemanship. When the term Rough Riders became associated with the First Volunteer Cavalry, Roosevelt initially claimed a dislike for the name because of its association with Buffalo Bill's Wild West ("rough rider" had been used to describe western horsemen even before Cody created his international coterie), but after the sobriquet stuck, the connection between Cody's spectacle and Roosevelt's heroics became definitive.[6] As discussed in chapter 1, Roosevelt lauded his regiment as diverse, but the ethnic and racial boundaries he ascribed both to his soldiers and to American memory contradicted the breadth of Cody's international project. Regardless, this international project had an undeniable imperial slant. When the Congress of Rough Riders of the World paraded, Cody inevitably led the procession, thus depicting the centrality of American power in an international arena.[7]

As the American West became an integral part of official culture, helping to delineate U.S. national identity during the late nineteenth and early twentieth centuries, Buffalo Bill's Wild West manifested the vision so necessary to a nation striving for greater political power internationally and greater social cohesion internally. Cody turned U.S. conflicts—and U.S. history—into racially charged struggles played out on a gladiatorial battlefield. Though his Congress of Rough Riders remained racially diverse and cohesive in purpose, Cody set up antagonistic situations based on racial difference throughout the rest of his show. Commonly, the Wild West presented conflicts and skirmishes between Native Americans and white settlers, cowboys, miners, stagecoach drivers, or soldiers in order to rationalize the violence of Manifest Destiny and the conquest of the West. Thus Cody's history, as well as his implied projections into the United States's future, rested on the demonization of those forces interrupting westward (and more generally, U.S.) expansion.

PLAYING INDIAN

Central to understanding Buffalo Bill's image of U.S. history is his presentation of Native Americans, particularly since he set Native Americans up as the central obstacle impeding American civilization and development. Primarily, Indians played roles in which they attacked various outposts of white civilization: "Attack on a Settler's Cabin," "Attack on the Emigrant Train," "The Battle of Summit Springs" (figures 13 and 14). Thus Cody generally presented whites, especially settlers, as passive victims of Indian aggression. But Native Americans also presented themselves as ethnographic curiosities by performing tribal dances and songs within the Wild West as well as allowing paying spectators to wander within their encampment after the shows finished for the day (figure 15). Cody also capitalized on the employment of certain Native American performers, particularly those who had been actively involved in conflicts with the U.S. military. For example, in 1893 Cody hired Plenty Horses, Painted Horse, and Rocky Bear, three Sioux Indians who fought at

FIGURE 13 Attack on Settler's Cabin in Buffalo Bill's Wild West (from a show in London between 1890–1900). Denver Public Library, Western History Collection, Collection of E. Vandyk, X-33465.

FIGURE 14 Attack on Stagecoach in Buffalo Bill's Wild West (1908). Denver Public Library, Western History Collection, F. J. Hiscock, X-33900.

Little Bighorn (Kasson 113). Thus Cody could claim that his reenactments of "Custer's Last Stand" might include surviving members from both sides, proving again that the Wild West was but one step removed from that battle itself. But Cody's use of Native Americans and his focused imagery played directly into the images and stories that American popular culture had already created. From the novels of James Fenimore Cooper to cartoons, from George Catlin's Indian shows to lithographs and serials, Americans expected Indians to be mysterious, reverent, noble, and savage. Thus when Native Americans in the Wild West played their various roles, they spoke immediately to the sensibilities of an expectant audience.

FIGURE 15 Postcard from Buffalo Bill's Wild West (1909). The back of the postcard reads: "Friend May: Here is a picture of one of the Indians with the Buffalo Bill show. How do we look. We had one taken with Cody [but] it isn't very good. Yours Mrs. S." Denver Public Library, Western History Collection, photographer unknown, X-31728.

In *The National Uncanny* Renée Bergland argues that nationalist narratives of triumph necessarily need ghosts to sustain them. Within the development of the United States, Native Americans took on spectral qualities—ghostly, ephemeral, and, most importantly, dead—providing an unspoken (and unspeakable) base for the narrative of imperial expansion. She argues that Indian ghosts inhabit U.S. national narratives concurrently with their physical removal from the American landscape: "By writing about Indians as ghosts, white writers effectively remove them from American lands, and place them, instead, within the American imagination" (4). As noted earlier in the introduction, Donald Pease similarly presents a U.S. national consciousness produced through the imagined separation of (white) Americans from those whom they believed their structural opposites: "these subject peoples were not a historical aberration but a structural necessity for the construction of a national narrative" (4). Thus the ghosts of America's Native dead—culturally or physically—shore up that very narrative that helped kill them. Bergland finds an "obsession" with Native Americans in American literature (particularly of the nineteenth century) and determines that "In American letters, and in the American imagination, Native American ghosts function both as representations of national guilt and as triumphant agents of Americanization" (4).[8]

Within this framework, we can see that Cody engaged within the Wild West the very tactics and ideology described by Bergland and Pease. He removes Indians from their lands (literally, in terms of his earlier association with the military, and through his physical disengagement of Native Americans from reservations for employment in his show) and places them "within the American imagination," where they act as what Jonathan Martin calls "a yardstick against which spectators measured white superiority and civilization" (95). Thus Native Americans in Cody's show could be nothing but wild Indians. They could not be farmers, schoolteachers, shopkeepers, cowboys, or even sharpshooters for that matter. Their primary role in this projection of U.S. history and in the official culture of the American West was to represent untamable wildness. In the imagined space of Native American identity projected by the Wild West, Indians could play only two roles to this end: they were either exotic savages or they were dead, the latter often following the former in many of Cody's historical plays.

But as workers employed by Cody, the Wild West offered Native Americans roles as productive subjects in American society that took them off reservations (or contested lands, for those Native Americans who still refused reservation living) and placed them in American and European cities. Cody's relationship with Native Americans was complicated in that while he publically presented them as villains in his historical tableaux, he ensured that they had equal rights and fair pay as employees. Though Native Americans remained vilified in the arena, Joy Kasson notes that the audience understood the Wild West as theatrics; they knew that after the imagined slaughter of marauding Indians, "the enemy 'other' would rise from the dust, wave to the crowd, and sell souvenir photographs at the end of the day" (265). This dual projection of Native American identity then allowed for audience members to perceive Indians simultaneously as a historical threat—a part of U.S. history—and as entertainers, but never as entertainers playing historical threats. By seeing the dead rise from the ground, Americans could pretend that the Indian wars waged over land and Native American autonomy shed no blood and

that those displaced natives could transform themselves happily into historical curiosities after the battles ended. By accepting the Wild West as theater,
audiences also allowed Native Americans to take on roles as actors. That is,
Native Americans might not only portray themselves, or at least what audience members believed to be Indian, but they might also dramatize Indianness: they would play Indian.

Cody offered Show Indians a kind of Americanization that most reformers, government officials, and military men scorned. Cody's drive to use Native Americans in his show was primarily selfish and driven by his desire for
popular and financial success, but by employing Native Americans as actors
he provided an avenue for those actors to become useful and productive
American citizens. Though Cody chose to exhibit Native Americans as spectacles, he also treated them as laborers and performers not unlike the other
cowboy or sharpshooter performers or the traveling laborers of the show itself. Starting in 1886 all Native American actors with the Wild West held employment contracts. Initially the terms of the contracts were vague, specify-
ing that the Indian employees were "to give public exhibitions of frontier life"
(quoted in Moses 32), but later these contracts more carefully stipulated working conditions, salary, and length of employment. Primarily this requirement
was forced on Cody by the Bureau of Indian Affairs (BIA) out of a fear that
Cody (and the owners of other shows) might abandon these Native American
actors if hard times befell him. In addition, the bureau insisted that shows employing Indians post a bond for their return to the reservation, as the government viewed Native Americans at this point as their charges rather than as individual citizens with the abilities to create their own contracts and obligations.

Employment in the Wild West allowed for Native American performers to
integrate partially into American society as both productive citizens and consumers. As Vine Deloria Jr. notes in an essay for the Brooklyn Museum's 1981
exhibition *Buffalo Bill and the Wild West*, "Instead of degrading the Indians and
classifying them as primitive savages, Cody elevated them to a status of equality with contingents from other nations" (53), pointing specifically to their participation in the Congress of Rough Riders of the World. Most Native Americans employed by Cody made more money in a single season than they might
see in many years of work on a reservation (if they could find work there at all).
During the 1886 season, Native American actors were paid twenty-five dollars
per month, about half the monthly salary of a white reservation day-school
teacher, and had their transportation paid both to and from Rushville, Ne-

braska, a town south of the Pine Ridge Reservation (Moses 31, 284 n. 22). Cody also claimed to have purchased a new suit of clothes for each Native American performer at the close of each season (Moses 116). Indeed, Luther Standing Bear, who acted as an interpreter and a kind of supervisor for Native American performers during the 1902 season, notes that each male performer received a hand-tailored suit and each woman a gingham dress; in Chicago after the close of the show Standing Bear helped a group of Indian performers buy twenty-seven fur overcoats at Marshall Field & Company's store, evidencing their recent acquisition of relatively disposable income (*My People* 267–68).[9]

Native American actors in the Wild West understood their roles as both actors and laborers. Black Elk tells us that he "liked the part of the show we made, but not the part the Wasichus [whites] made" (217), and Standing Bear writes that "I might take the part of a cowboy if I choose" and discusses two Indians "who were playing the parts of chiefs" (256, 258).[10] The role of Native Americans in the Wild West was twofold. They demonstrated Native customs such as song and dance, but they also took on other personas: ordinary men playing chiefs, for example. Most of the Native Americans employed by Cody came from the Pine Ridge Reservation and thus were Sioux, primarily Oglala. But they often had to present themselves as from multiple tribes. Thus just as cowboys might double as settlers in a certain sketch, Oglala Sioux might portray Cheyenne or Arapaho (Standing Bear, *My People* 252–54). Yet Show Indians knew that as actors in Cody's show they were also employees. First of all, they signed contracts with terms and specifications of employment. Also, they recognized themselves as being in the same position with reference to labor as other performers, if not the American white majority in general. In 1890, Rocky Bear, an actor in the Wild West, told the acting commissioner of Indian affairs, Robert V. Belt, "If the great father wants me to stop [working with the Wild West], I would do it. That is the way I get money. If a man goes to work in some other place, he has some for his children" (quoted in Moses 101; Moses also notes that Rocky Bear was carrying with him that day three hundred dollars in gold coin, presumably from his pay). In the same session with Acting Commissioner Belt, Black Heart, another Native American from Cody's show, explained that he saw Indian employment in Wild West shows as an extension of their lives on the Great Plains:

We were raised on horseback; that is the way we had to work. These men furnished us the same work we were raised to; that is the reason we want to work for these kind of men. . . . If Indian wants to work at any place and earn money, he wants to do so; white man got privilege to do the same— any kind of work that he wants. (Quoted in Moses 103)

While both Rocky Bear and Black Heart recognized their theatrical roles in Cody's show, they also recognized that employment with the Wild West provided them an income, to which they felt as entitled as any white American.

As early as 1879 Cody argued that Native American employment in shows and exhibitions outside of reservations was socially constructive. In hiring a group of Pawnee Indians for his stage show, the Buffalo Bill Combination, he claimed in opposition to reformers and the Bureau of Indian Affairs that their employment was "benefitting the Indians as well as the government" (quoted in Russell 262). In 1891, Cody did provide a direct service to the federal government when he agreed to take on twenty-three Native Americans imprisoned at Fort Sheridan for their association with the Ghost Dance. General Miles, who was in charge of the prisoners at Fort Sheridan, praised Cody's employment of the incarcerated Sioux, writing, "It would give them occupation for a year and a half without expense to the Government; they would be away from the Sioux country during that time" (quoted in Moses 109–10). The federal government did not force these prisoners to join the Wild West, though they certainly could do so in lieu of a possible prison sentence. These twenty-three prisoners were to remain with Cody in Europe until the fall of 1892, but they returned almost six months early, declaring that they had served enough time with Cody (Moses 119); arriving in America, about one-third of these Indians remained in military custody while General Miles allowed the others to return home.

Part of the Americanization process that allowed for Show Indians to become representative members of society lies in their status not only as culture producers (even if some of their production could be designated as prison labor), but as consumers as well. In the course of their employment, Show Indians, not only purchased trinkets and clothes to take home with them, but they also played tourist, seeing the sights of strange lands, both domestic and foreign. In Europe, for example, Native American employees used their free time to wander around new cities. They visited the Congregational Chapel in West Kensington and saw a production of Goethe's *Faust* in London (Moses 47, 48); in Barcelona they had their picture taken in front of a statue of Christopher Columbus (where a member of the group supposedly uttered, "It was a damned bad day for us when he discovered America" [Moses 86–87]); they attended the coronation of Pope Leo XIII in Rome (Moses 87); in Venice they took a gondola ride and visited St. Mark's Cathedral (Moses 91). In 1893 many of Cody's Indians partook of the events and shows at the Columbian Exhibition, just next door to their own show; in their off time they toured Chicago, taking boat tours, riding the newfangled Ferris Wheel, eating popcorn, and quite literally whooping it up on nearby merry-go-rounds (Moses 140; Havighurst 167–68). Admittedly, some of this tourism was planned and encouraged by Cody, who used the appearance of his Indian employees in public as advertisements for the show (see figure 16), but much of the wanderings were driven by the desires of these Native Americans to see new cities and new sights. Luther Standing Bear notes, "I was sorry to leave [London], because I had been given a chance to see many wonderful things and visit many wonderful places," including Westminster Abbey, the king's palace, and "the house where all the toys were kept with which Queen Victoria had played as a child" (*My People* 259). Upon returning from his tour with the Wild West, Black Elk noted in a 1889 letter to *Iapi Oaye*, a Sioux-language newspaper, "Across the ocean is where they killed Jesus; again I wished to see it but it was four days on the ocean and there was no railroad" (DeMallie 10), indicating that his taste for tourism and sightseeing had been established while with Buffalo Bill in England.

Reformers and many of the Bureau of Indian Affairs commissioners deemed Indian employment with Wild West shows inappropriate and exploitative. They refused to recognize the stability that employment with shows like Cody's provided. As Native Americans were essentially charges of the federal government, various commissioners attempted to halt Indian employment in shows.[11] Generally, reformers and the BIA could not suppress the practice of Native American employment, but they could at least regulate it. Initially the bureau insisted on contracts and bonds, but later, especially under Commissioner Thomas Jefferson Morgan (1889–93), it simply refused to acknowledge Show Indian employment as legitimate and disallowed any BIA assistance to Native Americans who participated in the shows.[12] BIA Commissioner Morgan strongly advocated Native American assimilation through education, agricultural pursuits, and the end of tribal identification. With no patience for the celebration of Native customs—in the Wild West arena or on the reservation—he wrote to the secretary of the interior, "Indians must conform to 'the white man's ways,' peaceably if they will, forcibly if they

FIGURE 16 Native American employees of Buffalo Bill's Wild West in front of a poster for the Wild West, Bodmin, Cornwall, England (1904). Denver Public Library, Western History Collection, Collection of John James, X-33496.

must. . . . They cannot escape it, and must either conform to it or be crushed by it" (quoted in Moses 74). Of particular concern to many reformers was the effect of travel and access to new, and possibly immoral, experiences for these performers. But according to Moses the real problem reformers had with Indian employment in shows lay not so much in the possibilities of exploitation or immoral influences, but rather in the image of Native Americans portrayed in those shows, which ran counter to the reformers' desires and conceptions. Reformers (and BIA commissioners alike) wanted public presentations of assimilated Indians: educated, studious, hardworking, and with vocations rather than traditions. Cody's presentations of Native Americans highlighted not only tribal customs, but also their supposed savage nature, even if only in theater, and thus, supposed the reformers, their more appropriate image of assimilated and anglicized Native Americans was not getting publicized.

The battle for Indian imagery took place on a tripartite battleground where reformers, show operators like Cody, and Native Americans themselves fought to establish identities within a complicated tension of political desires, popular conceptions, and ticket sales. From Cody's construction of savage exotics and the BIA's desire for autonomous and assimilated individuals we can turn to the images of Native Americans constructed by Native American performers themselves to best understand the complicated forces in this struggle for identity. Of the hundreds or possibly thousands of Native Americans who traveled with Cody's show, few left enduring artifacts through which we might interpret their experiences. But from the few autobiographies and a few pictures, we can try to understand not so much the actual experiences of those Show Indians, but rather, like Charging Elk's fictional narrative, the importance of their experiences in Buffalo Bill's Wild West for forging their identities both as American Indians and as Americans.

PERFORMING AMERICANNESS; AUTHENTICATING INDIANNESS

The concept of the Show Indian likely got its start with George Catlin and his exhibitions. Of course, Native Americans were taken to Europe, sometimes forcibly, and showcased there as early as Columbus and first contact. But the popular theatrical production focusing on Native American customs can be traced to Catlin's attempt to simultaneously highlight Native culture and profit from it personally. Primarily Catlin painted portraits and exhibited them across the East and then later in Europe, but he did periodically include "real" Native Americans in his shows. He would incorporate their presence into his lectures about Indian life, often posing questions to them through an interpreter. Occasionally he would highlight certain customs of these dioramic participants by having them engage in traditional rituals such as smoking or dancing. In Europe, where no Indians were to be found (many of the Indians who participated in Catlin's shows in the United States appeared coincidentally between their political meetings in Washington, D.C., and various sightseeing tours while on the East Coast; see Reddin 18, 20), Catlin and his associates sometimes dressed in various Native American garments to drum up excitement—though they were often exposed as frauds (Reddin 32).

Soon, Catlin began to present Indian tableaux vivants, in which white actors portrayed Native American scenes on a stage (Reddin 33). By 1843 Catlin had begun to engage Native American performers for his overseas productions. That year Catlin hired a group of Canadian Ojibways for his lectures and shows in England, later using other Native Americans for similar exhibitions. But in 1846 eight Indians working for him contracted smallpox and two of them died, thus ending Catlin's relationship with the exhibition of Native Americans. None of the Native Americans under Catlin's employ left any writings or pictures through which we might attempt to understand their position within his shows. In fact, most of the Native Americans Catlin employed were associated with other travelers who engaged them for European exhibition and then effectively leased them to Catlin.

One of the first self-representative narratives from a Native American involved in performances such as Catlin's or Cody's comes from the first published autobiography of a Native American woman, Sarah Winnemucca Hopkins's *Life among the Piutes: Their Wrongs and Claims* (1883). Oddly enough, her narrative of self-representation that is useful for a discussion of staged Native American identity comes to us here as an absence. Though Sarah Winnemucca (later Sarah Winnemucca Hopkins) became widely known for her autobiography and through her lectures on East Coast reformer circuits concerning both the history of her people and the present conditions of Native Americans more generally, she fails to address in her autobiography the months that she spent in tableaux vivants and other exhibitions with her family in Virginia City and San Francisco during 1864.

Life among the Piutes details Sarah Winnemucca's initial encounters with whites, the complicated confrontations with the U.S. Army in the 1870s, including the Paiute relocation, and the reestablishment of the Paiutes on a reservation encompassing their original lands. Within her autobiography, which mixes personal narrative, sentimentalism, and sometimes outright indignation, Sarah Winnemucca pleads for her white audience to realize the human cost laid upon Native Americans by the conquest of the West. She concludes her narrative by directly confronting her readers: "For shame! for shame! You dare to cry out Liberty, when you hold us in places against our will, driving us from place to place as if we were beasts" (243–44). Though she demands sympathy and anger from her readers, she calls for action as well: "I pray of you, I implore you, I beseech you, hear our pitiful cry to you, sweep away the agency system; give us homes to live in, for God's sake and for humanity's sake" (242–43). *Life among the Piutes* served as a political tool by providing a first-person account of wrongs done in the name of U.S. progress, but it also established through the logic of autobiography that Sarah Winnemucca—as representative of Native Americans generally—had a life worth living and a story worth telling. And within that story lay her carefully constructed image of Indian identity.

Apparently Sarah Winnemucca's father, a Paiute chief, enjoyed ceremony and performance a great deal, and his children generally followed suit. When her father appeared on stage in Virginia City in the early 1860s, generally to orate on the Paiutes and their relationship with whites, Sarah Winnemucca would translate and thus become part of the show (since most audiences saw the elder Winnemucca's speeches as performances rather than lectures). Then in 1864 Sarah Winnemucca, along with her father and other family members, performed in a series of tableaux vivants at Sutliff Music Hall in Virginia City, illustrating scenes such as "The Indian Camp," "Scalping the Prisoner," "The Coyote Dance," and a series depicting Pocahontas saving Captain John Smith (Zanjani 75). Because she spoke English quite well, Sarah Winnemucca's primary job was translation, though in a recent biography Sally Zanjani claims that the young Sarah may have been more than a mere linguistic conduit. According to Zanjani, Sarah may have in fact orchestrated these events and then used the money raised to help her destitute tribe (72). Even so, the Winnemuccas were soon whisked off to San Francisco under the safeguard of James Miller, a coonskin-capped hustler who presented himself as a well-connected agent for the family's theatrical enterprise. But after only a few weeks he abandoned Sarah Winnemucca and her family, who, now broke, painfully straggled home (Zanjani 77).

While later in life Sarah Winnemucca would use the (lecture) stage as a primary tool for reform, she might have eliminated these earlier memories from her autobiography because she found these stage experiences distasteful. Local reporters in San Francisco, for example, wrote patronizing reviews of the Winnemuccas' show, calling them "The Royal Family" and translating Chief Winnemucca's speech as "Rub-a-dub, dub! Ho-daddy, hi-daddy; wo-hup, gee-haw Fetch water, fetch water, Manayunk!" (Canfield 41). Perhaps the bitterness of her family's penniless abandonment by their sponsor also aided in her careful deletions. Or conceivably she chose to forget this short period due to an aversion to the theatrical exploitation of her identity merely for pecuniary aid (even if the idea had been her own). But more important than discovering on a personal level why Sarah Winnemucca chose to expunge these early theatrical moments from her narrative, we might ask what their removal tells us about Sarah Winnemucca's self-representation and its place within personal and tribal identity, as well as American identity more generally.

Sarah Winnemucca's early theater relied on tropes of Indianness that whites expected: they spoke nonsense (Rub-a-dub, dub!) and were primitive but noble and colorful as well (The Royal Family). Zanjani claims that Sarah Winnemucca capitalized on precisely these preconceptions and strove to give the audience exactly what they anticipated. By age fourteen, the gregarious Sarah had found that she could gain public popularity by presenting herself as a willing participant in saloon and square dances when white women were unavailable (Zanjani 52; see also Canfield 15). She learned that whites treated her differently and that she could manipulate their expectations to her benefit. Thus, in her stage productions we can assume that she produced an easily consumed Indian (specifically Paiute) identity for the sake of popularity and ticket sales. Such a construction would not sit neatly within her autobiography, which purports to present an authentic view of Indian life and the tragic results of conquest.

Through her participation in (and possible masterminding of) these tableau vivant shows, Sarah Winnemucca engages in the construction of Indianness. Each tableau meant to give the audience images of Indian life that they had grown to expect from other sources of popular culture—images produced by white authors. Thus Sarah Winnemucca's stage presentations disrupted any notion of authentic Indian identity, particularly precontact identity, and instead set her up as precisely one of those authors of the white idealization of Native American culture. What we see in *Life among the Piutes*, when mixed carefully with the absence of her tableau vivant performances, is a careful construction of identity centered on the expectations of the consumer (or reader) rather than on the details of the producer. The narrative absence of this twenty-year-old's foray onto the stage within her autobiography reminds us that the production of authenticity often proceeds with lapses and exclusions, even when emanating from the source of that authenticity.

SITTING BULL: CAPITALIZING ON THE (WILD) WEST

Not all Native Americans who performed in exhibitions, from tableaux vivants to Wild West shows, chose to ignore those experiences in order to produce more supposedly authentic narratives of Indian experience. Probably the most famous Native American to appear in any Wild West show was the Hunkpapa Sioux chief Sitting Bull. Widely known by the American public for his association with the Battle of Little Bighorn, Sitting Bull traveled with Cody's Wild West during the 1885 season, his appearance often accompanied by hisses and boos from the audience. The American public generally despised Sitting Bull, prompted by newspapers and magazines that branded him the "killer of Custer." Searching for a demon to blame for the obliteration of a large part of the United States Seventh Cavalry at Little Bighorn, Sitting Bull became a prime target for Americans' outrage. The Bismarck, North Dakota, *Tribune* labeled him the leader of a "band of murderers, refugees and outlaws" a full six months before the infamous battle, while other papers placed him at the center of the battle, claiming that the Indians from "Sitting Bull's main camp" made up "Sitting Bull's forces," who, of course, had then killed Custer (Coward 163, 167). Sitting Bull, in fact, did not kill Custer. For that matter, his participation in the fight at Little Bighorn was decidedly limited, for, as Robert M. Utley observes, "No one expected chiefs to expose themselves recklessly if there were enough young men to handle the tasks" (*The Lance and the Shield* 152). Regardless, after Little Bighorn Sitting Bull's notoriety grew in the American press. He was reported to speak French, to have studied the military tactics of Napoleon, to have graduated from West Point, or to not even be an Indian at all but rather a Sandwich Islander, all of which were patently untrue (Coward 164).

In early May of 1877, in the same week that the Oglala Sioux Chief Crazy Horse surrendered to the U.S. military at Fort Robinson in Nebraska, Sitting Bull, along with roughly one thousand other Lakotas, fled the United States for Canada after almost a year of heavy military retaliation for the deaths of Custer and his men. Four months later military guards at Fort Robinson killed Crazy Horse in a fuzzily understood altercation, which sent even more Sioux northward to Canada. Sitting Bull remained in Canada until July of 1881, when he surrendered to the U.S. military, primarily due to hunger and a lack of support from his own people, and returned to the United States and incarceration at Fort Randall in Dakota Territory and then later to life under military surveillance at the Standing Rock Agency.

In many ways, Sitting Bull's incarceration represented the beginnings of his career in show business, which he carefully coupled with presentations of injustices done to his people. Sitting Bull sat for at least two studio photographs

FIGURE 17 Sitting Bull upon his return from Canada, August 1881. Photos by Orlando Scott Goff. Reproduced from the Collections of the Library of Congress. LC-US262-116265/LC-US262-122855.

for the Bismarck photographer Orlando S. Goff, either in Bismarck immediately upon his return to the United States or soon thereafter while imprisoned at Fort Yates, just outside the Standing Rock Agency (figure 17). Though the purpose of these early photographs seems to be their inclusion in *Campaigns of General Custer in the North-West, and the Final Surrender of Sitting Bull* (1881), a sensational book about Custer and the Indian Wars, Sitting Bull's astronomical fee of fifty dollars for the session points toward a savvy understanding of his own marketability. He soon sat for many very similar portraits, which he sold along with his autograph. At Fort Randall, where Sitting Bull was under military watch for nineteen months before he returned to Standing Rock, he marketed his photographs as well as various pieces of his personal property and thus began a trade in his now well-known identity (Lindner 40).[13]

Sitting Bull had received so much publicity in the years following the Battle of Little Bighorn that he returned from his exile in Canada a celebrity, albeit a notorious one. After disembarking the aptly named steamer *General Sherman* at Bismarck, the town fêted him and the other returning chiefs with a lavish dinner complete with, apparently much to Sitting Bull's bewilderment, ice cream. Robert Utley reports that Sitting Bull sold his autograph, pipes, and "other 'trinkets'" at this event and "boarded the *Sherman* [to Fort Yates] richer in coin and wiser in the strange ways of his captors" (*The Lance and the Shield* 237). Then just a day later, even before disembarking at Fort Yates, Sitting Bull again sold his autograph to the curious, as Robert Utley reports, "free to the ladies, from one to five dollars for the men" (*The Lance and the Shield* 239). Sitting Bull continued to use his notoriety to his personal and financial advantage and toured Bismark again in 1883 during the celebrations of its new status as the capital of Dakota Territory, and then St. Paul, Minnesota in 1884, both trips under the supervision of James McLaughlin, the agent for the Standing Rock Agency. During these primarily sightseeing excursions Sitting Bull had occasion to sell both his autograph and photographs, even engaging in a contract with photographers in St. Paul for the sole manufacture and distribution of his portraiture (Lindner 41). Thus by manipulating his image and its circulation, Sitting Bull engaged his renown to increase his popular acceptance as well as to make extra money in a U.S. social economy that effectively disallowed Indian enterprise and employment. As Joy Kasson writes on Sitting Bull's newfound trade, "Commercial exchange and mutual cultural tourism thus marked his post-surrender relationship with the non-Sioux world" (173). With little to trade in a white world, Sitting Bull turned toward the popular creation of himself.

By the early 1880s, less than a decade after the Battle of Little Bighorn, Sitting Bull had become an American celebrity and no longer held the status of Custer's "red devil" murderer (Coward 163); the press did not inveigh against him, as they did in the late 1870s, as the Indian threat to western stability had begun to lessen. Once Sitting Bull arrived at Standing Rock, requests for him to join traveling exhibitions poured in, so many that McLaughlin felt the requests had "become considerable of a bore" (quoted in Utley, *The Lance and the Shield* 262). McLaughlin refused all employment requests, including an appeal from his predecessor at the Standing Rock Agency, a priest who now headed the Bureau of Catholic Indian Missions in Washington, D.C., who wished to use Sitting Bull at fundraisers for his organization (Pfaller 20–21; see also Utley, *The Lance and the Shield* 264). Eventually, McLaughlin agreed to Sitting Bull's appearance in a show run by Alveran Allen, McLaughlin's personal friend and the proprietor of the Merchants Hotel in St. Paul where Sitting Bull and his fellow Indian travelers just recently had lodged. He rationalized his approval by saying, "There is money to be made from this if properly managed" (quoted in Utley, *The Lance and the Shield* 264). Sitting Bull agreed to the tour only after protracted negotiations in which McLaughlin reported, "he talks of 'millions' as you or I would talk of 'hundreds' and he says he must have big money to go & that he knows he is worth untold fortunes" (quoted in Pfaller 21). Obviously, Sitting Bull was developing into a savvy showman with an understanding of his own cultural capital. The Sitting Bull Combination, as this tour with Allen was billed, consisted of Sitting Bull, seven other Indians, and two interpreters. They opened in New York City to six thousand people on the first day alone (Utley, *The Lance and the Shield* 263), but the novelty soon passed and the show closed roughly a month later, despite McLaughlin's financial predictions.

Sitting Bull proved to be little more than a prop for McLaughlin and Allen's entertainment venture. In the Sitting Bull Combination, Sitting Bull and the other members of the show presented themselves on stage in traditional dress, sometimes engaged in cooking or smoking, and lectured to the audience in Lakota on their impressions of Anglo culture and their relationships with Americans, which were then translated by one of the interpreters; thus Allen's show appeared to mimic quite closely Catlin's earlier exhibitions. Luther Standing Bear, an Oglala Sioux who later toured with Buffalo Bill's Wild West, attended a show of the Sitting Bull Combination in Philadelphia while there on summer employment away from the Carlisle School. The local newspaper advertised Sitting Bull as "the Indian who killed Custer," which, of course, struck Standing Bear as ridiculous, though no more absurd than Americans' passionate desire to witness the apparent killer of their golden-haired hero and shake his hand (*My People* 184–85, 186). Though the Sitting Bull Combination traveled with two interpreters, they in fact did very little actual translating, at least according to Standing Bear. Instead, the interpreters merely supplied narratives that met white expectations. Standing Bear writes that Sitting Bull spoke to the audience in Lakota, telling them of an impending visit to Washington to meet the president (which never happened) and delivering messages of peace such as "it makes me glad to know that some day my children will be educated also. There is no use fighting any longer" (*My People* 185). According to Standing Bear, Sitting Bull's message in Philadelphia was primarily conciliatory, and he notes that the man publicized as Custer's killer never once uttered the general's name. When the interpreter stood to translate Sitting Bull's speech, he instead related the story of the "Custer massacre" and "how [the Sioux] had swooped down on Custer and wiped his soldiers all out"; Standing Bear wryly notes that "[the interpreter] told so many lies I had to smile" (*My People* 185).

When Standing Bear visited Sitting Bull and the other Sioux performers in their hotel room after the show, he witnessed another blatant deception when the interpreter told Sitting Bull that they would visit Washington on their way home, though they apparently had already passed the nation's capitol. Somewhat paternalistically, Standing Bear muses about Sitting Bull's tour, "I wonder . . . what sort of Indian agent it could have been who would let these Indians leave the reservation without even an interpreter, giving them the idea they were going to Washington, and then cart them around to different Eastern cities to make money off them advertising that Sitting Bull was the Indian who slew Custer!" (*My People* 187). This sort of agent, of course, was McLaughlin, who recognized that the "money to be made from this if properly managed," as he had rationalized his sanction of the chief's employment, came not from Sitting Bull's words or even his political position vis-à-vis assimilation, but rather from the Sioux leader's public reputation and quite literally his face and physical presence.

Though Sitting Bull still sold his pictures and autographs while on this tour (he remained under agreement with the St. Paul photographers), he became little more than a cardboard curiosity, his audience likely to hear no more than the "Rub-a-dub, dub!" of Chief Winnemucca's speeches and appeals, which the interpreters freely translated into quite whatever they felt the audience wanted. If Sitting Bull felt exploited on this tour, we may never know, but during the next winter Cody strove to have Sitting Bull join the Wild West, and with Sitting Bull's—and possibly McLaughlin's—likely increased business acumen, Sitting Bull agreed to travel with Cody during the 1885 Wild West summer season. Cody had made earlier attempts to have Sitting Bull join him, but his requests were consistently rebuffed by McLaughlin and his higher-ups. Even as late as April of 1885, Cody's requests continued to fall on deaf ears in Washington: Secretary of the Interior Lucius Lamar wrote "Make a *very* emphatic *No*" on Cody's telegram in which the showman described Sitting Bull's desire to join the Wild West (Moses 27). Within a month, though, Secretary Lamar acquiesced to Cody's petitions and allowed Sitting Bull to sign on to Cody's venture.

Though Sioux author and onetime Pine Ridge Reservation physician Charles Eastman rather scornfully indicts Sitting Bull's association as "an advertisement for [Cody's] 'Wild West Show'" in his hagiographic essay on the Sioux leader in *Indian Heroes and Great Chieftains* (126), Sitting Bull's negotiations with Cody demonstrate an increasing self-awareness of the value of his cultural capital. In the Wild West of 1885 most Indian performers were paid twenty-five dollars per month per the broad employment contract Cody engaged to collectively cover numerous Indian performers, but Sitting Bull negotiated his own contract with specific stipulations. Sitting Bull would earn fifty dollars per week (paid on Saturday nights). He would also bring with him five other Indian men and three Indian women, paid at twenty-five and fifteen dollars per month, respectively. He could choose his own interpreter, to be paid sixty dollars per month, and all of their traveling expenses to the show from Standing Rock and returning to the agency at the end of the show would be paid in full. On top of all this, Sitting Bull demanded a 125 dollar signing bonus and two weeks' pay in advance. As an addendum, quite literally a postscript, Sitting Bull shrewdly had added to the contract, "P.S. Sitting Bull is to have sole right to sell his own Photographs and Autographs" (figure 18).[14] Less than a week later, Sitting Bull and his entourage arrived in Buffalo, New York, for their first appearance in Buffalo Bill's Wild West.

Sitting Bull's reception was often chilly, despite Cody's refusal to paint him as Custer's killer. (Canadian audiences, unlike U.S. ones, tended to cheer and embrace the Sioux chief when the Wild West toured there.) Cody presented Sitting Bull as the leader of a defeated nation, though still a military maestro. The program for the 1885 season even designated Sitting Bull the "Napoleon of the Indian Race" (Reddin 79) and announced his appearance as "The Renowned Sioux Chief, Sitting Bull, and Staff" (Kasson 177). Sitting Bull generally headlined just beneath Buffalo Bill on the 1885 Wild West handbills.

Newspapers that covered the show demonstrated the ambivalence toward Sitting Bull harbored by most U.S. audiences. John M. Coward notes that the same articles that might name Sitting Bull a "notorious chief" or "noted murderer" also hailed him as a "great chieftain" (Coward 183). One reporter wrote that Sitting Bull "yearned for cleaning," even though his face reminded that same newsman of the honored statesman Daniel Webster (Coward 183). Bluntly, Americans did not know what to do with this supposed enemy. But Sitting Bull knew his role. He accepted the attention that local politicians and dignitaries often lavished on him and even stopped by the White House in an attempt to meet with President Grover Cleveland. As an employee of Cody's

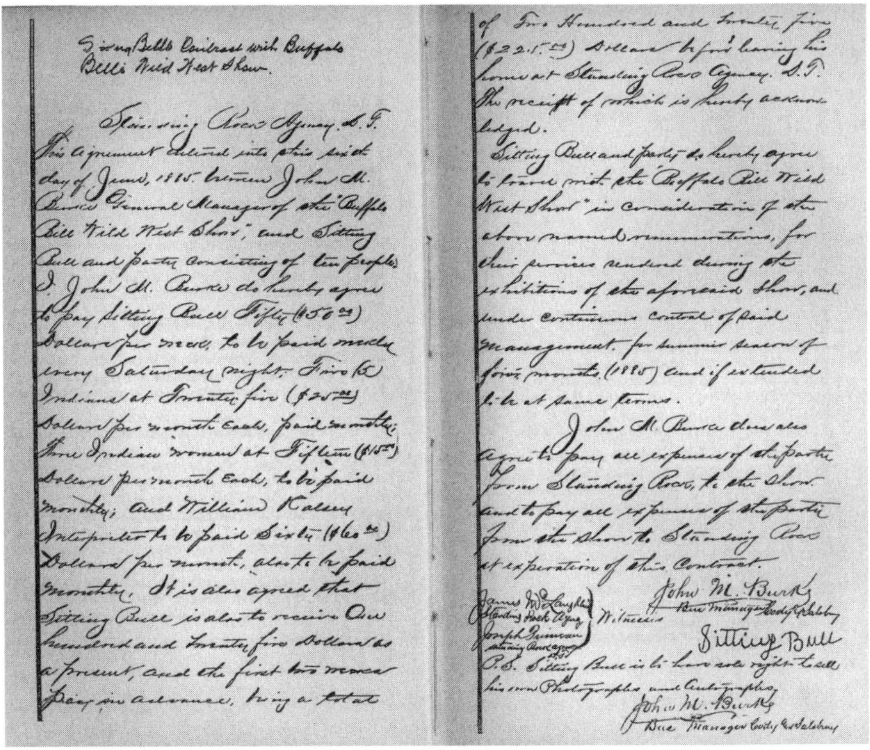

Sitting Bull's Contract with Buffalo Bill's Wild West Show.

Standing Rock Agency, D.T.

This agreement entered into this sixth day of June, 1885, between John M. Burke General Manager of the "Buffalo Bill Wild West Show," and Sitting Bull and party consisting of ten people. I, John M. Burke do hereby agree to pay Sitting Bull Fifty ($50.00) Dollars per week, to be paid weekly every Saturday night. Five Indians at Twenty five ($25.00) Dollars per month each, paid monthly; Three Indian women at Fifteen ($15.00) Dollars per month each, to be paid monthly; and William Halsey Interpreter to be paid Sixty ($60.00) Dollars per month, also to be paid monthly. It is also agreed that Sitting Bull is also to receive One hundred and Twenty five Dollars as a present, and the first two weeks pay in advance, being a total of Two Hundred and Twenty five ($225.00) Dollars before leaving his home at Standing Rock Agency, D.T. The receipt of which is hereby acknowledged.

Sitting Bull and party do hereby agree to travel with the "Buffalo Bill Wild West Show" in consideration of the above named remunerations, for their services rendered during the exhibitions of the aforesaid Show, and under continuous control of said management, for summer season of four months (1885) and if extended to be at same terms.

John M. Burke does also agree to pay all expenses of the party from Standing Rock, to the Show, and to pay all expenses of the party from the Show to Standing Rock at expiration of this Contract.

James McLaughlin
Standing Rock Agency
Joseph Primeau
Standing Rock Agency
D.T.
Witnesses

John M. Burke
Bus Manager Cody & Salsbury

Sitting Bull

P.S. Sitting Bull is to have sole right to sell his own Photographs and Autographs.

John M. Burke
Bus Manager Cody & Salsbury

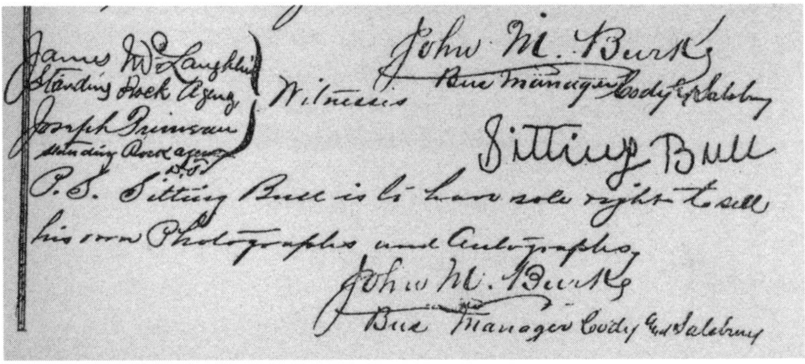

James McLaughlin
Standing Rock Agency
Joseph Primeau
Standing Rock Agency
D.T.
Witnesses

John M. Burke
Bus Manager Cody & Salsbury

Sitting Bull

P.S. Sitting Bull is to have sole right to sell his own Photographs and Autographs.

John M. Burke
Bus Manager Cody & Salsbury

FIGURE 18 Sitting Bull's contract with Cody's Wild West. Detail: addendum regarding Sitting Bull's rights to sell his image and autograph. From Usher L. Burdick, *The Last Days of Sitting Bull, Sioux Medicine Chief* (Baltimore: Wirth Brothers, 1941).

in the Wild West, Sitting Bull did not "play" Indian, at least in the sense that he never appeared in Cody's melodramas or reenactments. Rather, Sitting Bull presented only himself, sometimes appearing in Cody's grand review of his actors but more often riding into the arena alone, allowing for the audience to focus their full attention upon him. By giving Sitting Bull this opportunity to introduce himself as a noble leader and diplomat from the Great Plains, Cody helped to build the image of Sitting Bull as a stoic and honorable man who represented the political future—as well as the demise—of Native Americans in an odd contradistinction to the shrieking actors who attacked the cabins and stagecoaches daily in the arena. In this way, U.S. audiences perceived the two-pronged image of Native Americans they had come to expect: the noble and defeated rising above those who insisted on going down screaming.

Sitting Bull's commercial role in the Wild West was also twofold. He was an exhibition and an advertisement, as well as a sideline entrepreneur. Sitting Bull created a sensation for Cody in the arena and also drummed up excitement for the show in carefully orchestrated events such as Wild West barbecues, where Sitting Bull held court while guests ate with sharpened sticks (Kasson 177), or the public induction of Cody's business partner, Nate Salsbury, into the Sioux tribe by the Hunkpapa Sioux chief himself. As advertisements, these public events certainly worked to increase ticket sales for Cody. But during his season traveling with Cody, Sitting Bull also honed his sideline enterprises. Once again he sold his autograph and pictures (figure 19), and he also apparently sold his pipe bag numerous times, always having extra stock of this cherished possession hidden somewhere (Russell 317). His authenticity, not just his notoriety, now distinctly helped his commercial ventures.

But Sitting Bull's success at selling himself would also prove to aid in his downfall. For example, Sitting Bull was deeply disturbed by what he saw while on tour with Cody. Stanley Vestal, Sitting Bull's first biographer, writes that Sitting Bull remarked during his tenure with the Wild West, "The white man knows how to make everything, but he does not know how to distribute it" (quoted in Moses 27). Indeed, while with the Wild West, Sitting Bull gave away much of his earnings to indigent children he saw on the streets and who also frequented his tipi. And upon returning to Standing Rock, he again dispersed his profits among his people, as would be expected of any Sioux who suddenly had found excess. At the close of the tour in October of 1885, Sitting Bull did not display much interest in returning the next year, declaring,

FIGURE 19 Souvenir cabinet card of Sitting Bull with his autograph. Library of Congress, Prints and Photographs Division, LC-USZ62-122858. Photograph by Palmquist & Jurgens, St. Paul, Minnesota (1884).

"The wigwam is a better place for the red man. He is sick of houses and the noises and the multitudes of men" (quoted in Pfaller 26). Even if he had desired to return to show business, when Cody inquired of McLaughlin the following year in an attempt to secure Sitting Bull for the 1886 tour, the Standing Rock agent spurned his requests, writing to John Burke (who signed Sitting Bull the year before):

> [Sitting Bull] is such a consummate liar and too vain and obstinate to be benefitted by what he sees, and makes no good use of the money he thus earns, but on the contrary spends it extravagantly among the Indians in trying to perpetuate baneful influences which the ignorant and non-progressive element are too ready to listen to and follow. Of the money and property that he brought home last fall, he did not have a dollar, or anything else except the gray horse [a gift from Cody] left . . . and I had a great deal of

trouble with him and through him with other Indians caused by his own bad behavior and arrogance. I, however, have him under control again and would dislike to run similar risks. (Quoted in Pfaller 27)

McLaughlin had never liked Sitting Bull, saying of him even during the first week of their association at Standing Rock, "He is pompous, vain, and boastful, and considers himself a very important personage" (Utley, *The Lance and the Shield* 250). Sitting Bull's perceived arrogance, along with his inability to handle his newfound financial success in ways acceptable to people like McLaughlin, gave the Bureau of Indian Affairs even more cause to restrict his activities and travels, as well as his employment.[15]

Sitting Bull's self-portrayals were intimately bound up with the representational needs of Cody's show during his tour in 1885. But from his arrival in Bismark from Canada until the end of the 1885 Wild West season, Sitting Bull meshed the expectations of his public with his own political needs as well as those of the Sioux. A well-known photograph taken in Montreal while the Wild West performed there depicts Sitting Bull standing with Cody in a pose of reconciliation and trust (figure 20). The studio, William Notman & Son, made an unknown number of plates with Sitting Bull, some of him alone, others with members of the show, apparently because Sitting Bull had run out of photographs to sell and his contract with the St. Paul photographers had expired (Lindner 41). While Cody exploited the Sioux defeat in the Indian Wars—one of the Montreal photographs of Sitting Bull and Cody appeared in the 1893 Wild West program with the caption "Sitting Bull and Buffalo Bill—Foes in '76—Friends in '85" (Lindner 42)—Sitting Bull used these photographic opportunities to present himself as noble, respectable, and an equal to Cody, thus disproving standard American conceptions of Indians as savages.

Sitting Bull's exposition to the white world was not his story, but rather his visage. He did not produce any narrative autobiography for presentation to white audiences, as did other Native American Wild West performers such as Nicholas Black Elk and Luther Standing Bear. However, sometime before 1870, long before Sitting Bull could have even fathomed that he might appear on a stage in Philadelphia or sell his autograph outside a tipi in Montreal, he produced a series of pictographs depicting various foundational moments in his life as a present for his adopted brother, Jumping Bull. These documents, both in terms of their content (imagery) and Sitting Bull's commentary upon

FIGURE 20 Sitting Bull with William F. Cody. Denver Public Library, Western History Collection, Photo by David Frances Barry, B345.

them, are about as close as we can get to Sitting Bull's conception of himself as he might want others to remember him. Most of these pictographs show Sitting Bull engaged with various enemies, killing or counting coup (a technique by which a warrior gets close enough to strike or touch an enemy but does not necessarily kill him), though almost a quarter of the drawings feature Jumping Bull. According to Sitting Bull, these drawings were composed as gifts, not as a series documenting Sitting Bull's life (see figure 21).

FIGURE 21 Sitting Bull's pictographs (Kimball record, no. 1 and no. 9). National Anthropological Archives, Smithsonian Institution, MS 1929-a, neg. 3199-D1, and neg. 3199-D9.

In December of 1881, while Sitting Bull was incarcerated at Fort Randall, a Presbyterian minister from the Yankton agency who was essentially fronting for the U.S. military approached him with these drawings in the hopes of gaining more information about their content. Utley explains that the U.S. military expressed particular interest in uncovering certain details of this history, especially now that they had immediate and safe access to the Sioux leader (*The Lance and the Shield* 243). Surprised to see the drawings (which were actually copies of the originals), Sitting Bull chose his words and his stories quite carefully.

A version of Sitting Bull's narratives had already become public well before this interview. On July 9, 1876, just two weeks after the Battle of Little Bighorn (June 25), the *New York Herald* published a number of Sitting Bull's photographs with accompanying copy that spoke of the viciousness of the chief and the Sioux in general. The article, entitled "The Life of a Savage," noted that within Sitting Bull's narratives "No record is made of the kindly or of the good; it is only the base or the brutal that they think worthy of telling" (quoted in Coward 165). The *Herald* called Sitting Bull's drawings a "curious autobiography . . . which Sitting Bull narrates in his rude and primeval way" (quoted Coward 165). Primarily the *Herald* 's purpose in presenting these pictographs was to prove Sitting Bull's monstrousness and truculence. The *Herald* noted that for all of the federal government's "efforts at [Indian] advancement . . . [they] have turned again and again to the wild" (quoted in Coward 165), thus evidencing the intractable ways of Plains Indians and justifying the U.S. military's vicious retaliations for Custer's death. When pressed for narratives or information about his pictographs in 1881 at Fort Randall, Sitting Bull remained strategically mute. His interviewer noted that within their exchange Sitting Bull was "rather reserved" and that "a better time to secure [Sitting Bull's interpretations] would be at some future date when his status is definitely determined" (letter in Stirling 7). It is difficult to know if Sitting Bull had any knowledge of the publication of his drawings, but his significant silence on their meaning evinces Sitting Bull's awareness that public knowledge of his autobiographical stories provided fuel for the case against him. As Joy Kasson notes, by 1882 "[Sitting Bull] had already learned the importance of exerting whatever control he could over his self-representation" (173). At the time of the interview concerning his drawings, Sitting Bull remained under military supervision and thus must have known that self-incrimination would not contribute to sympathetic presentations of himself. In fact, according to Utley the only two drawings that Sitting Bull would discuss with the probing minister were depictions of himself at fourteen counting coup and a specific clash with a Ree, both situations that could not be seen as threatening to his military wardens (*The Lance and the Shield* 243). He said nothing of the illustrations concerning his encounters with white soldiers (figure 22).[16]

But Sitting Bull allowed his problematic acclaim to work for him with the discovery of these pictographs, as he would a few years later in the Wild West. In 1882, after the visit by the military's Presbyterian representative, Sitting Bull composed three sets of pictographs as gifts for two U.S. military officers and the trader at Fort Randall. In these collections, he decreased the emphasis on violence compared to his earlier depictions, consciously expunging images of himself or other Native Americans killing white soldiers (Utley, *The Lance and the Shield* 243–44). Utley claims that Sitting Bull may have produced these collections in hopes of commercial return, though apparently none was realized (*The Lance and the Shield* 243). In these pictographs Sitting Bull transforms feats of bravery against encroaching white civilization into deeds of honor with no references to his former U.S. enemies. Thus he manipulates ideals not only to increase the favor of his public image but also to depict the history of his people in a light favorable to Americans' imaginations.[17] Struggling against both bodily imprisonment and the media's construction of his life, Sitting Bull knew that his silence, though it might not help him, would likely do him no harm either. Regardless, the dearth of lurid tales to accompany Sitting Bull's pictographic autobiography likely contributed to the lack of commercial interest in its reproduction.

Sitting Bull's pictographs, particularly the ones he produced for Jumping Bull that were subsequently published by the *New York Herald* as damning evidence of Indian savagery, did not present a cohesive picture of the Sioux leader, particularly one that might stand in perpetuity. Instead they presented discrete events that proved Sitting Bull's bravery and honor as a Sioux warrior. The pictographic compilations that he made in 1882 more closely represent the imagery that Sitting Bull wished to present to the white world, evidenced by his mindful construction of these collections for three different white men. But again, these pictographs, individually or collectively, do not represent an autobiography, but rather a series of vignettes put together with rather careful and conscious narrative inclusions as well as omissions. This self-construction of his image through not only the content of his pictographs, but the absence of certain narratives about them, points toward Sitting Bull's later

FIGURE 22 Examples of pictographs that Sitting Bull would not discuss (Kimball record, no. 13 and no. 23). National Anthropological Archives, Smithsonian Institution, MS 1929-a, neg. 3199-D13, and neg. 3199-D23.

conscious (and savvy) construction of identity in Cody's show. Though together we cannot consider these constructions as clearly autobiographical, we can look to Sitting Bull's various manipulations of his image and story to understand his complicated public identities and their various purposes.

NATIVE AMERICAN AUTOBIOGRAPHY: CALLS FOR INCLUSION

Sitting Bull never endeavored to produce an autobiography, at least in the literary sense. But many other Native Americans born in the latter half of the nineteenth century used this genre to inform a U.S. reading public of their troubled Native American culture, then in flux. These autobiographies, often produced by Native Americans who had attended federal Indian schools, such as Luther Standing Bear (*My People the Sioux*, 1928), Gertrude Bonnin ([Zitkala-Sa] *American Indian Stories*, 1921), and Charles Eastman (*Indian Boyhood*, 1902; *From Deep Woods to Civilization*, 1916), were not only linear retellings of a life story, but appeals to non-Native audiences for an acknowledgment of Native American intelligence, creativity, and social and political rights. Yet in most Native American cultures there is no context for autobiography. The idea that a single individual's story might be of such importance that it ought stand out from all other narratives of the group seems senseless or even, as Brian Swann and Arnold Krupat write, possibly "repugnant" (ix). Feats of valor and bravery, as well as important political moments, may be remembered and presented through a medium such as Sitting Bull's pictographs, but these individual items are meant to attach significance and memory specifically to those moments, not to aid in building a coherent and linear narrative of the individual who participated in them. Thus Native American authors carefully constructed their autobiographies to match their readers' sense of the genre: each would depict a discrete and singular life, and, like the life narratives presented by Micheaux, Anderson, or Love, a life worthy of its presentation.

During the 1920s and 1930s, anthropologists (and others) published numerous "as-told-to" Native American autobiographies, many of which bear the mark of heavy editing and rewriting by white editors. Besides the aforementioned *Black Elk Speaks, Crashing Thunder: The Autobiography of an American Indian* (ed. Paul Radin, 1926), *Yellow Wolf: His Own Story* (ed. Lucullus Virgil McWhorter, 1940), and *Wooden Leg: A Warrior Who Fought Custer* (ed. Thomas B. Marquis, 1931) are representative examples. These Indians produced their life stories, specifically directed at white audiences, to provide possible, if small, sources of revenue to the narrator and to highlight the continuing injustices suffered by Native Americans in the United States. Some Native American autobiographies assert that they present the author's words and stories without the intervention of white editorship, as do Charles Eastman's writings for example. But others remain a mélange of the subject's words and the thoughts and desires of the amanuensis, who of course was necessary when an illiterate Native American (or the often white ethnographer) desired to produce his or her story. Thus, to read Native American autobiography one must employ interpretive tools for unpacking the motivation behind the publication of a particular story as well as the mechanics behind the production of that narrative. Native American autobiographies, particularly in the nineteenth and early twentieth centuries, were obviously meant for literate, educated, and primarily white audiences. By default, this reading constituency would also include those people with access to power and public opinion. These same audiences might find that the coherent narrative of a marginalized individual could also allow them access to a culture otherwise unavailable to them and thus, as atomistic readers, they could place themselves into another's individual life. As Swann and Krupat also point out, because of the radical changes in Native American life in the latter half of the nineteenth century, particularly for those tribes in the West and the Great Plains, the drive for Native American autobiographical production changed from providing a kind of historical record of contact and Indian wars to a desire to establish an ethnographic record of tribal life now fading from view (thus the many autobiographies piloted by anthropologists in the first half of the twentieth century; see Swann and Krupat x). Therefore, when we turn to Indian autobiographies to understand the intersection of Native American and American identities, we must take into account the social and political engines driving their production.

Autobiography is problematized when filtered through various levels of mediation. Still, in weighing the various autobiographical expressions of Native Americans, including the apparently "authentic" as well as the clearly manufactured, we can perceive Native Americans' sense of themselves within the larger ideological space of U.S. national citizenship and belonging. Two well-known autobiographies, *My People the Sioux*, by Luther Standing Bear, and *Black Elk Speaks*, by Black Elk and John G. Neihardt, include sections in which the authors discuss their experiences in the employ of Cody and his Wild

West show. These autobiographies are very much like the Wild West show that they describe: they are fabrications of the real, the authentic clothed in the garb of fiction, or sometimes out and out fiction dressed up as truth. In understanding Native American self-representation with respect to Buffalo Bill's Wild West, both autobiographies provide access to the lives of these performers and also act as representations themselves, not unlike their authors' presence in Cody's arena performing tribal dances, feigning to scalp make-believe settlers or soldiers, or even standing idly on the sidelines waiting for the next act.[18]

CARLISLE, CODY, AND AUTHENTICITY:
LUTHER STANDING BEAR

Luther Standing Bear's *My People the Sioux* relates his life story from his earliest memories as a boy learning traditional Lakota practices and preparing for life as a warrior to his years in Hollywood appearing in films in the 1910s and 1920s. He published his autobiography in 1928, giving thanks to E. A. Brininstool and Clyde Champion for "assistance in the preparation of the manuscript" (v).[19] As with most autobiographies, *My People the Sioux* opens with Standing Bear's birth and childhood. Standing Bear then relates, again following standard autobiographical form, various coming of age rituals that signal his movement toward adulthood; his education; and key moments that establish him in his community, thus investing his narrative of self with particular importance. Standing Bear wrote three other books before his death in 1939: *My Indian Boyhood* (1931), *Land of the Spotted Eagle* (1933), and *Stories of the Sioux* (1934). All of his books proved quite popular, garnering reviews in the *New York Times* as well as other papers upon their publication.

In the preface to *My People the Sioux* Standing Bear writes, "The preparation of this book has not been with any idea of self-glory. It is just a message to the white race; to bring my people before their eyes in a true and authentic manner" (v). Thus Standing Bear opens his narrative with a claim toward cultural integrity, one to which he has especial access since, as he writes, "no one is able to understand the Indian race like an Indian" (v). Standing Bear also insists on the authenticity of experience and identity when he writes, "White men who have tried to write stories about the Indian have either foisted on the public some blood-curdling, impossible 'thriller'; or, if they have been in sympathy with the Indian, have written from knowledge which was not accurate and reliable" (v). Yet in the first edition of *My People the Sioux* Standing Bear includes an introduction by none other than the lead actor of 1910s and early 1920s western "blood-curdling, impossible thriller[s]," William S. Hart (figure 23).

Hart rather astonishingly patronizes Standing Bear and evokes the supremacy of American Manifest Destiny in his introduction, where he writes, "The author of this book may be a bit short on education . . . but he has a story to tell. . . . It is a tale of a people whipped by a stronger race—like dumb animals—for deeds beyond their understanding" (xiv [1928 edition]). But, following Standing Bear's assertion that one must be an Indian to understand Indians, Hart legitimizes Standing Bear's experience as primary to his position as spokesperson by declaring, "To write of the West, one must know the West," thus favorably comparing Standing Bear to self-proclaimed westerners such as Owen Wister, Theodore Roosevelt, and Frederic Remington whom Hart considers "shy on only one thing—KNOWLEDGE GAINED BY ACUTAL [western] EXPERIENCE" (xiii [1928 edition]). Thus Hart, who signs his introduction with the Lakota name Ta-Sunke-Witko (Crazy Horse), adds legitimacy to Standing Bear's narrative by providing a voice of western authenticity to vouch for both the western and the Indian character of Standing Bear's stories. Of course, the addition of introductions by white authorities is not a new tactic within autobiographies of marginalized peoples. Nineteenth-century slave narratives generally exhibited letters and forewords from white authorities that verified their tales. Early Native American autobiographies, such as Black Hawk's 1833 *Life of Black Hawk* and even Sarah Winnemucca's *Life among the Piutes*, also contained such legitimations. By engaging Hart to write the introduction to his life story, Standing Bear sets himself not only within the tradition of white-legitimized autobiography, but also within the tradition of espousing western American authenticity through experience, albeit oddly verified here by a master of western cinematic fictions.

My People the Sioux is a personal narrative more than the narrative of a people, despite Standing Bear's title. In traditional autobiographical form, Standing Bear relates his early years, turn to manhood, education at Carlisle Indian School, and later endeavors toward assimilation into American culture. In this narrative, Standing Bear's attendance at Carlisle presents a clear thematic shift in *My People the Sioux*. In the pages before he discusses his schooling in Pennsylvania, Standing Bear presents a picture of Sioux life on the Great Plains unsullied by white contact or its corrupting forces; after his

FIGURE 23 Standing Bear and William S. Hart (ca. 1920s). Denver Public Library, Western History Collection, photo by D. F. Barry, B-708.

return from the East, Standing Bear, who works as an assistant teacher on the Rosebud Reservation, a post office manager, a store clerk, a rancher, and even an impromptu minister before joining Buffalo Bill's Wild West in 1902, expresses an assimilationist and accommodationist position centered on his acting as a mediator between white and Native cultures. Like Buffalo Bill's Wild West, *My People the Sioux* depicts an idealized Native American identity, though his actors are not disgruntled challengers to the development of white western civilization, but rather noble Americans (as Standing Bear often calls Indians)—who were nobler still before contact.

In the first third of *My People the Sioux*, before Standing Bear attends Carlisle Indian School, he presents the Sioux as honest, thrifty, and noble, qualities that seem to disappear after contact, the subsequent loss of land, and the introduction of alcohol by whites. In describing this early life, Standing Bear writes on a single page alone that "there were no idlers in our camp" and "there was no gossiping"; he then notes that upon first contact he found whites physically repulsive and apparently degenerate due to their hair and desires to live in dugouts; and he condemns the senseless slaughter of the buffalo by white hunters, especially since "Indians were never such wasteful, wanton killers of this noble game animal" (67; see also 52–53). In the early chapters of the book, Standing Bear describes how to build a tipi, including the preparation of the buffalo skins, numerous Indian games, and his first buffalo hunt. He presents here a picture of pre-contact Sioux life. But as his narrative nears his story of Carlisle, evidence of white civilization begins to appear. Standing Bear notes, for example, that on his first buffalo hunt with his father, "we left the agency without a permit" (60). He also begins to mention rations from the government, including the general bewilderment at flour and green coffee, both foods that the Sioux apparently did not know how to use, the appearance of beef cattle, and the establishment of his father's store.

Standing Bear's early narrative also contains numerous glitches or narrative hiccups that betray the constructedness of these early years and their interconnectedness with the white world. For example, Standing Bear was born on the Pine Ridge Reservation and appears in census records as early as 1863, though he does not mention this fact. Rather he writes that he was born "in the year of 'breaking up of camp'" (3) and discusses his people's camps and travels as if no boundary defined their movements. In fact, his first reference to the white administration of Native American life is his permitless buffalo hunt. Of course, outside knowledge of Standing Bear's birth is necessary to place his carefully constructed birth in this critical context. Within the narrative itself, one particular moment stands out in which the pre-contact story dissolves into a lace of white influences that go unspoken by the author. Standing Bear relates a story about an altercation during a traditional Sioux buffalo hunt with a group of Pawnees who have entered the Sioux's hunting grounds. Given that the preceding chapters related traditional Sioux games and coming of age rituals, the narrative of the buffalo hunt fits seamlessly into the kind of Plains Indian ethnology that Standing Bear creates. Describing the victory dance following the clash, Standing Bear observes the red paint that marks those warriors and horses wounded in the battle. He writes, "If a horse had been wounded, the animal was brought into the dance and painted where it had been struck by a bullet" (57). Strikingly, the mention of a bullet wound brings white contact into a narrative so far driven by descriptions of Sioux life without white incursion. Not until two chapters later does Standing Bear finally introduce the rifle to his narrative, calling them "long sticks which made a great noise" (68), thus suggesting the rifle's foreignness and unintelligibility, though his earlier remark illustrates that it was the very tool by which the Pawnees had shot the Sioux horses. Attaching particular significance to firearms, Standing Bear also locates the appearance of rifles as "the beginning of our hatred for the white people" (68). The manifestation of shot horses and bullets before white contact in Standing Bear's narrative appears very much like Sarah Winnemucca's silence on her tableaux vivants. The careful attention to narrative inclusion and omission builds stories that aid in the construction of identity, an identity that played upon white readers' desire to seek access to authentic Native American life.

In 1931 Standing Bear wrote *My Indian Boyhood*, an ethnographically styled autobiography of his youth directed at children. He rewrote much of his material from the first part of *My People the Sioux* for this book in an attempt to again present a picture of authentic pre-contact Native American life. He prefaces *My Indian Boyhood* with a simple statement: "I write this book with the hope that the hearts of the white boys and girls who read these pages will be made kinder toward the little Indian boys and girls" (vi). He then writes chapters on "Bows and Arrows," "Hunting and Fishing," "Games," and the like, producing for white adolescents a sketch of a "real" Indian's youth. Throughout the book, Standing Bear describes Native American effects and events with reference to white contact. In fact, the second sentence of the book begins "But before the white man came . . ." (1). As in *My People the Sioux*, Standing Bear here endeavors to produce a narrative of pre-contact life against which he can set his mediated position within the white world.

At Carlisle Indian School, Standing Bear begins to clearly define his views on Native American assimilation and his adaptation to the white world. Of course, Standing Bear wrote all of his autobiography well after attending Carlisle and thus comprehends the necessary negotiations involved in presenting himself as a Native American who has bridged the gap of pre-contact and post-contact culture. Regardless, he presents Carlisle as a turning point where he learns to navigate in the white world, an important skill for his later participation in the Wild West. His desire to travel east to Carlisle grows from his father's admonition to face bravery and not hope for death from old age (124). Since trusting in white authority and traveling toward the sun, where "they would dump us over the edge of the earth," seemed a most intimidating task, Standing Bear honored his father by undertaking this great feat of bravery (131). Not long before Standing Bear traveled east to Carlisle, his father explained to him that "the white men were pushing toward the West, and that sooner or later they would occupy the whole country. . . . the only recourse was [for Indians] to learn the white man's ways of doing things, get the same education, and thus be in condition to stand up for his rights" (98). Later, when his father visits Carlisle, he repeats this advice to his son (even though Standing Bear writes that "This was the first time my father had ever spoken to me regarding acquiring a white man's education" [152]). Revering his father, Standing Bear endeavors to adapt to the white world as he sees the Anglo presence in the Indian world as now inevitable.

After Carlisle, where Standing Bear and other students were forced to cut their hair, squelch their language, and engage in seemingly ridiculous vocational training (Standing Bear learned tinsmithing, which he thought rather silly because "the Government was already giving the Indians all the tinware they wanted" [175]), Standing Bear returned to the reservation and undertook various employments that enabled him to use not so much his vocational training but his cultural skills in mediation. Upon his return, Standing Bear found that many of his relatives now lived in wooden houses, drove buggies, bought goods in a store, and ate frybread as a staple. In a few short years, the Sioux world had changed radically, at least within Standing Bear's narrative. Standing Bear constantly moves back and forth between identification with his fellow Lakotas who had little experience with whites outside of military and reservation administrators and those whites charged with the supervision of those Lakotas. He arrives with a letter of recommendation from Captain Pratt, the founder of the Carlisle School, and is immediately given work as a teacher. Like Booker T. Washington in *Up from Slavery*, Standing Bear pays an inordinate amount of attention to cleanliness upon his return, noting his (white) fellow teacher's slovenliness and rejecting an Indian woman he begins to court (and spies on as she bathes in a stream) because "she wore an underskirt that was far from clean" (198). But he also acts as an arbitrator between the Native Americans on the reservation and the government agent, averting various troubles and helping to form bonds and agreements between the residents and their wardens. In his chapter on the Ghost Dance and the massacre at Wounded

Knee, however, Standing Bear loses all conciliatory postures and damns white culture, even as he argues for its importance for Native Americans:

> When I heard of this, it made my blood boil! I was ready myself to go and fight then. There I was, doing my best to teach my people to follow in the white men's road—even trying to get them to believe in their religion—and this was my reward for it all! The very people I was following—and getting my people to follow—had no respect for motherhood, old age, or babyhood. Where was all their civilized training? (224)

But Standing Bear soon resumes his amiable stance and continues with his presentation of life as a Native American rancher, store clerk, postal manager, and then interpreter for the Indians employed in Buffalo Bill's Wild West during the 1902 season.

During his first days at Carlisle, Standing Bear sets forth a position that informs his entire narrative and is particularly appropriate for understanding Native American self-representation in Buffalo Bill's Wild West. Pondering his father's advice and his own position that he ought not return home "unless I had done something very brave," Standing Bear writes, "Now after having my hair cut, a new thought came into my head. I felt that I was no more Indian, but would be an imitation of white men. And we are still imitations of white men, and the white men are imitations of the Americans" (141). Standing Bear's observation allows for multiple readings, though primarily we can see here the constructedness of his identity. Standing Bear sets up a dichotomy between whites and Indians and then claims that each are truly neither. Standing Bear is no more Indian than white men are themselves; in fact, each of these markers belies the interconnectedness of identities such that Indians become "imitations of white men" and whites are little but simulations of Indians. The foundational character of each side of the dichotomy relies on identity requiring its opposite. Thus at least part of Standing Bear's presentation of himself rests on his narrative ability to fit into those ideals of Native American identity generated within white culture. As he claims, he is an imitation of a white man, yet he is not white. But as such an imitation, which is also an "[imitation] of the Americans," Standing Bear becomes less of an authentic individual identity and more of a trope.

While Standing Bear worked for Cody, he understood this mediated position of identity. Within Buffalo Bill's Wild West, Native American performers produced just such constructed identities. They presented themselves as whites believed them to be while simultaneously demonstrating an ability to operate within the dominant culture defined by white America. They became not just "imitations of white men," but imitations of themselves: they played Indian. During the 1902 season in England, Standing Bear had roles and duties as a manager, chaperone, official interpreter, and actor. In the arena, he played himself, various other Indian identities, and possibly even a cowboy. Sometimes he sat on the sidelines in full regalia, while other times he danced traditional dances, as he did one day for the king of England. And behind his presence on stage, Standing Bear interpreted for the seventy-five Sioux actors in the Wild West while also acting as a steward for the Native American performers.

Standing Bear's vision of himself in the Wild West is twofold. He is a full-blooded Lakota in the arena, playing Indian for the English audiences, but he is also a manager concerned little with identity and instead sharply focused on the care and conduct of his charges. Standing Bear is well aware of the props and narrative templates necessary to produce the Indian image in the Wild West. He notes that before leaving Rushville, Nebraska, where the Show Indians gathered for their departure, Cody's operation "provided costumes for those of the Indians who had none themselves" (246). Thus "authentic" Native American attire came not from those Indians playing themselves, but rather quite clearly from a costume shop. Standing Bear also describes how Johnny Baker, a marksman close to Cody, told him not to wear his best costume on days when attendance was light; rather, "on such days [he] might take the part of a cowboy if [he] chose" (254). He also reveals that even though Cody's program for the year lists the presentation of chiefs from Cheyenne and Arapaho tribes, all the Indian actors were actually Sioux.

As a manager for part of Cody's show, Standing Bear dedicates himself to the straight (and temperate) path he sees as necessary for his people as well as his actors. In his first formal interaction with the Sioux actors in New York City, Standing Bear admonishes them in a brief speech:

> My relations, you all know that I am to take care of you while going across the big water to another country, and all the time we are to stay here. I have heard that when any one joins this show, about the first thing he thinks of is getting drunk. I understand that the regulations of the Buffalo Bill show requires that no Indian shall be given any liquor. You all know that I do not drink, and I am going to keep you all from it. Don't think that because you may be closely related to me I will shield you, for I will not. I will report to Colonel Cody immediately any one I find drinking. (249)

In his discussion of the Wild West within *My People the Sioux*, Standing Bear relates many other stories centered around alcohol and Native American performers. He devises a monitoring system so Indians cannot steal out of the encampment or hotel for a nip; he tracks down three missing Indians to a below-street-level bar; he withholds half of the actors' pay for the balance of the tour when he finds he cannot control liquor consumption; and he threatens the loss of a month's pay to any Native American who drinks during the voyage back to the United States. He sets himself apart from other Show Indians quite clearly with his pronoun usage when he writes, "Not very long after this, we began to have trouble with the Indians" (256). And before the show sailed back home to America, Cody awards Standing Bear a fifty-dollar bonus because, in Standing Bear's words, Cody "was in appreciation of the good work I had done in keeping the Indians sober and in good order" (268).

Thus within his discussion of employment with Buffalo Bill's Wild West, Standing Bear creates various images of Indianness within a book specifically written for a white audience. Of course not all Native Americans traveling with the Wild West drank to excess. But since Standing Bear can paint this picture of intemperance along with his quite pointed control of the problem, he endeavors to show white Americans that whatever Native American problems might exist—even stereotypical ones like drunkenness—good Indians like himself can overcome the issues and lead stragglers to the right path. Joy Kasson argues that "Luther Standing Bear played the role of Indian performer with gusto, apparently finding it morally acceptable and financially remunerative" (189). While I agree wholly with Kasson's judgment of Standing Bear's performativity, I would argue that Standing Bear does not play the role merely of Indian performer but of the Indian himself. Standing Bear markets himself as an "authentic" Indian, particularly within the first part of his autobiography, as well as in *My Indian Boyhood*, even though breaches appear in this account. And he creates an identity through an embracing of his education and a successful career in show business off the reservation to appear in a new authenticity, one that now corresponds easily to the white world. *My People the Sioux* narrates—for its white readership—this shift as an imminent and desirable transformation in Native American identity.

But Standing Bear was very conscious of his constructions. He adopts the role of "Indian" to further his cause where necessary. He puts on a costume within the narrative as he does in Cody's show. At the close of his autobiography, after discussing travels with other shows highlighting Native Americans, various lectures, a brief stint with the Miller Brothers 101 Ranch Wild West Show, and his film career, Standing Bear addresses his activism in California, where he served as president of the American Indian Progressive Association, an aid and information organization, and launched the Indian Employment Agency. During these later years, Standing Bear lectured to white audiences and acted as mediator for California tribes who were looking to Washington for aid. Speaking directly to his white readership, Standing Bear closes his autobiography with a call for white America to pull Native Americans into the social economy and the workplace, implicitly asking whites to drop their suppositions of savagery and intractability (despite his descriptions of drinking Show Indians): "As I am writing these last lines . . . I am starting an Indian Employment Agency, which I trust will be for the betterment of the whole race. The Indian is bright, and he is capable of holding good, responsible positions if he is only given a chance. And why not give the Indian a chance?" (288). Thus Standing Bear caps his autobiography—and his autobiographical construction—with a call for white recognition of Native American talents.

By playing "Indian," that is, an image built on white expectations, Standing Bear authenticates himself to his readership. Then, after giving his audience what they expect, he turns and bids them to hear his plea and see that something worthwhile exists underneath the facade. Standing Bear uses the same techniques in his autobiography that many Native Americans used within Buffalo Bill's Wild West in order to forward both themselves and their people more generally. When Standing Bear's son dressed up "in a full costume of buckskin," with his hair braided and his face painted, and stood outside the family's tipi as audience members toured the Wild West Indian camp, the spectators would ogle him and hand him coins until his pockets were full (266). Standing Bear's son dressed up for the stage and took home with him more money than his pockets could carry; his father also learned to adorn himself for others' expectations, so that he too could find power through this identity and the new cultural capital it thrust upon him.

EDITED INTO BEING: BLACK ELK

Black Elk, who writes briefly about his experiences with Buffalo Bill's Wild West in *Black Elk Speaks*, likewise plays with the construction of his identity in his autobiography. Tellingly, his references to the Wild West are peripheral. His engagement with the show sits uneasily with the larger project of his narrative: to present the life and wisdom of an "authentic" Native American, unsullied by prolonged contact with the white world. Even more than the other narratives discussed here, *Black Elk Speaks* mixes Native American identity with white ideals about Indian life to produce a composite narrative. The overlay of white editorship is so thorough, however, that one cannot clearly distinguish between Black Elk's self-representation and the constructions of his white editor, the American poet John G. Neihardt. Despite this authorial complication, *Black Elk Speaks* has become a staple within Native American autobiography in the last thirty years. Neihardt interviewed Black Elk in the summer of 1931 and produced *Black Elk Speaks* from the transcriptions of those interviews. The book did not receive much press initially and soon went out of print, but in the 1960s *Black Elk Speaks* was rediscovered and became exceedingly popular during a period in American culture when not only were Native American rights coming to the forefront of U.S. politics, but a large youth culture sought new kinds of spirituality distinct from conventional forms. Black Elk's narrative, republished in the United States in 1961, provided apparent access to tenets of Plains Indian spirituality and also an image of a wronged and noble people that appealed to the social and political climate of the day. *Black Elk Speaks* has remained popular over the last forty years and in academic circles has received more scholarly attention than any other Native American autobiography.[20]

Black Elk Speaks is constructed as an oral narrative in which Black Elk literally speaks and is occasionally interrupted by Fire Thunder, Iron Hawk, or Standing Bear (not Luther), three other men present during Neihardt's interviews. Thus the structure of the narrative allows readers to feel as if they are present at the annunciation of these memories. Like most autobiographies, including Luther Standing Bear's, *Black Elk Speaks* opens with the holy man's birth and earliest memories. His discussion of his early years, following a pattern of numerous Indian autobiographies, presents a Native American world yet untouched by white influences. But unlike Standing Bear, Black Elk ends his narrative just after the massacre at Wounded Knee, claiming pithily and with great gravity, "And so it was all over" (270). Black Elk differs from Luther Standing Bear in that he is a traditional healer who received visions at age nine and eighteen that structured the rest of his life. Thus *Black Elk Speaks* has often been cited as an important text on Sioux spirituality. Black Elk is often lauded as an important religious figure, though, as William Powers points out, only a minor portion of the book deals directly with spiritual matters, while the bulk of the narrative focuses on "the growing up of an average Lakota" (Powers 45).

For the purposes of understanding Native American self-representation, *Black Elk Speaks* provides a fascinating and complicated study. The words within the text are rarely Black Elk's but are more generally Neihardt's manipulations of Black Elk's stories. Neihardt initially became interested in Black Elk while doing research for the final section of his five-part epic poem, *The Cycle of the West*. Since this last section, *The Song of the Messiah*, was to focus on the Ghost Dance and Wounded Knee, Neihardt went to the Pine Ridge Reservation in the hopes of talking with older Native Americans who had participated in the Ghost Dance or knew intimately of the 1890 massacre. He was pointed toward the aged and somewhat reclusive Black Elk, who lived alone in the hills. Black Elk agreed to the interviews, and Neihardt eventually produced *Black Elk Speaks* from the transcripts, a radical departure from his initial research plans.

Black Elk's narrative arrives to its readers through numerous linguistic and cultural filters. During the interviews, for which Black Elk had constructed a tipi in which Neihardt and his daughters could live, the holy man spoke to the poet in Lakota, which was then translated into English by Black Elk's son, Ben Black Elk. Neihardt's daughter, Enid, then took down this English translation in shorthand, and from these transcriptions Neihardt built his story of Black Elk's life and his visions. Most critics do not focus on these various layers of interpretation, but they instead laud Neihardt for pulling from Black Elk's discourse the tone and kernel of his narrative, if not the exact words. For example, Michael Castro finds that Neihardt produces "a moving human story of declining fortune and ultimate fall from power" (86), in which Neihardt's "editorial decisions tended to reduce ambiguity and enhance clarity and power of what he interpreted as Black Elk's essential teachings" (94–95). In Vine Deloria Jr.'s introduction to the 1979 edition of *Black Elk Speaks*, he argues that critics need not concern themselves with Neihardt's editing because "The very nature of great religious teachings is that they encompass everyone who understands them and personalities become indistinguishable from the transcendent truth expressed" (xiv). Thus, according to both Castro and Deloria, Black Elk and Neihardt stand on equal footing in the construction of this Black Elk's story—Deloria declares it "perhaps the only religious classic of this century" (xi)—and the desire to uncover editorial designs and creations is misguided. But Neihardt's manipulations are unquestionable and heavy handed. He in fact has admitted to writing both the beginning and the ending of the book, claiming "they are what [Black Elk] would have said had he been able" (quoted in McCluskey 238). In discussing his motives, Neihardt remarked, "the translation—or rather the *transformation*—of what was given me was expressed so that it could be understood by the white world" (quoted in McCluskey 239). With these claims, Neihardt presents Black Elk's words as mystical and unintelligible to non–Native American audiences and sets himself up as their only possible spiritual interpreter. In fact, Neihardt claims that even though Black Elk had recently refused to be interviewed by a woman interested in Crazy Horse (Black Elk's cousin), when Neihardt arrived unannounced to ask for an audience, he sensed that Black Elk had been expecting him. After sitting with Neihardt and a few aged Lakota neighbors, Black Elk turned to the interpreter (here a man named Flying Hawk) and said, "As I sit here, I can feel in this man beside me a strong desire to know the things of the Other World. He has been sent to learn what I know, and I will teach him" (Black Elk xvii). From this acceptance speech by Black Elk, Neihardt felt that he was the predetermined translator for Black Elk's story. Many critics, apparently hesitant to criticize Neihardt's role or the authentic conduit of the amanuensis, agreed.

In 1984, Raymond J. DeMallie published *The Sixth Grandfather: Black Elk's Teachings Given to John G. Neihardt*, a book which, although laudatory of Neihardt's work, prints for the first time the transcriptions of Neihardt's interviews with Black Elk. Since no audio tapes of these interviews exist, nor any Lakota transcriptions, *The Sixth Grandfather* presents the closest possible account of Black Elk's words (barring a rereading of the shorthand documents themselves). DeMallie notes quite clearly in the preface that most readers and critics "have failed to recognize that the books were written by Neihardt, not Black Elk" (xxi), and he consistently refers to Neihardt's two books on Black Elk (the other is *When the Tree Flowered* [1951]) as the poet's constructions, not merely as unaltered presentations of Black Elk's story. Even so, DeMallie echoes Neihardt's own words when he praises the poet for "the sincerity of [his] commitment to make the books speak for Black Elk faithfully, to represent what Black Elk would have said if he had understood the concept of literature and if he had been able to express himself in English" (xxii). Apparently, DeMallie, like other critics, believes that Black Elk's words can only make sense through their active manipulation by white editors. Indeed, as David Murray points out in *Forked Tongues: Speech, Writing, and Representation in North American Indian Texts*, "[Neihardt] creates a style which successfully incorporates what we have come to expect a dignified old Indian to sound like" (71). And within this style, then, Neihardt tends to make Black Elk speak in an over-simplified manner, in abstractions, and, when describing his years off the plains or the reservation, often through the stylized perspective of an unlearned and bewildered stranger in a strange land.

Note, for example, the differences between Black Elk's description of his travels east to join Buffalo Bill's Wild West in 1886 and Neihardt's "transformation" of those words. From the transcriptions, here is Black Elk's description of his journey east with the Wild West:

> The trains were awaiting our arrival and we had everything ready to leave. We got on the train and I began to think about my people and I felt very bad—I was almost sick—I felt like turning back but I went anyway. The train hooked on to our car and started off. We ran all that night and had breakfast at Long Pine and arrived at Omaha that evening. Right there I could compare my people with the white's ways and right there I felt bad again and was sorry that I had left my people behind.
>
> The train proceeded eastward now from Omaha. We arrived at Chicago next morning and stayed all day and all that night here. Then we went eastward and we arrived in New York soon. Then we got off the train and walked to Madison Square Garden. . . . I was surprised to see those skyscrapers there in New York. (DeMallie 246)

In a simple and coherent narrative made up mainly of compound sentences, Black Elk relates his homesickness, the details of his journey, and his wonder at the New York skyline with little descriptive language, certainly nothing that would characterize it distinctly as Native American, except for the phrase "my people." While these experiences are new to Black Elk, he does not inject superlatives to describe a sense of perplexity or astonishment.

Neihardt then rewrites Black Elk's journey with more adjectives, a repetition of words ("big" and "roared/roaring" for example), and consciously awkward sentences to produce a sense of distance and alienation from the event:

> That evening where the big wagons [train passenger cars] were waiting for us on the iron road, we had a dance. Then we got into the wagons. When we started it was dark, and thinking of my home and my people made me very sad. I wanted to get off and run back. But we went roaring all night

long, and in the morning we ate at Long Pine. Then we started again and went roaring all day and came to a very big town in the evening.

Then we roared along all night again and came to a much bigger town. There we stayed all day and all night; and right there I could compare my people's ways with Wasichu [white] ways, and this made me sadder than before. I wished and wished that I had not gone away from home.

Then we went roaring on again, and afterwhile we came to a bigger town—a very big town. We walked through this town to the place where the show was. . . . I was surprised at the big houses and so many people, and there were bright lights at night, so you could not see the stars, and some of these lights, I heard were made with the power of thunder. (Black Elk 216–17)

Neihardt manipulates Black Elk's story so as to create in it a sense of bewilderment at the "big towns," "big houses," "big wagons," and lights made from thunder. Yet apparently Black Elk was quite cognizant of the names of the cities through which he traveled, the nature of locomotive travel, and the existence of skyscrapers as well as Madison Square Garden. A bit later in the narrative, where Black Elk discusses his stay in London, he tells Neihardt, "They took us to London where the fire-boat stops. . . . We stayed there six months" (DeMallie 248). Keeping up character, Neihardt transforms Black Elk's information: "they took us to a place where the show was going to be. The name of this very big town was London. . . . We stayed in this place six moons; and many, many people came to see the show" (Black Elk 220). Admittedly, we do not know the role of the interpreter in modifying Black Elk's words or the variations occurring through the stenographic transcription, but the reconstruction of Black Elk's story from a lucid and descriptive narrative to that of a vague, bewildered, and even slightly childish traveler, complete with the stock mumbo-jumbo of "big wagons," "iron roads," and magical lights, ought to point scholars away from Neihardt's work and toward, if nothing else, the actual transcriptions of Black Elk's words.

The project of Native American autobiography produced in conjunction with white editors, anthropologists, philanthropists, or even poets was never completely one-sided in terms of either the seemingly irrational Native American desire for the public presentation (and publication) of an individual life or the amanuensis's desire for "anthropological salvage" (Krupat 116). We might turn to DeMallie's publication as something closer to the truth and write off Neihardt's construction as pure fantasy, but to do so merely substitutes one translation for another. The transcriptions appear to us a raw data, while the published text of *Black Elk Speaks* is essentially a finished, if fabricated, product. Exactly what Black Elk expected from these interviews we do not know. Black Elk was certainly aware of the imminent publication of his memoirs because Neihardt wrote to him after his first fortuitous interview, "My publisher is eager to have me do [this book], for I have told him all about it" (Black Elk 278). In fact, as H. David Brumble has pointed out, many Native Americans who produced autobiographies in conjunction with white translators and editors recognized that their stories were to be published and widely disseminated in a new print culture. Brumble notes that the Sioux chief Joseph White Bull told his biographer Stanley Vestal, who also wrote a biography of Sitting Bull, "When our book is published, my name will be remembered and my story read so long as men can read it" (quoted in Brumble 58). A contemporary of White Bull, the Crow warrior Two Leggings, also noted to his editor, "You are the one to tell about my life and it will soon travel all over the earth" (quoted in Brumble 58). Even Black Hawk's book, *The Life of Black Hawk* (1833), which is generally considered the first published autobiography of a non-Christian Indian, is prefaced with his editor's declaration that Black Hawk had "a great desire to have a history of his life written and published" (quoted in Murray 68). Thus the construction of these narratives is driven by forces emanating from the desires of the teller as well as the scribe.

Black Elk's tenure with Buffalo Bill's Wild West does not figure prominently in *Black Elk Speaks*. Primarily this period in his life operates within the narrative to explain his first major incursion into the white world. Black Elk joined the Wild West in 1886, at the age of twenty-three. By this point, Black Elk had established himself as a developing shaman, noting in his autobiography that before leaving with the Wild West he had been "curing the sick for three years more, and many came to me and were made over" (Black Elk 214). He sees employment with the Wild West as an experience through which he might find the answers to his people's despair by acquiring knowledge of the white world. Referencing his earlier visions, Black Elk says, "Maybe if I could see the world of the Wasichu, I could understand how to bring the sacred hoop together and make the tree bloom again at the center of it. . . . [My people] were traveling the black road, everybody for himself and with little rules of his own, as in my vision. I was in despair, and I even thought that if the Wasichus had a better way, then maybe my people should live that way" (Black Elk 214–15).

Hoping to discover the "secret of the Wasichu" (214), Black Elk joined the Wild West along with a number of his friends. They traveled to New York and performed for six months and then traveled to Europe, where just at the end of the season Black Elk and two other Indian performers became stranded for unknown reasons in Manchester. Black Elk says little about his day-to-day experiences with Buffalo Bill's Wild West, and he says almost nothing about the near two years he traveled and worked in Europe after he became lost from the Wild West. In fact, he quite jarringly records a long stretch of performances in London in one line: "We stayed here six months" (DeMallie 248). Black Elk does not discuss with Neihardt money, contracts, or material details of his tenure with Buffalo Bill, possibly because these items might detract from his presentation of himself as completely separate from the Wasichu world. In fact, his descriptions of life with the Wild West tend toward abstraction and distance, reading almost as if Black Elk were describing someone else's experiences there.

In a single moment, though, Black Elk does present his own interpretation of the Wild West. He tells Neihardt, "I enjoyed the Indian part of the shows that we put on . . . but I did not care much about the white people's parts" (DeMallie 246). Here Black Elk separates himself and other Indians from the cowboys, sharpshooters, and cavalrymen of the Wild West and thus distances himself from the show in general, presenting Native Americans as self-empowered components of a show of their own definition. Yet the sections of the show that Native Americans "made" were relatively small, as most of their acting was as aggressors toward Wasichu stagecoaches and cabins. Black Elk may be referring here to those "anthropological" moments of cultural exhibition (dances and songs, for example) that Cody included in some shows, or he may be referring to their playacting as scourges of white advancement. Either way, Black Elk presents himself as something outside of the white economy (both monetary and social) even as he was thoroughly embroiled within it. He presents Buffalo Bill's Wild West as an opportunity for him to discover the white world in the hopes that something there might help his people, yet he neglects most mentions of money, the mechanics of travel (except through what seems like a massive abstraction of fire boats), contracts, and day-to-day life in a foreign world.[21]

While part of the construction of Black Elk's identity undoubtedly comes from Neihardt's well-meaning manipulations, Black Elk himself also carefully chose information to include in his narratives. Most notably absent from both

Black Elk Speaks and the transcriptions are mentions of Black Elk's early conversion to Episcopalianism and later Catholicism. When he joined the Wild West, Black Elk had already converted to Christianity (all Native Americans employed with Buffalo Bill's Wild West were required to be Christian), and his letters home from the show contained biblical references and showed a devotion to his new religion. From Manchester, England, Black Elk wrote to the Sioux language newspaper *Iapi Oaye*, "Always in my mind I hold to the law and all along I live remembering God. . . . [N]ow I know the white men's customs well. One custom is very good. Whoever believes in God will find good ways—that is what I mean" (quoted in DeMallie 8). Upon returning from Europe, Black Elk became disenchanted with white culture after Wounded Knee, but he maintained his connections to Christianity, having three children baptized in the Catholic church between 1893 and 1907.

In the early 1900s, Black Elk himself converted to Catholicism and became a catechist, traveling to other reservations, where he "went to preach the gospel" (quoted in DeMallie 18) and serve occasionally as a priest when none other was available. Yet Black Elk mentions nothing of this part of his life in his interviews with Neihardt, even though his Catholic duties kept him quite busy traveling and preaching in the twenty or thirty years before the poet's visit. In fact, some on the reservation remembered Black Elk as an Indian who "never talked about the old ways. All he talked about was the Bible and Christ" (quoted in Murray 72). Possibly Black Elk—and Neihardt—knew that a book about a devout Native American convert to Christianity might not be unique (and thus less marketable). Or possibly Black Elk simply believed, following a classic western theme, that all that he had seen and known was now fading from view and thus he needed to record it. Undoubtedly, Black Elk continued much of his shamanistic practices, particularly in the years following his employment with the Wild West; he closes his narrative by sharing with Neihardt a Native American ritual on Harney Peak in the Black Hills, thus evincing his dual spiritual attachments to both Native American and Christian traditions. According to Frank Fool's Crow, Black Elk's nephew and a Teton Sioux holy man, Black Elk counseled him in the early part of the century to keep careful control of his sacred knowledge. When Fool's Crow traveled with Wild West shows in the early twentieth century, he noted that when he and other Native Americans danced in the shows, "the dances were social performances . . . and never sacred ones" (quoted in Kasson 191). Even after heartily embracing Catholicism, Black Elk obviously did not turn his back on his Lakota spirituality, producing a fluid hybrid identity that he could call upon according to the needs of a situation.

Black Elk's narrative, made up of his own carefully chosen tales combined with Neihardt's poetic license, presents a Native American who remains distant from white culture. But this supposed distance apparently contributed to the success of his autobiography. William Powers argues that "much of what passes for Lakota religion today is the product of the white man's imagination" (43), partially due to the Black Elk/Neihardt presentation. Powers also notes that of the numerous languages into which *Black Elk Speaks* has been translated, Lakota stands out as a glaring exception. Thus the circulation of this autobiography, as well as most other Native American autobiographies, continues only in non-Native circles. Like Luther Standing Bear, Black Elk sought to present a kind of authentic Indian narrative, with a particular focus on spirituality, and also like *My People the Sioux*, *Black Elk Speaks* draws outsiders to the cause of Native American rights. Oddly enough, within a U.S. model that demanded the assimilation of others, Native Americans who participated in the Wild West proved that the maintenance of difference—to a degree—helped their cause more than did a humbled deference. By establishing themselves as Other they called attention to their stories, and by playing Indian when necessary they kept their white audiences' attention. They simultaneously provided two narrative poles through which American audiences remained rapt: they were the savage specter and the dying race, both of which were Wild West show tropes. By imparting their narratives with both impressions, these outsiders made Americans (and Europeans) comfortable by reinforcing their expectations only to then provide narratives of possible salvation and assimilation.

AND THE SHOW GOES ON

In 1992, Lakota activist and one-time U.S. presidential candidate Russell Means appeared as Chingachgook in Michael Mann's blockbuster screen adaptation of James Fenimore Cooper's *Last of the Mohicans*. Means's portrayal of this noble savage figure, the apparent last of his tribe, appears paradoxical given Means's decades of political activism. Cooper enacts a nineteenth-century white fantasy (albeit tragic) of Native American eradication on American soil, whereas Means's activism directly contradicts this project in his affirmation of Native American presence and rights. But Means's portrayal of Chingachgook mirrors the theatrics of Standing Bear, Black Elk, and the many other Native Americans who portrayed themselves within exhibitions and Wild West shows earlier in the century. Means did not play himself on screen; rather, he played Indian. In a 1992 editorial in *News from Indian Country*, Means wrote, "I have been asked whether my decision to act in the *Last of the Mohicans* means that I've abandoned my role as an activist. On the contrary, I see the film as an extension of the path I've been on for 25 years—another avenue to eliminating racism" (Means). Like Standing Bear, who hoped that the young readers of *My Indian Boyhood* would find understanding and compassion for Native American peoples, Means claims that, despite the criticism, his role as Chingachgook might allow white viewers to see that "the Indians are depicted as equals with the white[s]—they interact both socially and economically" (Means).

In *Manifest Manners: Postindian Warriors of Survivance*, the Anishinabe (Chippewa) novelist and literary critic Gerald Vizenor argues that Native Americans must forge their images through the creation of stories and pictures that move beyond white stereotypes. But rather than merely knock down white standards, these new "warriors of survivance," as he calls them, must play within the terms created by white culture in order to disrupt and transcend those standards. He criticises Native American authors who embrace white mythologies about Indians such as their natural intimacy with the earth and inherent spirituality or nobility. These authors' rigid attachment to these ideals ultimately traps them within what Vizenor terms "manifest manners," that is, cultural, political, and social frameworks designed by non-Indians. Vizenor attacks the concept of "Indian," claiming that it, as well as specific tribal names, "are simulations in the literature of dominance" (10–11).

Working from Jean Baudrillard's notion that simulations enact symptoms and manifestations of signs rather than merely represent them, Vizenor reworks the concept of "survivance" as the creation of (often postmodern) counter-narratives to that literature of dominance. Vizenor praises Means as a "wise warrior of survivance" (19) and, though he qualifies his acclaim with reference to some of Means's public statements, he lauds Means's appearance in *The Last of the Mohicans*. In fact, Vizenor uses Andy Warhol's painting *The American Indian (Russell Means)* on the cover of the first edition of *Manifest Manners*. (Interestingly, the 1991 republication replaces Warhol's painting with the portrait of Cody and Sitting Bull taken in Montreal.) Vizenor writes that Means "countered manifest manners and the simulations of dominance in education, politics, and motion pictures, and he has created new stories about tribal rights, philosophies, and traditions" (19). Means's portrayal of a problematic Indian figure denotes his ability to work within the terms of white-defined mythologies about Native Americans—Cooper's enduring novels, for instance. Within such a performance, Means creates new affirmative narratives of Indian presence. Vizenor describes these "postindian" figures:

> The postindian warriors hover at last over the ruins of tribal representations and surmount the scriptures of manifest manners with new stories; these warriors counter the surveillance and literature of dominance with their own simulations of survivance. The postindian arises from the earlier inventions of the tribes only to contravene the absence of the real with theatrical performances; the theater of tribal consciousness is the recreation of the real, not the absence of the real in the simulations of dominance. (5)

The affirmative nature of progressive Native American identity is not static, nor is it merely the expression of some innate temperament. Rather it is performative. Theatrical constructions of the Indian self dispute the absence of Indian authenticity in the narratives of the dominant culture. Vizenor continues, "Postindian simulations arise from the silence of heard stories, or the imagination of oral literature in translation, not the absence of the real in simulated realities; the critical distinction is that postindian warriors create a new tribal presence in stories" (12).

Like Means, Show Indians—both within Wild West shows as well as within their written narratives depicting that experience—assert themselves through the silence inherent in their stories. Their very presence within the arena undermines the simulations of Cody's narratives. If Cody had employed white actors to portray Native Americans within his show, his representations would have carried more weight in the cultural arena and furthered the annihilation of both tribal identities and tribal people. The appearance of "real" Indians allowed the audience to attach significance to their presence rather than their absence. Their absence would have literally signaled their disappearance, be that a fantasy or not, and would thus validate those narratives of dominance, that is, Cody's manifest manners. When Native Americans play themselves in Cody's show, they brought into the arena, through their presence and their silence, their own histories and stories, which countered Cody's and those of official culture more generally.

According to Vizenor, the continued presence of Native Americans in shows, films, politics, and American culture in general allowed their stories to surface through the cracks within the white idealization of Indian culture. He writes, "The once bankable simulations of the savage as an impediment to developmental civilization, the simulations that audiences would consume in Western literature and motion pictures, protracted the extermination of tribal cultures" (6). Thus the simulation of Indians as savages ultimately worked to the advantage of Native Americans, giving them more time to fight the institutional policies of destruction. Cody's show, complete with howling and bloodthirsty aborigines, supported Indian extermination through its stories. But those stories also bought time for Native Americans. As employees of the show, these simulations allowed particular Native Americans to survive, giving them money, experience, careers, and escape from the surveillance and oppression of reservation life. Beyond the show, Indians such as Luther Standing Bear and Black Elk turned to their life stories to create new identities that appealed to white culture while at the same time demanding that their stories of injustices and their desires for legitimacy be heard.

In 1933, Luther Standing Bear wrote to President Franklin D. Roosevelt to propose a bill requiring the teaching of Native American culture and history in public schools. He wrote, "Today the children of our public schools are taught more of the history, heroes, legends, and sagas of the old world than of the land of their birth while they are furnished with little material on the people and institutions that are truly American" (quoted in Moses and Wilson 141). Certainly his autobiography might have figured prominently as an exhibit of those "truly American" materials. Regardless, Standing Bear was able to use the ideals of Native American culture produced within the official culture of the nation in an attempt to bring his stories to light. Vizenor writes that "Postindian warriors encounter their enemies with the same courage in literature as their ancestors evinced on horses" (4); Standing Bear confronts his enemies, the leaders and the institutional structures of Native American extermination, with the same terms used to create Indian imagery in the dominant culture.

Native Americans, particularly Plains Indians, have a place in the official narrative of the American West: they represent resistance, domination, destruction, and finally cultural extinction. Cody's show replayed this timeworn story to repeat audiences who could recite it by heart. But outside the arena, Native American actors could capitalize on those stories and force their audience to remember that even as actors playing a vanished people, they demanded recognition. Native Americans and William F. Cody were engaged in the project of the performance of western narratives, and both capitalized on gesturing toward "authentic" Indian identities. But the Wild West project attests to the constructedness not only of Native American identity, but of the American West, itself a region fundamentally important in building the national character of the United States. While these Indians could not fashion themselves into model pioneer citizens, they could use their marginalized and romanticized identities for all these were worth in establishing the Native American presence in the nation.

CONCLUSION

<hr/>

JUST A FEW MINUTES PAST NOON on January 10, 1917, William F. Cody died at his sister's home in Denver, Colorado. Although he had disappointed his fans with his publicly reported infidelity and subsequent marital crises and become a financial failure and a pawn of larger entertainment managers in recent years, in death Cody became a national hero. Even in the midst of a world war, telegraph companies cleared their lines to send the announcement of Cody's death worldwide. President Woodrow Wilson was one of the first to send condolences, followed by messages from England's King George V and Queen Mary, other international political and military leaders, and even a delegation representing the Oglala Sioux of Pine Ridge, South Dakota. The Colorado state legislature passed a special resolution to lay Cody's body in state in the rotunda of the capitol building on the day of his funeral. Cody's funeral procession included soldiers, Boy Scouts (fifty of them), Spanish–American and Civil War veterans, members of the National Order of Cowboy Rangers, and numerous associates of local Masonic and other secret fraternal societies (Russell 469–70). Twenty-five thousand people passed before his body, which lay guarded by soldiers from nearby Fort Logan. In Cody, Wyoming, stores closed and flags hung at half-mast.

Because the dirt road to Cody's requested resting place, on Lookout Mountain high above Denver, remained impassable until early summer, his body remained in a Denver mortuary—under armed guard—for five months. But even with the spectacle of his funeral over, Cody's June internment was anything but regular. Thousands more mourners drove up the winding Lariat Trail for his burial; the *Denver Post* urged motorists to drive "carefully and with due solemnity" for the sake of safety as well as "respect for the departed frontiersman" (Fowler, "Western World"). On Lookout Mountain, Cody's wife Louisa reopened the casket for additional viewing before finally entombing her husband's body in a steel vault placed inside a cement-lined granite crypt. Cody's grave was soon covered with a twenty-ton cement slab and steel rails; watchmen guarded the site "to frustrate attempts by ghouls or vandals from tampering with the vault" (Fowler, "Western World").

In death, Cody became a national icon, a thing of wonder, and an indigenous treasure. In February of that year, Theodore Roosevelt, the honorary vice-president of the newly formed Buffalo Bill Memorial Association, commemorated Cody as "an American of Americans. . . . He embodied those traits of courage, strength, and self-reliant hardihood which are vital to the well-being of the nation" (quoted in Russell 469). Besides standing in for the entire narrative of western history—at least the kind he brought to the stage for over thirty years—Cody became the apotheosis of Americanness, a symbol of national identity. As a condensation of this identity, Cody's body became in turn a fetish. Almost immediately upon his death, the towns of North Platte, Nebraska (the site of Cody's Scout's Rest Ranch), and Cody, Wyoming (which Cody founded), vied with Denver for Cody's remains. While police and volunteers protected his body immediately after his burial, by 1921 threats of exhumation and theft became so serious—and so ingrained in Cody mythology—that the Colorado National Guard felt it appropriate to station a tank immediately next to his grave (figure 24).[1] The public—embodied in the federally funded tank—laid claim to Cody's legend, distilled now into his remains: exhibited by order of a state legislature, memorialized by an ex-president, and protected by an arm of the U.S. military. Evidenced by the National Guard presence at the grave site, the United States, rather than protecting western property, insuring national sovereignty, or even effecting a campaign of expansion, was defending—through Cody's body—the myth of the West and its corresponding connection to American character.[2]

In death, Cody represented the successes of the western American spirit (regardless of his failures while living). The mythic Cody now symbolized the mythic West, including the narratives of people like Roosevelt and Turner as well as those westerners who embraced this story of conquest and accomplishment. Yet Cody's story ought not be disregarded merely because of its Triumphalist cast. When Richard White declares that Old Western Historians write only comedies with happy historical resolutions (Limerick's "happy face history") and that the present generation of western historians produces primarily tragedies where "Things don't end well," he establishes a prescriptive scholarship that limits the content of those narratives available for consideration ("Trashing the Trails" 33). While White considers the need for

FIGURE 24 Tank at William F. Cody's grave. The Buffalo Bill Museum and Grave, Lookout Mountain, Golden, Colorado.

more tragedies as antidotes to the progress-centered narratives of the West, his discursive demarcation characterized by outcome disallows narratives of western success (real or perceived) that collide with those same ideological structures that New Western Historians condemn. White claims that New Western tragedies often "find people attempting one thing and very often achieving another," thus highlighting the achievement of the historical actor over the endpoint of the narrative ("Trashing the Trails" 33). But the African American, Mormon, and Native American writers addressed in *Outside America* sought to embody the comedies of the Old West just as Cody had; they proved themselves hardy pioneers, self-sufficient workers, and boosters of western mythologies. Yet their narratives show that they very much were "attempting one thing and . . . often achieving another." They sought to prove their belonging in the story of the American West and subsequently that of the nation through the very narratives that excluded, erased, and even annihilated them. But despite adopting these triumphant narratives, many of these westerners experienced failed mortgages, broken marriages, religious persecution, and even cultural genocide. Their attempts at establishing a western identity led them, in New Western historical fashion, to an ideological space where the limits of that identity became palpably clear. These writers' decisions in presenting themselves to both their neighbors and the nation reflect the mutability of the terms of western mythologies as well as their sometimes seemingly mismatched appropriation.

Cody manipulated his Wild West's presentation of comedic westward expansion to meet the expectations of his audience as well as the ideological needs of the nation at the time. The confluence of mythic narratives of the West, whether patently false or simply subjective, and the lives of actual westerners proves much more complicated than either New or Old Western Historians have presented. Cody's venture was driven not by a desire to reveal the truth of recent western history, but by a desire to create a pageant that might stand in for history as well as draw crowds and profits. Similarly, other westerners sought popular acceptance through their establishment of "true" western narratives, ones that seemed to reflect the historical desires of the nation. But while narratives such as Cody's or Roosevelt's sought popular success, nothing less than national belonging was at stake in the presentations of African Americans, Native Americans, Mormons, immigrant Chinese, Hispanics, and a slew of other western outsiders that might also include homesteading wives, laborers, prostitutes, Catholics, and Jews, among others. As westerners they could become Americans, given that other avenues to cultural citizenship appeared closed to them. If the traits of western culture defined U.S. nationality, then, they believed, becoming more western mitigated their outsider status.

Admittedly, not all western outsiders chose this route of identification; some even rejected American identification altogether. Yet the narratives of marginalized people who sought national belonging through western mythology are conspicuously missing from the historical narratives of New and Old Western Histories. New Western Historians reject these westerners for their implicit sanction of (ironically) white-washing and Triumphalist history. But these actors also rarely appeared within Old Western History except to occasionally serve as evidence of the grand opportunities the West provided to all peoples regardless of race, religion, or ethnicity. Including these figures who sought refuge from injustice within those very myths that sought to disassociate them provides a more complicated picture of western history, western identity, and the role of the American West in forging national belonging.

Though the fiction of Oscar Micheaux or the autobiographies of other western African Americans display an affinity to the comedies of Old Western History, the tragedies of racism emanate from their words, if not their conclusions. These writers insisted that reliance on the western myths could bring them closer to prosperity and cultural acceptance. Mormon writers also used western tropes to their advantage, but in ways that more clearly aided their assimilation into American culture. Though their narratives held their share of tragic components—exile, slander, murder, and war—they turned to the pioneer myth to establish, quite successfully, their role as true westerners and thus ideal U.S. citizens. The western narratives of Native Americans were by definition tragic. But actors and employees within Buffalo Bill's Wild West turned their horrific presentation of self-extermination to their ideological and material advantage by supplying the world with their version of western history—rising from the arena's battleground and waving to the crowd. Not all Show Indians embraced the Americanization offered by such work, but their association with Cody's show allowed them more power to manipulate the terms through which they demanded acceptance into—or consciously rejected—the nation.

These various westerners did not merely accept or reject the terms of Americanization offered through regional identification. Instead they engaged in a complex mediation in which they leveraged the terms of western mythologies to their advantage while reflecting upon their positions as marginalized citizens. Often their lives differed drastically from their presentations. To this end these western outsiders shared in the project of myth-making with Cody, Roosevelt, and Turner. Unlike these men, however, the degree to which their particularity clashed with the hegemonic narratives of the West and the nation reflected the limits of both narratives in defining U.S. cultural citizenship.

NOTES

INTRODUCTION

1. Amy Kaplan argues in *The Anarchy of Empire* (2002) that turn-of-the-century domestic representations of the United States necessarily reflect the nation's imperial designs. The mythology of the West (and particularly the Western), she argues, restructures itself through a kind of colonial look backward so as to reflect growing U.S. global power. Thus the new Americanness that grows from the apparent loss of the frontier is also formulated by "feeding on the outposts of the American empire" (120); see in particular pp. 92–120. Her study complicates the work of historians such as David M. Wrobel in *The End of American Exceptionalism: Frontier Anxiety from the Old West to the New Deal* (1993), where he argues that Americans' anxiety about the "close" of the frontier fueled changes in domestic policy, the growth and expansion of pioneer and wilderness narratives, and the search for "frontiers" (generally overseas) to replace the now frontier-less American West.

2. General texts, including collections, that elaborate the position of New Western History include Limerick, *Legacy of Conquest* (1987), as well as her collection *Something in the Soil* (2000); Limerick, Milner, and Rankin, eds., *Trails Toward a New Western History* (1991); Nash, *Creating the West* (1991); White, *"It's Your Misfortune and None of My Own"* (1991); Cronon, Miles, and Gitlin, eds., *Under an Open Sky* (1992); and Milner, ed., *A New Significance: Re-envisioning the History of the American West* (1996).

3. For a critique of just such an elimination of the concept of the frontier, see Glenda Riley's "Airbrushing Western History" (1992), published just one year after White's textbook.

4. Influential titles in these areas include, on Native Americans, Hurtado, *Indian Survival on the California Frontier* (1988), and Utley, *The Indian Frontier of the American West* (1984); on African Americans, Taylor, *In Search of the Racial Frontier* (1998); on Latino/as, Ruiz, *Cannery Women, Cannery Lives* (1987), and Gutiérrez, *When Jesus Came the Corn Mothers Went Away* (1991); on Asian Americans, Nomura, "Significant Lives: Asia and Asian Americans in the History of the U.S. West" (1994), and Takaki, *Strangers from a Different Shore* (1989); on western women, Kolodny, *The Land before Her* (1984), and Riley, *The Female Frontier* (1988); on western children, West, *Growing Up with the Country* (1989); on western environmental history, Worster, *Rivers of Empire* (1985) as well as his *Under Western Skies* (1992).

5. See the special issue of the *Arizona Quarterly*, "The New Western History: An Assessment," 53:2 (Summer 1997), for a series of discussions on the structural similarities between New and Old Western History, particularly with reference to New Western Historians' claims that they are telling untold narratives ignored by the fictions of the Triumphalists.

6. A number of recent scholars focus on the relationship of American culture around the turn of the century to America's conception of itself as a nation. In her recent study of turn-of-the-century American literature and intellectual life, *The Uses of Variety* (2001), Carrie Tirado Bramen locates the eruption of a rhetoric of cultural variety in the late nineteenth and early twentieth centuries as definitive of American culture. She finds that the concept of cultural variety "operated within American culture to alleviate two apparently contradictory sources of anxiety: first, concerns about the crisis of individuality due to the encroaching homogeneity of modernity; and second, concerns about the excessive heterogeneity of the metropolitan centers" (9). Thus her figuration of turn-of-the-century America produces a nation of conflicts, but one in which polarized ideological factions turn to a similar concept to process change. Setting herself against other Americanists such as Amy Kaplan and T. J. Jackson Lears, who find in literary realism and American culture more generally "hetero-phobic" narratives and standards, Bramen discerns within American culture a tension between the ideals of homogeneity and separation and the desire for difference (Bramen 20). Likewise, Wald's *Constituting Americans* (1995) characterizes American culture as conflicted. Wald finds that American authors often walk an ideological line between "conforming to cultural prescriptions and refusing comprehensibility" (3). Thus, Americans of the late nineteenth and early twentieth centuries were caught between official narratives of national identity and a conflicting sense of cultural alienation. Other scholars such as Alan Trachtenberg have argued that around the turn of the century American society had become molded by corporate models so that the "texture of daily life" (4) reflected the machinations of business life and capitalist culture. His *Incorporation of America* (1982) sketches a nation conflicted by the principles of capitalist progress and what he terms "the moorings of familiar values," (7) where American life of the late nineteenth century (and, I would argue, the entire twentieth century) was defined by "the invasion of the marketplace into human relations" (144). Lears, Richard Wightman Fox, and others, in *The Culture of Consumption* (1983), locate a change in American culture from a focus on production to a celebration of consumption around the turn of the century. As Americans entered the twentieth century, consumption became not merely a mode of expression for middle-class America, but an ideology connected with the rhetoric of rights and an expression of quality of life (Fox and Lears ix–x). See also Lears's *No Place of Grace* (1981).

1. I am indebted to Patrick Dooley for pointing out this exchange between Crane and Roosevelt at the 2001 Western Literature Association conference. See his *The Pluralistic Philosophy of Stephen Crane* (1993), 161 n. 10.

2. Roosevelt has rather strong words concerning sheep, as well as their stewards, in the American West. In *Hunting Trips of a Ranchman*, Roosevelt writes, "Cattlemen hate sheep. . . . The sheep-herders are a morose, melancholy set of men, generally afoot, and with no companionship except that of the bleating idiots they are hired to guard. No man can associate with sheep and retain his self respect" (120–21). Finding sheep to be an active disruption of the natural social progression of the West (of which cattle and cattlemen seemingly held a most important, if only temporary, part), Roosevelt writes in his autobiography, "The large migratory flocks of sheep, each guarded by the hired shepherds of absentee owners, were the first enemies of the cattlemen; and owing to the way they ate out the grass and destroyed all other vegetation, these roving sheep bands represented little permanent good to the country" (*Theodore Roosevelt* 95). See also his correlation between "granger" and "sheep-owner," both of whom drive cattlemen off the open range, in *Hunting Trips of a Ranchman* (21).

3. Roosevelt's *Winning of the West* (1889–96) ended in the early nineteenth century with the explorations of Lewis and Clark to the Pacific Coast and Zebulon Pike's meanders into the Spanish southwest. Before this series, Roosevelt had already published other historical texts, including *The Naval War of 1812* (1882) and biographies of Thomas Hart Benton (1887) and Gouverneur Morris (1888).

4. Though the cowboy myths of Roosevelt abound, see Hagedorn's *Roosevelt in the Badlands* (1921) for the most reasonable narrative account of Roosevelt's ranching days. Collins's *That Damned Cowboy* (1991), while a scholarly study, relies heavily on Hagedorn's stories but adds quotations from Roosevelt and others who knew him while in Dakota Territory; Collins's book, like Hagedorn's, is still a cowboy hagiography.

5. For Roosevelt's discussion of the losses to ranchers that winter, see his *Ranch Life and the Hunting Trail* 77–79, published only a year after that devastating season. While Roosevelt does not mention his own losses here, he does declare that "Easterners who invest their money in cattle without knowing anything of the business, or who trust all to their subordinates, are naturally enough likely to incur heavy losses" (8). Possibly to exorcize his losses in print, Roosevelt invokes his ranching story again only two pages later: "Probably during the last few years more than half of the young Easterners who have come West with a little money to learn the cattle business have failed signally and lost what they had in the beginning. The West, especially the far West, needs men who have been bred

on the farm or in the workshop far more than it does clerks or college graduates" (10). Roosevelt—the Eastern college graduate—definitively signals here the close of his ranching career.

6. Besides *The Winning of the West*, which Roosevelt completed in 1896, a complete list of Roosevelt's books published before he became vice president includes *The Naval War of 1812* (1882), *Hunting Trips of a Ranchman* (1885), *Thomas Hart Benton* (1887), *Ranch Life and the Hunting Trail* (1888), *Gouverneur Morris* (1888), *New York* (1891), *The Wilderness Hunter* (1893), *Hero Tales from American History* (with Henry Cabot Lodge, 1895), and *The Rough Riders* (1899).

7. Many scholars have noted the shift in the characteristics associated with American masculinity at this time. While in the latter half of the nineteenth century, masculinity—particularly middle-class masculinity—was generally associated with self-restraint, self-mastery, gentility, and the possession of strong character, by the turn of the century masculinity came to be defined by physical strength, virility, adventurousness, vigorous exercise, and sports. See Bederman, *Manliness & Civilization* (1995), esp. 1–44; Kimmel, *Manhood in America* (1996); and Nelson, *National Manhood* (1998), esp. 1–28. For an excellent discussion of Roosevelt and "manliness," see Bederman, 170–216. On the connections between this new masculinity and the U.S. wars of the turn of the century (within which Roosevelt was especially central), see Hoganson, *Fighting for American Manhood* (1998).

8. Roosevelt published an essay entitled "True Americanism" in the *Forum* in April 1894 where he argued that immigrants must give up their Old World customs, language, and even "habits of thought." In Roosevelt's vision of hypernationalism, he writes that "[The immigrant] must revere only our flag; not only must it come first, but no other flag should even come second. He must learn to celebrate Washington's birthday rather than that of the Queen or Kaiser, and the Fourth of July instead of St. Patrick's Day. . . . Above all, the immigrant must learn to talk and think and *be* United States." The essay is collected in Roosevelt's *American Ideals, and Other Essays, Social and Political* (1897), 14–32 (quote is from 28–29, emphasis in original). See also Roosevelt, *The Americanism of Theodore Roosevelt* (1923), esp. 199–210.

9. According to Samuels and Samuels, some regular army officers and soldiers declined to serve under Wood because, though he was a career military man, he was viewed primarily as a physician, not a soldier (14).

10. The term "rough rider" was used to describe skilled horsemen of the American West as early as the mid-nineteenth century, and William F. Cody labeled his contingent of international equine performers the Congress of Rough Riders in 1893. Thus the colloquial name for the First Volunteer Cavalry echoed

both the citizens of the American West and their mythical stories as embodied by Cody through his Wild West. Roosevelt initially disliked the appellation, worrying that the name would connect his mission and his men to a "hippodrome affair" (qtd. in Reddin 133).

11. Initially *The Rough Riders* was published serially in *Scribner's* from January to June 1899; Roosevelt received one thousand dollars per installment (Morris, *The Rise of Theodore Roosevelt* 686–87). Charles Scribner's Sons then published the complete text in 1905.

12. Unless otherwise noted, the version of *The Rough Riders* cited hereafter is in *The Works of Theodore Roosevelt*, National Edition (vol. 11).

13. On the history of African American soldiers prior to the Spanish-American War, see Steward, *The Colored Regulars in the United States Army* (1904); Billington, *New Mexico's Buffalo Soldiers, 1866–1900* (1991); Fowler, *The Black Infantry in the West, 1869–1891* (1971); Leckie, *The Buffalo Soldiers: A Narrative of the Negro Cavalry in the West* (1967); and Schubert, ed., *On the Trail of the Buffalo Soldier* (1995). For a broader study of African Americans and turn-of-the-century American imperialism, see Gatewood, *Black Americans and the White Man's Burden, 1898–1903* (1975).

14. See Gerstle, *American Crucible*, 36. See also the letters collected in Washington, Wood, and Williams, *A New Negro for a New Century* (1900). Gatewood's collection "*Smoked Yankees*" prints many letters that reconstruct the events in Cuba from the generally unheard African American perspective. Roosevelt himself notes that during the night atop San Juan Hill "some [Rough Riders] went back to the buildings in our rear and foraged through them, for we had now been fourteen hours charging and fighting without food" (*Rough Riders* 95), thus calling into question his own assumptions about the retreating black soldiers earlier in the day.

15. Presley Holliday, in his earlier cited letter to the *New York Age*, writes that Fleming was the one who sent two men to the rear "to go for rations and entrenching tools," which led Roosevelt to assume that the black soldiers were fleeing the front line (Gatewood, "*Smoked Yankees*" 94). In *Letters of Theodore Roosevelt*, editors Morison and Blum do not specify exactly what letter of Fleming's it is to which Roosevelt is responding; regardless, Roosevelt never sent this letter to Fleming. See Roosevelt, *Letters* 2: 1315 (letter to Albert Leopold Mills, May 26, 1900).

16. This appendix does not appear in the version of *The Rough Riders* collected in the National Edition of the Works of Theodore Roosevelt, but rather in the *Scribner's* 1905 publication.

17. Unwilling to let the heroics of his cowboy soldiers fade after 1898, Roosevelt tried to convince President Woodrow Wilson to allow him to regroup the Rough Riders for participation in the First World War. Wilson declined.

18. Remington includes a single African American soldier in *The Charge of the Rough Riders at San Juan Hill*, located almost dead center on the canvas, with all but his head hidden by the bodies of the Rough Riders surrounding him. Though his inclusion may be an attempt at historical accuracy by Remington, Alexander Nemerov believes that this soldier's scarce visibility and effective occlusion by the other members of the charge alludes to an American desire to keep African Americans as followers and to disrupt racial progress in favor of white racial ideals. Nemerov writes that Remington's painting "evinces a fear of the racial progress it ostensibly endorses. . . . [T]he very vigor with which Remington conceals the black man indicates his importance. Screaming up the hill, Remington's Rough Riders protest too much. Each Rough Rider occluding our view functions as an individual denial of the black man's role and symbolism, as though at this central point the picture issues a suspiciously loud chorus of nos." See Nemerov, *Frederic Remington and Turn-of-the-Century America* (1995), 91 and 93.

19. The recording of Cody's speech is available at the Library of Congress's American Memory website, <http://memory.loc.gov>.

20. See Turner's "The First Official Frontier of the Massachusetts Bay" (1920).

21. "The Significance of the Frontier in American History" was originally published in *Annual Report of the American Historical Association for the Year 1893* (1894): 199–227.

22. Turner began teaching at Harvard intermittently in 1904 and then took a permanent position there from 1910 to 1923. In an autobiographical letter in 1928, Turner lists Roosevelt as one of his scholarly friends, along with the historian and president of the United States, Woodrow Wilson; the *Atlantic Monthly* and *World's Work* editor and ambassador to England under President Wilson, Walter Hines Page; and the historian and director of the Wisconsin Historical Society, Reuben Gold Thwaites. Turner qualifies his relationship with Roosevelt, writing that he knew him "less intimately" than the others listed; Ray Allen Billington notes that the relationship between Turner and Roosevelt "was based on [Turner's] reviews of Roosevelt's *The Winning of the West* and apparently did not progress beyond the corresponding stage." See Billington, *The Genesis of the Frontier Thesis: A Study in Historical Creativity* (1971), 295 n. 21. The evidence concerning an actual meeting of Turner and Roosevelt appears unclear, though Roosevelt warmly offers a lunch invitation to Turner during a stay in New York in December of 1896 (Roosevelt, *Letters* 1: 572; this letter was Roosevelt's last to Turner). They were to sit on a panel together at the 1896 meeting of the American Historical Association, but Roosevelt canceled due to commitments in New York as police commissioner (Bogue 128). For Turner's repast brushes with Roosevelt at Harvard, see Bogue, 128.

1. A cursory list of scholarship on Micheaux's cinema includes Bowser, Gaines, Musser, eds., *Oscar Micheaux and His Circle* (2001); Bowser and Spence, *Writing Himself into History* (2000); Cripps, *Slow Fade to Black* (1977), esp. 183–202 (one of the earliest books to discuss Micheaux in any significant fashion); Gaines, "Fire and Desire: Race, Melodrama, and Oscar Micheaux" (1993); Green, *Straight Lick* (2000) and *With a Crooked Stick* (2004); Musser, "To Dream the Dreams of White Playwrights" (1999); Regester, "The Misreading and Rereading of African American Filmmaker Oscar Micheaux" (1995).

2. See Elder, "Oscar Micheaux: Melting Pot on the Plains" (1976); Fontenot, Jr., "Oscar Micheaux, Black Novelist and Film Maker" (1982); and Herbert, "Oscar Micheaux: A Black Pioneer" (1973–74), who calls Micheaux "a unique homesteader" (62).

3. Illuminating correspondence concerning some of his early motion picture productions can be found in the George P. Johnson Negro Film Collection, Department of Special Collections, University of California, Los Angeles; also, correspondence with Charles Chesnutt concerning Micheaux's desire to purchase the film rights to Chesnutt's *The Conjure Woman* and *The House Behind the Cedars* is in the Charles Waddell Chesnutt Papers, Western Reserve Historical Society, Cleveland, Ohio. Presently, the only biography of Micheaux is VannEpps-Taylor's *Oscar Micheaux: A Biography* (1999), a comprehensive, though often uncomplicated, hagiography.

4. Micheaux states that out of twenty-four thousand claims, the odds for acquiring one were one in forty-four. See *Conquest*, 57–58; see also Schell's *History of South Dakota* (1968), 254.

5. Micheaux uses Greeley's words as a chapter title in *The Conquest* (48; see also 47); the *Chicago Defender* also uses Greeley's words in the header to Micheaux's 1910 article "Where the Negro Fails."

6. In 1904 the federal government arranged a treaty by which the eastern edge of the Rosebud Sioux Reservation would come open to non–Native American homesteading in exchange for a cash settlement with the tribe. After the settlement, all land acquired by the U.S. government would open up to settlement through a lottery system in which potential homesteaders' names were pulled from a jar to determine his or her allotted quarter section, if any. For Micheaux, the Rosebud Reservation land was practically free, but only if he could get a title to a section through this lottery.

7. The states and territories included in this count are west of—or include—the hundredth meridian.

8. Boley had a reputation as a rough-and-tumble western town and was even the site for some early black Westerns, notably the Norman Film Manufacturing Company's *The Crimson Skull* (1921) and *The Bull-Dogger* (1923), both featuring the renowned black cowboy Bill Pickett. (Another Norman Company film *Black Gold* featured "the entire all-colored city of Tatums, Oklahoma"; see poster in Kisch and Mapp (1992), 4.) Washington notes, however (and apparently through hearsay), that Boley "is one of the most peaceful towns in that part of Oklahoma. When I was in Topeka, Kansas, in 1907, I was told that not a single citizen of Boley had been arrested for two years." See *Story of the Negro*, 2: 251.

9. On the site near Brownlee, see Taylor, *In Search of the Racial Frontier* 153. On the more well-known Dearfield Colony, see Taylor, *In Search of the Racial Frontier* 153–55; Norris, *Dearfield, Colorado — The Evolution of a Rural Black Settlement* (1980); and Johnson, "Agricultural Negro Colony in Eastern Colorado" (1915). All-black towns were established in many other parts of the West during the early twentieth century. For example, near the turn of the twentieth century, Francis Boyer and Dan Keyes, two African American men from Georgia, founded Blackdom sixteen miles south of Roswell, New Mexico. At its height around 1915, Blackdom was home to about twenty-five families. In 1908, Colonel Allen Allensworth founded the town of Allensworth, California, thirty miles north of Bakersfield. Allensworth attempted to build a "Tuskegee of the West" but failed to win the confidence of the state legislature, through which a bill had to pass to form the school. By 1914, thirty-five families resided in Allensworth, which now covered nine hundred acres. But with the death of Colonel Allensworth in September of 1914, Allensworth's population began to decline. By World War II, the town was almost empty; in 1966, arsenic was discovered in the water and the town folded for good. On Blackdom, see Gibson, "Blackdom" (1986); on Allensworth, see Bunch, "Allensworth: The Life, Death and Rebirth of an All-Black Community" (1987), and Hamilton, *Black Towns and Profit* (1991), 138–48. For general discussions of all-black towns in America, see Crockett, *The Black Towns* (1979); Hamilton, *Black Towns and Profit* (1991); and Pease and Pease, *Black Utopia* (1972). For a comprehensive listing of all-black towns throughout the United States, see <http://www.soulofamerica.com/towns.>

10. For more on Groves, besides Washington's chapter on him in *The Story of the Negro* (1909), see Hawkins, "Hoeing Their Own: Black Agriculture and the Agrarian Ideal in Kansas, 1880–1920" (1999). In the world of Micheaux's fiction, Baptiste visits Groves and his family to lament his bad decision in not marrying the "Potato King's" daughter; see *The Homesteader* 409–35.

11. Gibbs's autobiography sheds light on the connections between his life and Washington's beliefs. While Gibbs consciously presents the West as a peculiar region that provides prospects not found elsewhere, Washington, in his short in-

troduction to the book, writes only two lines concerning the West, pointing to "the development of lawlessness there and its results." See Gibbs, *Shadow and Light* (1902), xxiii.

12. In 1913, Washington wrote a series of articles for the *New York Age* sketching his observations of African American life in certain western states during his "extensive tour of the Northwest." He finds that since the western African American population is significantly less than in other parts of the country, "racial solidarity, racial oneness" is missing ("Booker T. Washington Tells About Conditions" 1). Washington's articles establish the American West as a white locale, with African Americans barred from western trade unions, discriminated against in education past grade school, and segregated or barred from various public establishments. Washington writes as his final assessment, "I am more convinced than ever that the Negro in the South is doing better than any group of colored people that I have found in this part of the world, and I am still further convinced that the Negro in the South has a better future in the South than in any part of the world that I have yet visited" ("Negro in South" 2). For Washington, the frontier was surely not colorblind. See "Booker T. Washington Tells About Conditions of Negro in Northwest," *New York Age* 20 March 1913: 1ff; "Intelligent and Cultured," *New York Age* 3 April 1913: 1ff; "Negro in South Has Brightest Future," *New York Age* 10 April 1913: 2; "There are Colored Mormons Out in Utah," *New York Age* 17 April 1913: 1ff; and "Creed of Mormon Church," *New York Age* 24 April 1913: 2.

13. Though no print of *The Betrayal* exists today, the script for the film can be found in the New York State Archives (Motion Picture Scripts Collection), Albany, New York.

14. Almost all of the films discussed here have been lost, so the narratives have been gleaned from reviews, posters, and screenplays where available. For the lost films, I have taken synopses from Sampson's *Blacks in Black and White* (1995); see also Richards, *African American Films through 1959: A Comprehensive, Illustrated Filmography* (1998). *The Symbol of the Unconquered* was recently located in Belgium; a copy of *The Exile* can be found in the Library of Congress.

15. Bowser and Spence argue in *Writing Himself into History* that Micheaux consciously reworks his own persona through his novels and films. That is, Micheaux becomes a construct in much the same way as do Oscar Devereaux, Jean Baptiste, Martin Eden, Sydney Wyeth, or even Hugh Van Allen, the homesteading protagonist of *Symbol of the Unconquered* (for which the working title was *The Wilderness Trail*; see Bowser and Spence 175). They write, "Writing himself into history, [Micheaux] used his own life in his films and novels (a selection of actual and imaginary events), which gave credibility to his role as an entrepreneur

and pioneer" (5). Just as Micheaux created reflections of himself in his productions, those phantasms, in turn, mediated their maker.

16. On Micheaux's masculinity and its relationship to his western identification, see M. K. Johnson, *Black Masculinity and the Frontier Myth in American Literature* (2002). Johnson argues that "The South Dakota frontier serves as a place where Micheaux hopes black manhood can be reconstituted" (70).

17. Micheaux's choice of name for Eden's unfaithful lover is quite odd, given that Micheaux thinly disguises his characters. The historical Jesse Binga was a successful (male) real estate developer who opened Chicago's first black-owned bank in 1908. Binga Bank was known for providing loans and mortgages to African Americans when other banks refused. Binga's bank failed in the 1930s, and Binga was indicted on charges relating to financial irregularities. He served three years of a ten-year sentence. Given that Binga represents Washingtonian principles and business ethics (barring his possibly illegal activities), Micheaux's linking of Binga with Eden's weak-willed lover appears somehow inappropriate. Binga gets a short mention in Washington's *Story of the Negro* 2: 223–24.

3 RECASTING THE WEST

1. Before historians began to undertake a serious reconsideration of Turner's Frontier Thesis, which effectively whitewashed both the process and the place of the West, the only booklength studies that broadly attempted to understand western African American history were Porter, *The Negro on the American Frontier* (1971); Savage, *Blacks in the West* (1976); and Katz, *The Black West* (1987). For more recent studies, see Billington and Hardaway, eds., *African Americans on the Western Frontier* (1998), and Taylor, *In Search of the Racial Frontier* (1998). An early book of significance for presenting the history of African Americans in the West is *The Negro Trail Blazers of California* (1919), by African American amateur historian Delilah Beasley.

2. Besides the more general histories of Porter, Katz, Savage, Billington and Hardaway, and Taylor indicated in note 1, see, on cowboys: Durham and Jones, *The Negro Cowboys* (1965), Porter, "Negro Labor in the Western Cattle Industry, 1866–1900" (1969), Massey, ed., *Black Cowboys of Texas* (2000); on miners: Savage, "The Negro on the Mining Frontier" (1945), Lapp, *Blacks in Gold Rush California* (1977); on homesteaders: Littlefield and Underhill, "Black Dreams and 'Free' Homes" (1973), Painter, *Exodusters* (1977), Athearn, *In Search of Canaan* (1978), Ravage, *Black Pioneers* (1997); on fur traders and mountain men: Porter, "Negroes in the Fur Trade" (1934) (reprinted in Porter, *The Negro on the American Frontier*), Wilson, *Jim Beckwourth* (1972); on U.S. soldiers: Leckie, *The Buffalo Soldiers* (1967), Carroll, *The Black Military Experience in the American West* (1971), Fowler, *The Black Infantry in the*

West: 1869–1891 (1971); on lawmen: Littlefield and Underhill, "Negro Marshals in the Indian Territory" (1971), Williams, "Black Men Who Wore the 'Star'" (1981). For comprehensive bibliographies of scholarship about African Americans in the West, see Hardaway, "The African American Frontier: A Bibliographic Essay" (1998), and Taylor, "Bibliographic Essay on the African American West" (1996).

3. Jeffries's singing cowboy Westerns are *Harlem on the Prairie* (1938), *Two Gun Man from Harlem* (1938), *Bronze Buckaroo* (1938), and *Harlem Rides the Range* (1939). On Jeffries's story see *Midnight Ramble* (1994) and also Jeffries's autobiographic oral history in Govenar, *African American Frontier*, 217–40.

4. For a wide-ranging, though incomplete, list of western black writers, see Abajian's *Blacks and Their Contributions to the American West* (1974).

5. Detter and Micheaux will be discussed in this chapter; on the other writers in this list see Beckwourth's *The Life and Adventures of James P. Beckwourth* (1856); Flipper's *The Colored Cadet at West Point* (1878); Gibbs's *Shadow and Light* (1902); and Griggs's *Imperium in Imperio* (1899) and *The Hindered Hand, Or, The Reign of the Repressionist* (1905), among others. This list is decidedly male; my research has turned up no evidence of African American women writers publishing in the West around (or before) the turn of the century. However, more recovery work may produce just such prose. By the 1940s, though, African American women were beginning to produce narratives about and from the American West. See, for example, Ida Bell Thompson's *American Daughter* (1946), a narrative of a black family farm in North Dakota, and Elizabeth Laura Adams's *Dark Symphony* (1942), the celebrated spiritual autobiography of a California-born Catholic woman.

6. Since the details of Micheaux's prose have been outlined in the previous chapter, I will turn here to the aspects of both his fiction and his life specific to self-publication and investigate how they add to his ideological narrative of the West as a rejuvenating and enterprising space.

7. Though a number of African Americans produced stories of the American West, fictional and otherwise, few of these writers actually wrote and published west of the hundredth meridian. The American West was the birthplace of such well-known black writers of the early twentieth century as Sutton E. Griggs (Chatfield, Texas), Wallace Thurman (Salt Lake City, Utah), Langston Hughes (Joplin, Missouri, raised in Topeka and Lawrence, Kansas), Gwendolyn Brooks (Topeka, Kansas), and Ralph Ellison (Oklahoma City, Oklahoma). Yet none of these writers remained in the West. Various opportunities (many of them literary) called all of them east. Many writers, such as Jim Beckwourth, Mifflin Wister Gibbs, Sutton E. Griggs, and even W. E. B. Du Bois, wrote about the West but published their works outside of its boundaries.

8. Besides hosting the more widely known *Pacific Appeal* and *Elevator*, San Francisco was also home to the *San Francisco Vindicator* (1884–1906). Between 1889

and the mid-1920s at least six successful African American newspapers were published in Omaha, Nebraska, alone: *Afro-American Sentinel, The Enterprise, The New Era, Omaha Monitor, Omaha Whip,* and *Progress.* During this same period, African American newspapers appeared in Colorado, New Mexico, Utah, Kansas, and Oklahoma, though none were established in South Dakota, North Dakota, or Wyoming. For a comprehensive listing of African American periodicals, see Danky and Hady, eds., *African American Newspapers and Periodicals* (1998).

9. On Micheaux's papers, see chapter 2, note 3.

10. Robert Ball Anderson joined the Union army a few months before the end of the Civil War. He and Daisy Graham were married in 1922; she was twenty-one, he was seventy-nine. When Daisy Anderson died on September 19, 1998, she was one of three surviving Civil War widows. See Johnston, "A Widow's Legacy" (1997). See also Daisy Anderson's obituary by Jim Kirksey in the *Denver Post* 24 Sept. 1998: A-1. (Kirksey also includes a sales pitch for Anderson's book, though the cost of the book had doubled from the 1997 price to $20.) Her obituary also appeared in the *New York Times,* 26 Sept. 1998.

11. While the *Dallas News* notes that Micheaux's book was to appear from A. C. McClury in Chicago, the rejection letter to Baptiste in *The Homesteader* comes from A. C. McGraw & Co. (406). At the time that Micheaux sent out his manuscript, two publishing houses with very similar names existed in Chicago, the aforementioned A. C. McClury, a small house that produced books ranging in topic from women composers to western railroads, and the larger A. C. McClurg Company, which first published W. E. B. Du Bois's *Souls of Black Folk* (1903). Micheaux generally thinly disguises place names and people within his novels (Oscar Devereaux from *The Conquest* is quite obviously a fictionalized Oscar Micheaux; the cities of Attalia and Effingham in *The Forged Note* represent Atlanta and Birmingham). Without knowledge of the *Dallas News* article, a reader could easily infer from Baptiste's letter that Micheaux was separating himself from Du Bois—and strengthening his alignment with the principles of Booker T. Washington—by depicting Du Bois's publisher (A. C. McGraw/A. C. McClurg) as rejecting this narrative of a self-made western man. On the history of African American publishing, see Joyce, *Gatekeepers of Black Culture: Black-Owned Publishing in the United States, 1817–1981* (1983).

12. Micheaux lists Lincoln, Nebraska, as the home of the Western Book Supply Company on the title page of *The Forged Note,* though the copyright to *The Forged Note* is held by the Woodruff Bank Note Company, also of Lincoln. With the publication of *The Homesteader,* Micheaux has changed the location of the Western Book Supply Company to Sioux City, Iowa, where he intermittently resided from possibly as early as 1914 to 1919 (see VannEpps-Taylor 82–89). Iowa was also home to the black-owned Iowa State Bystander Publishing Company

(1894–1974), which published the African American weekly *Iowa State Bystander*. This firm also occasionally published books dealing with African American history, but Micheaux apparently had no business dealings with the publisher, likely already devoting himself to his own publishing venture by 1916 with the publication of *The Forged Note*. On the Iowa Bystander Publishing Company, see Joyce, *Gatekeepers of Black Culture* (1983), 59, 195.

13. At one point in *The Forged Note*, Wyeth sells books that he had previously purchased and read. While not exactly an attempt at distribution, Wyeth allows that this practice forms part of his venture as a book salesman. See *The Forged Note*, 301.

14. Micheaux's *The Conquest, The Homesteader, The Wind from Nowhere, The Case of Mrs. Wingate,* and *The Masquerade* are currently available from various publishers, *The Conquest* and *The Homesteader* as relatively inexpensive trade paperbacks from the University of Nebraska Press; *The Story of Dorothy Stanfield* and *The Forged Note* are both out of print. Thomas Detter's *Nellie Brown* is also available from the University of Nebraska Press, though only in cloth; Nat Love's *Life and Adventures* is widely available in both paper and cloth as well as on audiocassette. Robert Ball Anderson's *From Slavery to Affluence* is not currently in print.

15. In all of the "homesteading" productions after *The Conquest*, (*The Homesteader* [novel], *The Homesteader* [film, 1919], *The Exile* [film, 1931], *The Wind from Nowhere* [novel, 1941], and *The Betrayal* [film, 1948]), Micheaux's neighbor discovers her black ancestry so that the she and the homesteader can finally acknowledge and consummate their love. Micheaux published *The Conquest* after his homesteading venture had effectively failed, though given the thinly veiled nature of his narrative, neighbors who could recognize themselves could undoubtedly also identify Micheaux's illicit lover. Her presence in this book, however, is quite minor.

16. In 1909, South Dakota passed a law that prohibited "intermarriage or illicit cohabitation of persons belonging to the African race with any person of the opposite sex belonging to the Caucasian race." This act labeled such miscegenation a felony punishable by up to one thousand dollars and/or up to ten years in prison. See *Enabling Act and Constitution* (House Bill 362 [Session Law Chapter 196]). In 1913, this law was repealed and replaced with a more restrictive miscegenation law that prohibited "intermarriage or cohabitation of any persons belonging to the African, Corean, Malayan, or Mongolian Race, with any person of the opposite sex, belonging to the Caucasian or White Race." See *Enabling Act and Constitution* (House Bill 204 [Session Law Chapter 266]). Miscegenation under this law became a misdemeanor, though the punishment did not change. Both acts declared null and void any marriages entered into before the passage of the bills. The 1913 law was not repealed until 1957.

17. Passed in 1873, the Timber Culture Act grew from the logic that rain follows the plow. In an attempt to produce lumber on the treeless plains, the Timber Culture Act allowed citizens to acquire up to a quarter section (160 acres), provided that the settler plant trees on at least forty acres of the claim. In 1878, this number was reduced to ten acres, though the act demanded that 2,700 trees be planted on each of those acres. The act was repealed in 1891 after significant abuse by land speculators and ranchers.

18. Wax has written two studies of Anderson. The first ("Robert Ball Anderson" [1983]) discusses Anderson's homesteading in western Nebraska, while the second ("The Odyssey of an Ex-Slave" [1984]) illustrates Anderson's life up to 1884 when he moved to Nebraska to build his homestead.

19. Some of the more popular autobiographies remain in print today. See, for example, Andy Adams's *Log of a Cowboy* (1903) or Charlie Siringo's *A Texas Cowboy: or, Fifteen Years on the Hurricane Deck of a Spanish Pony* (1885).

20. In *The Negro Cowboys*, Durham and Jones speculate that Love's story of the acquisition of his name may be part of the larger hyperbole found throughout Love's narrative. They note, "Love said that in 1875, he 'was known all over the cattle country as "Red River Dick"' and he added that 'many cattle kings of the West as well as scores of bad men all over the western country have at some time or another had good reason to remember the name "Red River Dick."' Perhaps. But it is remarkable that none of these rather articulate men did remember. The cattlemen for whom [Love] claimed to have worked do not appear in the records, and none of the cowboys he worked with seem to have ridden with other crews" (193). While not questioning Love's narrative as a whole, Durham and Jones are willing to suspect the veracity of any of Love's particular yarns.

21. Allmendinger incorrectly notes that Love's autobiography went out of print in 1968 (see *Ten Most Wanted* [1998], 29, and "Deadwood Dick" [1993], 88, as well as n. 12); in fact, Love's book disappeared soon after its publication and then did not come back *into* print until 1968.

4 THE MAKING OF AMERICANS

1. Mormon is the colloquial name for The Church of Jesus Christ of Latter-day Saints. The designations Mormon Church and LDS Church will be used interchangeably within this chapter.

2. Section 20 of the Edmunds-Tucker Act reads: "That it shall be unlawful for any female to vote at any election hereafter held in the Territory of Utah . . . and any and every act of the legislature assembly of the Territory of Utah providing for or allowing registration or voting by females is hereby annulled." Section 24 demanded that all male voters in Utah take an oath before voting that included

the voter's name, age, place of business, marital status, and a declaration that he "support the Constitution of the United States and will faithfully obey the laws thereof, and especially will obey the act of Congress approved March twenty-second, eighteen hundred and eighty-two, entitled 'An act to amend section fifty-three hundred and fifty-two of the Revised Statutes of the United States, in reference to bigamy and for other purposes,' and will also obey this act in re-spect of the crimes in said act defined and forbidden, and that he will not, di-rectly or indirectly, aid or abet, counsel or advise, any other person to commit any of said crimes." See *Statutes at Large of the United States of America*, chapters 397, 635, (1887).

3. Thomas Alexander argues that this early period of the twentieth century brought a change in the Mormon world view from unitary to pluralistic (14). Be-fore the Woodruff Manifesto (1890), in which the church officially denounced and distanced itself from polygamy (the single most important event in Mormon his-tory to date), the LDS Church demanded adherence to ideas of unity and com-munity. For the faithful, the Mormon religious sphere and the political world were necessarily linked. But after the disruption by federal law of this ideal of a political kingdom of God, and the subsequent entrance of Utah into the Union, church leaders saw that their presence in national politics and culture demanded a shift toward a pluralistic world view. The struggle of the first two decades after the Woodruff Manifesto consisted primarily of reconfiguring the LDS Church's politics toward a secular and pluralist nation. At this point in Mormon history, though, culture, doctrine, and political tendencies all became jumbled. Polyga-mous culture, for example, was distinctly at odds with the new doctrine; the cling-ing ideals of the Kingdom of God jarred harshly with American political plural-ism, and the body of the LDS Church suddenly found itself politically severed from its unitary head, leaving it adrift in a new, and still embittered, secular and pluralist United States (Alexander 11).

4. The last significant national attempt to deflect Mormon political power oc-curred upon the election of Utah Republican Reed Smoot to the U.S. Senate in 1903. At the time of his election, Smoot was a prominent Utah businessman as well as an Apostle in the LDS Church. All Apostles sit on the Quorum of the Twelve Apostles, the highest ruling body of the church, and are potential candi-dates for the next church presidency. After Smoot's election, a group of Salt Lake City businessmen, lawyers, and non-Mormon clergy protested to unseat Smoot, arguing that his role as an LDS Church leader could not possibly make him im-partial to secular political concerns. Folded into these grievances were veiled (and unsubstantiated) rumors of Smoot's polygamy. A senate committee considered this petition and finally concluded in 1907 that Smoot could occupy his seat, which he had held throughout the investigation. Smoot served Utah in the senate

for thirty years. See Merrill, *Reed Smoot: Apostle in Politics* (1990), and Flake, *The Politics of American Religious Identity* (2004).

5. Besides Vexler, *Chronology and Documentary Handbook of the State of Utah* (1979), the original Utah state constitution can be found at <http://www.archives .state.ut.us/exhibits/Statehood/1896text.htm>; the current Utah state constitution can be found at <http://www.le.state.ut.us/~code/const/const.htm>; neither of these documents include the "Address to the People of Utah." The sections and articles concerning polygamy originally written into the 1895 constitution remain today.

6. Three other state constitutions have clauses forbidding polygamous marriages. All of these constitutions were accepted within roughly a decade of Utah's statehood, likely to protect those new states from the emigration of Mormon polygamists: Idaho (1890; article 1, section 4); Montana (1889; article 3, section 4); and Oklahoma (1907; article 1, section 2). See Antineau, Carroll, and Burke, 79–80.

7. Throughout the nineteenth century, the LDS Church was quite successful in finding converts, in Europe and Britain especially. During the late nineteenth and early twentieth centuries, the missionary program expanded into the Middle East, South America, and the Pacific Islands. See Alexander, 212–38. By the late 1950s, the majority of LDS Church members resided outside of Utah. By the mid-1990s, the majority of church members lived outside of the United States.

8. In the hierarchy of Mormon Church buildings, stake houses are administrative buildings that fall between ward buildings (which are used for weekly worship as well as community events) and tabernacles (buildings reserved for larger annual meetings). Generally these buildings are geographically located according to the density of church membership.

9. For more on Home Literature, see Cracroft's "The Didactic Heresy as Orthodox Tool: B. H. Roberts as Writer of Home Literature" (1996), as well as his "Seeking 'the Good, the Pure, the Elevating'" (1981, parts 1 and 2).

10. See, for example, Arrington, "Mormonism: Views from Without and Within" (1974), where he argues that Mormons did not "encourage or produce, for publication, a body of literature describing the variety, richness, and quality of pioneer life" (150). He concludes, however that by remaining literarily silent during the turbulent years of Mormon persecution and growth, "Latter-day Saints lost the image-battle during the period of their pioneering" (150). Also on this dearth of early Mormon literature see Geary, "Women Regionalists of Mormon Country" (1985), and Morgan, "Mormon Storytellers" (1996), esp. 4–5. This sense of Mormon literature's scarcity in the nineteenth century can also be read implicitly within other Mormon scholars' work through their valorization of nineteenth-century scripture, poetry, hymns, and religious discourse over fiction.

See in particular, Eugene England's "Good Literature for a Chosen People" (1999), "The Dawning of a Brighter Day" (1982) (see in particular the divisions in his bibliography of Mormon literature, 157–60), and "Mormon Literature: Progress and Prospects" (1995); and William Mulder's "Mormonism and Literature" (1954–55) and "Telling It Slant" (1993).

11. Bruce Jorgensen, in "Digging the Foundation" (1975), does not attribute the scarcity of "reprintable" Mormon literature to pioneer distractions but rather to an inability to integrate broader cultural changes in American literature into their work. He writes, "Perhaps the literary developments of the 1880s, the 1890s, and especially the 1920s, could not be assimilated by Mormon writers still committed to attachment to didacticism and waning literary fashions" (56).

12. According to the records of *Books in Print, The Giant Joshua* was apparently republished in 1966 as a paperback, though only for one year; it was again republished in 1976 by Western Epics Inc. because of "continuing demand for the book" (Whipple, *The Giant Joshua* ["Publisher's Foreword"]). A collection of Whipple's previously unpublished writings is forthcoming, entitled *Maurine Whipple: The Lost Works*, edited by Veda Tebbs Hale and Laura Fielding Anderson. Whipple's only other published book is a narrative history of Utah and Mormon culture entitled *This the Place: Utah* (1945), published in Knopf's series, the American Scene, which celebrates American landscape and place by state.

13. For a comprehensive overview of anti-Mormon writings from the nineteenth century, see Arrington, "Mormonism: Views from Without and Within" (1974). See also Givens, *The Viper on the Hearth* (1997). For a general comparison of anti-Mormon polemics with attacks on other religious minorities in the mid-nineteenth-century United States, see Davis, "Some Themes of Counter- Subversion" (1960).

14. Signature Books has no official connection to the LDS Church, but they are dedicated to "religious and non-religious books that relate to the Mormon Corridor . . . [including] southern Alberta, eastern Washington, Idaho, western Wyoming, Utah, Nevada, southwestern Colorado, Arizona, southern California, and Chihuahua." They also state, "Our religious books are scholarly rather than devotional in nature." See <http://www.signaturebooks.com/faq.htm>.

15. Besides *A Little Lower than the Angels* (1942), Sorensen's books include *On This Star* (1946), *The Neighbors* (1947), *The Evening and the Morning* (1949), *The Proper Gods* (1951), *Many Heavens* (1954), *Kingdom Come* (1960), *Where Nothing Is Long Ago* (short stories; 1963), and *The Man with the Key* (1974). She was awarded two Guggenheim Fellowships, with which she produced *The Proper Gods* and *Kingdom Come*. She also wrote children's and young adult fiction, including *Curious Missy* (1953), *The House Next Door; Utah, 1896* (1954; The Strength of the Union series), *Plain Girl* (1955; Child Study Award), *Miracles on Maple Hill* (1957;

John Newbery Medal of the American Library Association), *Lotte's Locket* (1964), *Around the Corner* (1971), and *Friends of the Road* (1978).

16. *The Peaceable Kingdom* was reviewed in non-Mormon journals, though not nearly as widely as the novels of Whipple and Sorensen; most reviews favored the book. One reviewer, clearly imbued with the nineteenth-century notion of the sexual sensationalism latent in polygamy, wrote that Kennelly's novel "is no peep-show, no 'exposé' on polygamy" (Wells 23). Virginia Sorensen reviewed *The Peaceable Kingdom* in the *New York Herald Tribune Weekly Book Review* and placed the novel within the framework of her own arguments concerning Mormon patriarchy, writing, "this is a Mormon story—living here and there, doing the best they could while they waited to find out what The Church would do about polygamy" ("Mormon Wife" 6). While Sorensen wrote nothing in the review that might antagonize the Mormon Church, by writing for the *New York Herald Tribune* she certainly did not represent a church-sanctioned position on the novel. I have not been able to uncover any reviews of *The Peaceable Kingdom* in official LDS Church publications.

17. See, for example, the poetry and short stories collected in Peterson, *Greening Wheat: Fifteen Mormon Short Stories* (1983); England and Clark, *Harvest: Fifteen Contemporary Mormon Poets* (1989); and England, *Bright Angels and Familiars* (1992), as well as the novels of Levi Peterson.

5 BUFFALO BILL'S OBJECT LESSONS

1. For recent and comprehensive studies of William F. Cody and the Wild West, see Blackstone, *Buckskins, Bullets, and Business* (1986); Brooklyn Museum of Art, *Buffalo Bill and the Wild West* (1981); Clark, "The Menace of Wild West Shows" (1994); Kasson, *Buffalo Bill's Wild West* (2000); Kramer, "The American Wild West Show and 'Buffalo Bill' Cody'" (1972); Martin, "'The Grandest and Most Cosmopolitan Object Teacher'" (1996); Mitterling, "Buffalo Bill and Carry Nation: Symbols of an Age" (1982); Moses, *Wild West Shows and the Images of American Indians* (1996); Reddin, *Wild West Shows* (1999); Rosa and May, *Buffalo Bill and His Wild West* (1989); Russell, *The Lives and Legends of Buffalo Bill* (1960); Schwartz, "The Wild West Show" (1970); Slotkin, "Buffalo Bill's Wild West and the Mythologization of the American Empire" (1993), as well as his chapter on Buffalo Bill in *Gunfighter Nation* (1992); Tompkins, "At the Buffalo Bill Museum" (1990); White, "Frederick Jackson Turner and Buffalo Bill" (1994); and Wilson, *Buffalo Bill's Wild West: An American Legend* (1998).

2. For a comprehensive examination of Cody's stage career, see Wickstrom, "Buffalo Bill the Actor" (1995).

3. While the 1893 summer performances drew record crowds, and thus

record sales, Cody claimed to be making almost $160,000 per month as early as 1886; see Blackstone, 18.

4. The tradition of Wild West shows continued sporadically into the 1940s, but they never reached the heights of popularity that Cody realized in the 1890s. While Wild West shows appear to be a thing of the past, their appeal has not disappeared altogether. Today, a company in California has retained the rights to the name Buffalo Bill's Wild West and reproduces Cody's show worldwide; see <www.buffalobill.com>. EuroDisney amusement park also has a twice daily Wild West show, complete with a fictional Cody, Annie Oakley, and Sitting Bull; see Wilson, 256, as well as EuroDisney's information at <http://www.dlp-guidebook .de/Village/Village_BuffaloBill.htm>. Additionally, numerous organizations and companies that produce Renaissance fairs often stage reenactments of Buffalo Bill's Wild West.

5. Ironically, displayed at the 1893 Chicago World's Fair, where the Wild West played just outside the grounds, were the cabin in which Sitting Bull had been shot, the Hunkpapa leader's sweat lodge, and two women who purported to be his widows, thus allowing viewers to meld together the ethnographic presentations of the Columbian Exposition and the supposed history of the "everything genuine" Wild West; see Reddin, 119, Utley, *The Lance and the Shield*, 312, and Moses, 139.

6. Christine Bold argues in "The Rough Riders at Home and Abroad" that the image of the Rough Rider was exploited for nationalist and imperialist projects, particularly by the three greatest proponents of its western imagery: "Cody, Roosevelt and Remington reformulated the frontier West according to certain organizational patterns, then set within this scene the part-military, part-Western figure of the Rough Rider. With this creation, they acted out a healing of domestic tensions, by presenting the Rough Rider as the harmonious meeting point of various regions, races, and classes in modern America. Then they demonstrated America's power abroad by pitting these national Rough Riders against an array of savage enemies, often in the context of a rule-bound game" (347).

7. Regardless of the general acceptance of Cody's international creation, the audience's approval of the various ethnic or national groups represented within the Congress of Rough Riders often shifted with changes in the international political climate. Richard Slotkin notes that while audiences initially cheered Filipino horsemen in the Congress of Rough Riders, the crowds hissed and jeered at them after the Filipino revolt against the U.S. presence on the islands (*Gunfighter Nation* 85).

8. See also Bellin, *Demon of the Continent* (2001). Bellin, like Bergland, looks to the Native American presence for determinants of American literature, invoking D. H. Lawrence's assertion that "The moment the last nuclei of Red life break

up in America, then the white men will have to reckon with the full force of the demon of the continent" (1). Bellin claims that, though the "the last nuclei of Red life" is far from gone, "the presence of Indian peoples in the land that is now the United States has been of profound significance in the shaping of American Literature—not only to texts that overtly engage this presence, but to the whole body of literature produced in a nation itself produced by encounter" (3). Thus Bellin stresses not so much the images of Native Americans in American literature, but the determinates of the encounter and its representation.

9. All subsequent references to Standing Bear's *My People the Sioux* are to the 1977 edition, unless otherwise noted.

10. Though I noted earlier that Native American performers were relegated to clearly Native American roles, Standing Bear here alludes to a possible crossing of those lines. This reference to Native Americans acting in non-Native roles seems to be singular and certainly not conclusive of such a practice.

11. See, in particular, Moses's chapter "Reformers and the Images of the Show Indian," 60–79; see also Kvasnicka and Viola, eds., *The Commissioners of Indian Affairs, 1824–1977* (1979), esp. 190, 200, 215.

12. In a circular to U.S. Indian Agents, Commissioner Morgan argued that Native American employment in shows and exhibitions destroyed both Indians themselves as well as any reform work undertaken by the BIA. Morgan claimed the these shows "[fostered] idleness and a distaste for steady occupation" and "brought [Indians] in contact with people of the lowest character," concluding "they frequently returned home wrecked morally and physically. . . . In such case . . . their influence and example among the other Indians is the worst possible." He closed his memo with an ultimatum to both his Indian agents and their charges: "You will therefore impress upon the Indians the importance of their remaining at home and devoting their time and energies to establishing comfortable homes, cultivating farms, building houses, and acquiring thrifty, industrious habits. . . . If, on the contrary, they ignore these suggestions, which are made wholly for their best interest, and join exhibitions, they must not look to this Office for favor or assistance." See Moses, 77–78.

13. The first photographs of Sitting Bull are in dispute. There may be two photographs taken earlier than the sitting at Bismark or Fort Yates, one a group picture taken at Fort Walsh in Canada that may include Sitting Bull and another in which Sitting Bull sat with Swift Bear, Spotted Tail, Julius Meyer, and Red Cloud for a studio picture; see Linder, 37–40, and Utley, *The Lance and the Shield*, 384 n6. Regardless, these 1881 photographs by Goff represent the beginning of Sitting Bull's saleable visage. The woodcut made from Goff's photograph that appears in *Campaigns of General Custer* includes Sitting Bull's signature, presciently pointing to the cabinet cards that Sitting Bull would eventually sell in the Wild

West. Besides Lindner's article, Watson, "The Photographs of Sitting Bull" (1949), provides an earlier cataloging of Sitting Bull's portraits.

14. Sitting Bull's contract is partially printed in Havighurst, 49; the full contract is printed in the *Middle Border Bulletin* 3:2 (Autumn 1943): 1–2; a photostat of the original is in Burdick 18–19.

15. Fifteen years after Sitting Bull returned from his tour with the Wild West, McLaughlin's contempt for the Sioux leader had only increased. In a letter to Commissioner of Indian Affairs Morgan (October 17, 1890), McLaughlin describes Sitting Bull as the "high priest and leading apostle of this latest Indian absurdity [Ghost Dance] . . . a man of low cunning, devoid of a single manly principle in his nature or an honorable trait of character . . . the most vain, pompous and untruthful Indian that I ever knew . . . a polygamist, libertine, habitual liar, active obstructionist and a great obstacle in the civilization of these people [who] is so totally devoid of any of the nobler traits of character and so wedded to the old Indian ways and superstitions that it is very doubtful if any change for the better will ever come over him at his present age of 56 years" (letter printed in Burdick 91–92).

16. Short Bull, a Lakota Ghost Dancer and federal prisoner who traveled with Cody in Europe during 1891 as part of his sentence deferral, also produced a number of pictographs of his life, though never apparently with the intent of publishing them. Primarily collected by folklorist Natalie Curtis, Short Bull's drawings depict numerous scenes of battles with other Indians, though not necessarily any with white soldiers. Some of Short Bull's material has been published or exhibited, but a notebook that includes drawings he made between 1891 and 1893, possibly while with the Wild West in Europe, rests unpublished in the Museum für Volkerkunde in Leipzig, Germany. See McCoy, "Short Bull: Lakota Visionary, Historian and Artist" (1992).

17. These pictographic collections have been published in Stirling, *Three Pictographic Autobiographies of Sitting Bull* (1938). Praus, *A New Pictographic Autobiography of Sitting Bull* (1955), presents a fourth series. The originals of the 1870 and one of the 1882 series can be found in the National Anthropological Archives in Washington, D.C.; the series presented by Praus is at the Fort St. Joseph Historical Association Museum in St. Joseph, Missouri.

18. One other autobiography by a Native American, *The Memoirs of Chief Red Fox*, describes his employment with the Wild West, though this book appears to be predominately a fabrication. Specific events in *The Memoirs of Chief Red Fox* seem preposterous, such as when Red Fox meets William McKinley in the company of Mark Hanna, Thomas Edison, and Alexander Graham Bell at a Wild West performance, or an anecdote about New York Police Commissioner Theodore Roosevelt stopping by Red Fox's tent at Madison Square Garden to

swap Western yarns. Apparently Cash Asher, who collected and edited Red Fox's stories, fabricated much of the narrative. See Red Fox, *The Memoirs of Chief Red Fox* (1971); for an overview of the Red Fox controversy, see Hale, "Exploiting the Native American Renaissance: The Chief Red Fox Memoirs Hoax" (2001).

19. E. A. Brininstool was an early-twentieth-century popular western historian (focusing primarily on George Armstrong Custer, the Battle of Little Bighorn, and Crazy Horse), journalist, and cowboy poet. I have found no information on Clyde Champion (save that one-half of the famous 1930s bankrobbing duo Bonnie and Clyde sometimes signed his name "Clyde Champion Barrow"— an unlikely connection).

20. See Castro, *Interpreting the Indian* (1983), esp. 71–97; DeMallie, *The Sixth Grandfather* (1984), especially the lengthy introduction (1–99); Krupat, *For Those Who Came After* (1985), particularly his chapter, "Yellow Wolf and Black Elk: History and Transcendence" (107–36); McCluskey, "Black Elk Speaks" (1972); Neihardt and Utecht, *Black Elk Lives* (2000); Powers, "When Black Elk Speaks, Everybody Listens" (1990); Rice, *Black Elk's Story: Distinguishing Its Lakota Purpose* (1991); Sayre, "Vision and Experience in *Black Elk Speaks*" (1971); Silvio, "*Black Elk Speaks* and Literary Disciplinarity" (1999); and Wong, *Sending My Heart Back across Years* (1992), particularly her chapter, "Oral and Written Collaborative Autobiography: Nicholas Black Elk and Charles Alexander Eastman."

21. Black Elk does mention that after he gets stranded in England he joins another Wild West show (run by Captain Mexican Joe Shelley) that paid him better than Cody's had. Also he notes that just three days after he was stranded, the local police detained him and his Indian compatriots for questioning, apparently concerning their seeming vagrancy; he tells Neihardt, "They probably blamed us with something that had happened" (DeMallie 252). Neihardt does not include any mention of Black Elk's encounter with the police in *Black Elk Speaks*.

CONCLUSION

1. Whether this placement of the tank reflected some immediate threat to Cody's grave or merely a generalized (and possibly imagined) peril of exhumation remains unknown. Some recent, though inconclusive, evidence points to the possibility that guardsmen stationed the tank at the grave while en route to a September 1922 celebration in Idaho Springs, Colorado, and not necessarily as a deterrent to an actual threat. Regardless, the mingling of the national military and the western imaginary remains significant. See Friesen (2005).

2. Threats against Cody's body did not stop after 1921. In the summer of 1948, the Cheyenne, Wyoming, American Legion declared that it would return Cody's body to Cedar Mountain, outside of Cody, Wyoming, a place Cody had

once said he wished to be buried. The Cheyenne American Legion wired the Cody American Legion, "The state of Wyoming has long rankled under the humiliation of Buffalo Bill's enforced absence from his chosen burial spot on Cedar Mountain. . . . [We] have taken a solemn pledge to return the remains of the great pioneer to the bosom of his chosen people." Acknowledging this vow, the Cody American Legion publicly offered a $10,000 reward for the return of Cody's body by August 19, the opening day of the Wyoming American Legion convention (which happened to be in Cody that year). The Cody American Legion declared in their offer, "No more heinous act was ever committed than to purloin the mortal remains of Cody's illustrious founder and sink him under twenty feet of concrete in the foreign soil of Colorado's Lookout Mountain for purely mercenary purposes." Not to be outdone by the Wyoming bluster, the Denver American Legion swiftly reacted to the threats and stationed a five-man armed guard over Cody's tomb, declaring, "If this be treason—and I think it is . . . [w]e are prepared to throw back any assault against Lookout Mountain. We are there and it will take more than palaver to get us out." Quotes from the Wyoming American Legion are from *Cody Enterprise*, 4 Aug. 1948: n.p.; the Denver reply can be found in the *Rocky Mountain News*, 1 Aug. 1948, and reprinted in *Colorado Prospector: Historical Highlights from Early Day Newspapers* 6:15 (1975): 1ff.

Abajian, James. *Blacks and Their Contributions to the American West: A Bibliography and Union List of Library Holdings Through 1970.* Boston: G. K. Hall & Co., 1974.

Alexander, Thomas G. *Mormonism in Transition.* Urbana: University of Illinois Press, 1986.

Allmendinger, Blake. "Deadwood Dick: The Black Cowboy as Cultural Timber." *Journal of American Culture* 16:4 (Winter 1993): 79–89.

———. "The Plow and the Pen: The Pioneering Adventures of Oscar Micheaux." *American Literature* 75:3 (2003): 545–69.

———. *Ten Most Wanted: The New Western Literature.* New York: Routledge Press, 1998.

Anderson, Benedict. *Imagined Communities: Reflections on the Origins and the Spread of Nationalism.* London: Verso Press, 1983.

Anderson, Robert Ball. *From Slavery to Affluence: Memoirs of Robert Anderson, Ex-Slave.* 1927. Steamboat Springs, Colo.: Steamboat Pilot Printer, 1988.

Andrews, William L. Introduction. *African American Autobiography: A Collection of Essays.* Ed. William L. Andrews. Upper Saddle River, N.J.: Prentice Hall, 1993. 1–7.

Antineau, Chester James, Phillip Mark Carroll, and Thomas Carroll Burke. *Religion under State Constitutions.* Brooklyn, N.Y.: Central Book Company, 1965.

Arrington, Leonard J. "Mormonism: Views from Without and Within." *Brigham Young University Studies* 14 (1974): 140–53.

Arrington, Leonard, and Jon Haupt. "The Mormon Heritage of Vardis Fisher." *Brigham Young University Studies* 18:1 (1977): 27–47.

Athearn, Robert G. *In Search of Canaan: Black Migration to Kansas, 1879–1880.* Lawrence: Regents Press of Kansas, 1978.

Baker Jr., Houston A. *Long Black Song: Essays in Black American Literature and Culture.* Charlottesville: University Press of Virginia, 1972.

Bancroft, Hubert Howe. *History of Utah, 1540–1886.* San Francisco: The History Company, 1889.

Beasley, Delilah. *The Negro Trail Blazers of California: A Compilation of the Records from the California Archives in the Bancroft Library at the University of California, in Berkeley; and from the Diaries, Old Papers, and Conversations of Old Pioneers in the State of California. It Is a True Record of Facts, as They Pertain to the History of the Pioneer and the Present Day Negro of California.* 1919. New York: Negro Universities Press, 1969.

Bederman, Gail. *Manliness and Civilization: A Cultural History of Gender and Race in the United Sates, 1880–1917*. Chicago: University of Chicago Press, 1995.

Bellin, Joshua David. *Demon of the Continent: Indians and the Shaping of American Literature*. Philadelphia: University of Pennsylvania Press, 2001.

Bergland, Renée L. *The National Uncanny: Indian Ghosts and American Subjects*. Hanover, N.H.: Dartmouth College Press/University Press of New England, 2000.

Berlant, Lauren. *The Anatomy of National Fantasy: Hawthorne, Utopia, and Everyday Life*. Chicago: University of Chicago Press, 1991.

Bernson, Sara L., and Robert J. Eggers. "Black People in South Dakota History." *South Dakota History* 7 (1977): 241–70.

"'Betrayal' Severely Criticized, A Bore." *Chicago Defender* 10 July 1948: 28.

Billington, Monroe Lee. *New Mexico's Buffalo Soldiers, 1866–1900*. Niwot: University Press of Colorado, 1991.

Billington, Monroe Lee, and Roger D. Hardaway, eds. *African Americans on the Western Frontier*. Niwot: University Press of Colorado, 1998.

Billington, Ray Allen. *The Genesis of the Frontier Thesis: A Study in Historical Creativity*. San Marino, Cal.: Huntington Library, 1971.

Black Elk, (Nicholas). *Black Elk Speaks*. As told through John G. Neihardt. 1932. Lincoln: University of Nebraska Press, 1988.

Blackstone, Sarah J. *Buckskins, Bullets, and Business: A History of Buffalo Bill's Wild West*. Westport, Conn.: Greenwood Press, 1986.

Bogue, Allan G. *Frederick Jackson Turner: Strange Roads Going Down*. Norman: University of Oklahoma Press, 1998.

Bold, Christine. "The Rough Riders at Home and Abroad: Cody, Roosevelt, Remington and the Imperialist Hero." *Canadian Journal of American Studies* 18:3 (Fall 1987): 321–50.

Bowser, Pearl, and Louise Spence. *Writing Himself into History: Oscar Micheaux, His Silent Films, and His Audiences*. New Brunswick, N.J.: Rutgers University Press, 2000.

Bowser, Pearl, Jane Gaines, and Charles Musser, eds. *Oscar Micheaux and His Circle: African-American Filmmaking and Race Cinema of the Silent Era*. Bloomington: Indiana University Press, 2001.

Bradford, Mary Lythgoe. Foreword. *A Little Lower Than the Angels*. By Virginia Sorensen. Salt Lake City: Signature Books, 1997. v–xx.

Bramen, Carrie Tirado. *The Uses of Variety: Modern Americanism and the Quest for National Distinctiveness*. Cambridge, Mass.: Harvard University Press, 2001.

Brooklyn Museum of Art. *Buffalo Bill and the Wild West*. Pittsburgh: University of Pittsburgh Press, 1981.

Brown, Jayna. "Black Patriarch on the Prairie: National Identity and Black Manhood in the Early Novels of Oscar Micheaux." *Oscar Micheaux and His Circle: African-American Filmmaking and Race Cinema of the Silent Era*. Ed. Pearl Bowser, Jane Gaines, and Charles Musser. Bloomington: Indiana University Press, 2001. 132–43.

Brumble III, David. *American Indian Autobiography*. Berkeley: University of California Press, 1988.

Bunch III, Lonnie G. "Allensworth: The Life, Death and Rebirth of an All-Black Community." *The Californians* (November/December 1987): 26–33.

Burdick, Usher L. *The Last Days of Sitting Bull, Sioux Medicine Chief.* Baltimore: Wirth Brothers, 1941.

Bush Jr., Lester E. "A Peculiar People: The Physiological Aspects of Mormonism, 1850–1975." *Dialogue: A Journal of Mormon Thought* 12:3 (Fall 1979): 61–83.

Canfield, Gae Whitney. *Sarah Winnemucca of the Northern Paiutes*. Norman: University of Oklahoma Press, 1983.

Carney, George O. "Oklahoma's All Black Towns." *African Americans on the Western Frontier*. Ed. Monroe Lee Billington and Roger D. Hardaway. Niwot: University Press of Colorado, 1998. 147–59.

Carroll, John M., ed. *The Black Military Experience in the American West*. New York: Liveright Publishing, 1971.

Castro, Michael. *Interpreting the Indian: Twentieth-Century Poets and the Native American*. Albuquerque: University of New Mexico Press, 1983.

Clark, Susan F. "The Menace of Wild West Shows" *The Cultures of Celebrations*. Ed. Ray B. Browne and Michael T. Marsden. Bowling Green, Ohio: Bowling Green State University Press, 1994. 145–55.

Collins, Michael L. *That Damned Cowboy: Theodore Roosevelt and the American West, 1883–1898*. New York: Peter Lang, 1991.

Coward, John M. *The Newspaper Indian: Native American Identity in the Press, 1820–90*. Urbana: University of Illinois Press, 1999.

Cracroft, Richard H. "The Didactic Heresy as Orthodox Tool: B. H. Roberts as Writer of Home Literature." *Tending the Garden: Essays on Mormon Literature*. Ed. Eugene England and Lavina Fielding Anderson. Salt Lake City: Signature Books, 1996. 117–33.

———. "Seeking 'the Good, the Pure, the Elevating': A Short History of Mormon Fiction" (Part 1). *Ensign* 11 (June 1981): 57–62.

———. "Seeking 'the Good, the Pure, the Elevating': A Short History of Mormon Fiction" (Part 2). *Ensign* 11 (July 1981): 56–61.

Crane, Stephen. *Complete Short Stories and Sketches of Stephen Crane*. Ed. Thomas A. Gullason. Garden City, N.Y.: Doubleday & Company, 1963.

———. *Correspondence of Stephen Crane.* 2 vols. Ed. Stanley Wertheim and Paul Sorrentino. New York: Columbia University Press, 1993.

Cripps, Thomas. *Slow Fade to Black: The Negro in American Film, 1900–1942.* 1977. Oxford: Oxford University Press, 1993.

Crockett, Norman L. *The Black Towns.* Lawrence: Regents Press of Kansas, 1979.

Cronon, William, George Miles, and Jay Gitlin. *Under an Open Sky: Rethinking America's Western Past.* New York: W. W. Norton, 1992.

Danky, James P., and Maureen E. Hady, eds. *African-American Newspapers and Periodicals.* Cambridge, Mass.: Harvard University Press, 1998.

Davis, David Brion. "Some Themes of Counter-Subversion: An Analysis of Anti-Masonic, Anti-Catholic, and Anti-Mormon Literature." *Mississippi Valley Historical Review* 47:2 (September 1960): 205–24.

Deloria Jr., Vine. "The Indians." *Buffalo Bill and the Wild West.* Brooklyn Museum of Art. Pittsburgh: University of Pittsburgh Press, 1981. 45–56.

———. Introduction. *Black Elk Speaks.* By Nicholas Black Elk, as told through John G. Neihardt. 1932. Lincoln: University of Nebraska Press, 1988. xi–xiv.

DeMallie, Raymond J. *The Sixth Grandfather: Black Elk's Teachings Given to John G. Neihardt.* Lincoln: University of Nebraska Press, 1984.

Detter, Thomas. *Nellie Brown, or The Jealous Wife, with other sketches.* 1871. Lincoln: University of Nebraska Press, 1996.

DiNunzio, Mario R. "Theodore Roosevelt: An American Life." *Theodore Roosevelt: An American Mind: A Selection from His Writings.* New York: Penguin Books, 1994. 1–21.

Doctrine and Covenants of the Church of Jesus Christ of Latter-day Saints / The Pearl of Great Price. Salt Lake City: The Church of Jesus Christ of Latter-day Saints, 1982.

Dooley, Patrick. *The Pluralistic Philosophy of Stephen Crane.* Urbana: University of Illinois Press, 1993.

Durham, Philip, and Everett L. Jones. *The Negro Cowboys.* New York: Dodd, Mead and Company, 1965.

Eastman, Charles A. *Indian Heroes and Great Chieftains.* 1918. Lincoln: University of Nebraska Press, 1991.

Elder, Arlene. "Oscar Micheaux: Melting Pot on the Plains." *Old Northwest* 2:3 (September 1976): 299–307.

Enabling Act and Constitution and Laws Passed by the Eleventh Session of the Legislature of the State of South Dakota. Sioux Falls, S.D.: Brown & Saenger, 1909.

Enabling Act and Constitution and Laws Passed by the Thirteenth Session of the Legislature of the State of South Dakota. Sioux Falls, S.D.: Brown & Saenger, 1913.

England, Eugene, ed. *Bright Angels and Familiars.* Salt Lake City: Signature Books, 1992.

———. "The Dawning of a Brighter Day: Mormon Literature after 150 Years." *Brigham Young University Studies* 22:2 (1982): 131–60.

———. "Good Literature for a Chosen People." *Dialogue: A Journal of Mormon Thought* 32:1 (Spring 1999): 69–89.

———. "Mormon Literature: Progress and Prospects." *Mormon Americana: A Guide to Sources and Collections in the United States.* Provo, Utah: Brigham Young University Press, 1995. 455–505.

England, Eugene, and Dennis Clark, eds. *Harvest: Fifteen Contemporary Mormon Poets.* Salt Lake City: Signature Books, 1989.

Esplin, Ross S. "A Survey of Fiction Written by Mormon Authors and Appearing in Mormon Periodicals between 1900 and 1945." Master's thesis. Brigham Young University, 1949.

"Excerpts from Bush's Remarks on Retaliation." *New York Times* 18 September 2001: A10.

Fabian, Ann. *The Unvarnished Truth: Personal Narratives in Nineteenth-Century America.* Berkeley: University of California Press, 2000.

Fisher, Vardis. *Children of God: An American Epic.* New York: Harper & Brothers, 1939.

Flake, Kathleen. *The Politics of American Religious Identity: The Seating of Senator Reed Smoot, Mormon Apostle.* Chapel Hill: University of North Carolina Press, 2004.

Fontenot Jr., Charles. "Oscar Micheaux, Black Novelist and Film Maker." *Vision and Refuge: Essays on the Literature of the Great Plains.* Ed. Virginia Faulkner with Frederick C. Luebke. Lincoln: University of Nebraska Press, 1982. 109–25.

Foster, Frances Smith. Introduction. *Nellie Brown or The Jealous Wife, with other sketches.* By Thomas Detter. Lincoln: University of Nebraska Press, 1996. vii–xxi.

Fowler, Arlen L. *The Black Infantry in the West: 1869–1891.* Westport, Conn.: Greenwood Publishing, 1971.

Fowler, Gene. "Western World to Journey to Crypt on Wildcat Point Standing Sentinel over Scout's Beloved Plains." *Denver Post* 3 June 1917, morning edition, n.p.

Fox, Richard Wightman, and T. J. Jackson Lears. *The Culture of Consumption: Critical Essays in American History, 1880–1980.* New York: Pantheon Books, 1983.

Friesen, Steve. "Tanks for the Memories." *Scout's Dispatch* (Newsletter of Buffalo Bill Museum and Grave). (Winter 2005): 1ff.

Gaines, Jane. "Fire and Desire: Race, Melodrama, and Oscar Micheaux." *Black American Cinema.* Ed. Manthia Diawara. New York: Routledge, 1993.

Gatewood Jr., William B. *Black Americans and the White Man's Burden, 1898–1903.* Urbana: University of Illinois Press, 1975.

————. "*Smoked Yankees" and the Struggle for Empire: Letters from Negro Soldiers, 1898-1902.* Urbana: University of Illinois Press, 1971.

Geary, Edward A. "Mormondom's Lost Generation: The Novelists of the 1940s." *Tending the Garden: Essays on Mormon Literature.* Ed. Eugene England and Lavina Fielding Anderson. Salt Lake City: Signature Books, 1996. 23–33.

————. "Poetics of Provincialism: Mormon Regional Fiction." *Dialogue: A Journal of Mormon Thought* 9:2 (Summer 1978): 15–24.

————. "Women Regionalists of Mormon Country." *Regionalism and the Female Imagination: A Collection of Essays.* Ed. Emily Toth. New York: Human Sciences Press, 1985. 139–96.

Gerstle, Gary. *American Crucible: Race and Nation in the Twentieth Century.* Princeton: Princeton University Press, 2001.

Gibbs, Mifflin Wistar. *Shadow and Light: An Autobiography.* 1902. Lincoln: University of Nebraska Press, 1995.

Gibson, Daniel. "Blackdom." *New Mexico Magazine* 64:2 (February 1986): 46–50.

Givens, Terryl L. *The Viper on the Hearth: Mormons, Myths, and the Construction of Heresy.* New York: Oxford University Press, 1997.

Gottlieb, Robert, and Peter Wiley. *America's Saints: The Rise of Mormon Power.* New York: G. P. Putnam's Sons, 1984.

Govenar, Alan. *African American Frontier: Slave Narratives and Oral Histories.* Santa Barbara, Cal.: ABC-CLIO, 2000.

Gramsci, Antonio. *Selections from the Prison Notebooks of Antonio Gramsci.* New York: International Publishers, 1971.

Green, Ronald J. *Straight Lick: The Cinema of Oscar Micheaux.* Bloomington: Indiana University Press, 2000.

————. *With a Crooked Stick: The Films of Oscar Micheaux.* Bloomington: Indiana University Press, 2004.

Gutiérrez, Ramón A. *When Jesus Came the Corn Mothers Went Away: Marriage, Sexuality, and Power in New Mexico, 1500–1846.* Stanford: Stanford University Press, 1991.

Hagedorn, Hermann. *Roosevelt in the Badlands.* Boston: Houghton Mifflin Company, 1921.

Hale, Frederick. "Exploiting the Native American Renaissance: The Chief Red Fox Memoirs Hoax." *European Review of Native American Studies* 15:1 (2001): 29–36.

Hamilton, Kenneth Marvin. *Black Towns and Profit: Promotion and Development in the Trans-Appalachian West, 1877–1915.* Urbana: University of Illinois Press, 1991.

Hardaway, Roger D. "The African American Frontier: A Bibliographic Essay."

African Americans on the Western Frontier. Ed. Monroe Lee Billington and Roger D. Hardaway. Niwot: University Press of Colorado, 1998. 231–57.

Havighurst, Walter. *Annie Oakley of the Wild West.* New York: MacMillan Company, 1954.

Hawkins, Anne P. W. "Hoeing Their Own: Black Agriculture and the Agrarian Ideal in Kansas, 1880–1920." *Kansas History* 22 (Autumn 1999): 200–213.

Herbert, Janis. "Oscar Micheaux: A Black Pioneer." *South Dakota Review* 11:4 (Winter 1973–74): 62–69.

Hoganson, Kristin L. *Fighting for American Manhood: How Gender Politics Provoked the Spanish-American and Philippine-American Wars.* New Haven: Yale University Press, 1998.

The Homesteader. Advertisement. *Chicago Defender* 22 February 1919: 14.

Hopkins, Sarah Winnemucca. *Life among the Piutes: Their Wrongs and Claims.* 1883. Reno: University of Nevada Press, 1994.

Howe, Susan Elizabeth. Foreword. *Where Nothing is Long Ago: Memories of a Mormon Childhood.* By Virginia Sorensen. Salt Lake City: Signature Books, 1998. v–ix.

Hurtado, Albert. *Indian Survival on the California Frontier.* New Haven: Yale University Press, 1988.

Johnson, Frederick P. "Agricultural Negro Colony in Eastern Colorado." *Western Farm Life* 1 May 1915: 5ff.

Johnson, M. K. *Black Masculinity and the Frontier Myth in American Literature.* Norman: University of Oklahoma Press, 2002.

Johnston, Michelle Dally. "A Widow's Legacy: Wife of Civil War Vet Going to Gettysburg." *Denver Post* 30 June 1997: A-1.

Jones, Virgil Carrington. *Roosevelt's Rough Riders.* Garden City, N.Y.: Doubleday & Company, 1971.

Jorgensen, Bruce W. "Digging the Foundation: Making and Reading Mormon Literature." *Dialogue: A Journal of Mormon Thought* 9:4 (1975): 50–61.

Joyce, Donald Franklin. *Gatekeepers of Black Culture: Black-Owned Book Publishing in the United States, 1817–1981.* Westport, Conn.: Greenwood Press, 1983.

Kaplan, Amy. *The Anarchy of Empire: The Making of U.S. Culture.* Cambridge, Mass.: Harvard University Press, 2002.

———. "Black and Blue on San Juan Hill." *Cultures of United States Imperialism.* Ed. Amy Kaplan and Donald E. Pease. Durham, N.C.: Duke University Press, 1993. 219–36.

Kasson, Joy S. *Buffalo Bill's Wild West: Celebrity, Memory, and Popular History.* New York: Hill and Wang, 2000.

Katz, William Loren. *The Black West.* Seattle: Open Hand Publishing, 1987.

Kennelly, Ardyth. *The Peaceable Kingdom*. Boston: Houghton Mifflin, 1949.

Kimmel, Michael. *Manhood in America: A Cultural History*. New York: Free Press, 1996.

Kirksey, Jim. "Civil War Veteran's Widow Dies at 97." *Denver Post* 24 September 1998, A-01.

Kisch, John, and Edward Mapp. *A Separate Cinema: Fifty Years of Black Cast Posters*. New York: Farrar, Straus and Giroux, 1992.

Kolodny, Annette. *The Land Before Her: Fantasy and Experience of the American Frontiers, 1630–1860*. Chapel Hill: University of North Carolina Press, 1984.

Kramer, Mary D. "The American Wild West Show and 'Buffalo Bill' Cody." *Costerus* 4 (1972): 87–98.

Krupat, Arnold. *For Those Who Came After: A Study of Native American Autobiography*. Berkeley: University of California Press, 1985.

Kvasnicka, Robert M., and Herman J. Viola, eds. *The Commissioners of Indian Affairs, 1824–1977*. Lincoln: University of Nebraska Press, 1979.

Lapp, Rudolph M. *Blacks in Gold Rush California*. New Haven: Yale University Press, 1977.

Lears, T. J. Jackson. *No Place of Grace: Antimodernism and the Transformation of American Culture, 1880–1920*. New York: Pantheon Books, 1981.

Leckie, William H. *The Buffalo Soldiers: A Narrative of the Negro Cavalry in the West*. Norman: University of Oklahoma Press, 1967.

Lewis, Alfred Henry. "The Viper on the Hearth. Part 1: Mormonism: Its Plots, Plans, and Intrigues Against American Homes." *Cosmopolitan Magazine* L:4 (March 1911): 439–50.

Limerick, Patricia Nelson. *The Legacy of Conquest: The Unbroken Past of the American West*. New York: W. W. Norton, 1987.

———. *Something in the Soil: Legacies and Reckonings in the New West*. New York: W. W. Norton, 2000.

———. "What on Earth Is the New Western History?" *Trails: Toward a New Western History*. Ed. Patricia Nelson Limerick, Clyde A. Milner II, and Charles E. Rankin. Lawrence: University of Kansas Press, 1991. 81–88.

———. "What Raymond Chandler Knew and Western Historians Forgot." *Old West—New West: Centennial Essays*. Ed. Barbara Howard Meldrum. Moscow: University of Idaho Press, 1993. 28–39.

Limerick, Patricia, Clyde Milner II, and Charles Rankin, eds. *Trails: Toward a New Western History*. Lawrence: University of Kansas Press, 1991.

Lindner, Markhus H. "Goggles, Family, and the 'Wild West': The Photographs of Sitting Bull." *European Contributions to Native American Studies* 15:1 (2001): 37–48.

Littlefield Jr., Daniel F., and Lonnie E. Underhill. "Black Dreams and 'Free'

Homes: The Oklahoma Territory, 1891–1894." *Phylon* 34:4 (December 1973): 343–57.

———. "Negro Marshals in the Indian Territory." *Journal of Negro History* 56 (1971): 77–87.

London, Jack. "Martin Eden." *The Collected Jack London: Thirty-Six Stories, Four Complete Novels, A Memoir.* Ed. Steven J Kasdin. New York: Barnes and Noble Books, 1991.

Love, Nat. *The Life and Adventures of Nat Love, Better Known in the Cattle Country as "Deadwood Dick," By Himself, A True History of Slavery Days, Life on the Great Cattle Ranges and on the Plains of the "Wild and Wooly" West, Based on the Facts, and Personal Experiences of the Author.* 1907. Lincoln: University of Nebraska Press, 1995.

Marsh, Fred T. "A New Novel by Vardis Fisher: *Children of God* Is the Story of the Great Mormon Migration." Review of *Children of God: An American Epic*, by Vardis Fisher. *The New York Times Book Review* 27 August 1939: 1.

Martin, Jonathan D. "'The Grandest and Most Cosmopolitan Object Teacher': Buffalo Bill's Wild West and the Politics of American Identity, 1883–1899." *Radical History Review* 66 (Fall 1996): 92–123.

Massey, Ara R., ed. *Black Cowboys of Texas.* College Station: Texas A&M University Press, 2000.

Mauss, Armand L. "The Mormon Struggle with Assimilation and Identity: Trends and Developments since Midcentury." *Dialogue: A Journal of Mormon Thought* 27:1 (Spring 1994): 129–49.

McCluskey, Sally. "Black Elk Speaks: And So Does John Neihardt." *Western American Literature* 6:4 (1972): 231–42.

McCoy, Ronald. "Short Bull: Lakota Visionary, Historian and Artist." *American Indian Art Magazine* 17:3 (1992): 54–65.

Means, Russell. "Acting Against Racism in Mohicans." <http://users.efni.com/~kristy/means.htm>. 15 November 2004.

Merrill, Milton R. *Reed Smoot: Apostle in Politics.* Logan: Utah State University Press, 1990.

Micheaux, Oscar. *The Case of Mrs. Wingate.* 1945. New York: AMS Press, 1975.

———. "Colored Americans Too Slow." *Chicago Defender* 28 October 1911 (vol 6, no. 43): 1ff.

———. *The Conquest: The Story of a Negro Pioneer.* 1913. Lincoln: University of Nebraska Press, 1994.

———. *The Forged Note.* Lincoln: Western Book Supply Co., 1915.

———. *The Homesteader.* 1917. Lincoln: University of Nebraska Press, 1994.

———. "Where the Negro Fails." *Chicago Defender* 19 March 1910 (vol. 5, no. 12): 1.

————. *The Wind from Nowhere*. 1941. Freeport, N.Y.: Books for Libraries Presses, 1972.

Midnight Ramble: Oscar Micheaux and the Story of Race Movies. Dir. Bestor Cram and Pearl Bowser. Northern Lights Production, 1994.

Milner II, Clyde A., ed. *A New Significance: Re-envisioning the History of the American West*. New York: Oxford University Press, 1996.

Mitterling, Philip I. "Buffalo Bill and Carry Nation: Symbols of an Age." *North Dakota Quarterly* 50:1 (1982): 62–71.

Morgan, Dale. "Mormon Storytellers." *Tending the Garden: Essays on Mormon Literature*. Ed. Eugene England and Lavina Fielding Anderson. Salt Lake City: Signature Books, 1996. 3–12.

"Mormons, Armenians, Boers, Lords, Lawyers, Chromosomes." Review of *Children of God: An American Epic*, by Vardis Fisher, and other titles. *New Yorker* 2 September 1939: 53–55.

Morris, Edmund. *The Rise of Theodore Roosevelt*. New York: Coward, McCann & Geoghegan, 1979.

————. *Theodore Rex*. New York: Random House, 2001.

Moses, L. G. *Wild West Shows and the Images of American Indians, 1883–1933*. Albuquerque: University of New Mexico Press, 1996.

Moses, L. G., and Raymond Wilson, eds. *Indian Lives: Essays on Nineteenth and Twentieth-Century Native American Leaders*. Albuquerque: University of New Mexico Press, 1985.

Mulder, William. "Mormonism and Literature." *Western Humanities Review* 9 (Winter 1954–55): 85–89.

————. "Telling It Slant: Aiming for Truth in Contemporary Mormon Literature." *Dialogue: A Journal of Mormon Thought* 26:2 (Summer 1993): 155–69.

Murray, David. *Forked Tongues: Speech, Writing, and Representation in North American Indian Texts*. Bloomington: Indiana University Press, 1991.

Musser, Charles. "To Dream the Dreams of White Playwrights: Reappropriation and Resistance in Oscar Micheaux's Body and Soul." *Yale Journal of Criticism* 12:2 (1999): 321–56.

Nash, Roderick. *Creating the West: Historical Interpretations, 1890–1990*. Albuquerque: University of New Mexico Press, 1991.

Neihardt, Hilda, and Lori Utecht. *Black Elk Lives: Conversations with the Black Elk Family*. Lincoln: University of Nebraska Press, 2000.

Nelson, Dana. *National Manhood: Capitalist Citizenship and the Imagined Fraternity of White Men*. Durham, N.C.: Duke University Press, 1998.

Nemerov, Alexander. *Frederic Remington and Turn-of-the-Century America*. New Haven: Yale University Press, 1995.

Nomura, Gail. "Significant Lives: Asia and Asian Americans in the History of the U.S. West." *Western Historical Quarterly* 25:1 (1994): 69–88.

Norris Jr., Melvin Edward. "Dearfield, Colorado—The Evolution of a Rural Black Settlement: An Historical Geography of Black Colonization on the Great Plains." Ph.D diss. University of Colorado, 1980.

Olney, James. "The Value of Autobiography for Comparative Studies: African vs. Western Autobiography." *African American Autobiography: A Collection of Essays.* Ed. William L. Andrews. Upper Saddle River, N.J.: Prentice Hall, 1993. 212–23.

Painter, Nell Irvin. *Exodusters: Black Migration to Kansas after Reconstruction.* New York: Alfred A. Knopf, 1977.

Pease, Donald. "National Identities, Postmodern Artifacts, and Postnational Narratives." *National Identities and Post-Americanist Narratives.* Ed. Donald E. Pease. Durham, N.C.: Duke University Press, 1994. 1–13.

Pease, William, and Jane Pease. *Black Utopia: Negro Communal Experiments in America.* Madison: State Historical Society of Wisconsin, 1972.

Peterson, Levi S., ed. *Greening Wheat: Fifteen Mormon Short Stories.* Midvale, Utah: Orion Books, 1983.

Pfaller, Louis. "'Enemies in '76, Friends in '85'—Sitting Bull and Buffalo Bill." *Prologue* 1:2 (1969): 16–31.

Poll, Richard D. "The Americanization of Utah." *Utah Historical Quarterly* 44:1 (1976): 76–93.

Porter, Kenneth W. "Negroes in the Fur Trade." *Minnesota History* 15 (1934): 421–33.

———. "Negro Labor in the Western Cattle Industry, 1866–1900." *Labor History* 10:3 (Summer 1969): 346–74.

———. *The Negro on the American Frontier.* New York: Anno, 1971.

Powers, William. "When Black Elk Speaks, Everybody Listens." *Social Text* (1990): 43–56.

Praus, Alexis A. *A New Pictographic Autobiography of Sitting Bull.* Smithsonian Miscellaneous Collections 123:6. Washington, D.C.: Smithsonian Institution, 1955.

Ravage, John W. *Black Pioneers: Images of the Black Experience on the North American Frontier.* Salt Lake City: University of Utah Press, 1997.

Red Fox. *The Memoirs of Chief Red Fox.* New York: McGraw Hill, 1971.

Reddin, Paul. *Wild West Shows.* Urbana: University of Illinois Press, 1999.

Rees, Robert A. "The Imagination's New Beginning: Thoughts on Esthetics and Religion." *Dialogue: A Journal of Mormon Thought* 4:3 (Autumn 1969): 21–25.

Regester, Charlene. "The Misreading and Rereading of African American Filmmaker Oscar Micheaux." *Film History* 7:4 (1995): 426–49.

Rennert, Jack. *100 Posters of Buffalo Bill's Wild West.* New York: Darien House, 1976.

Rice, Julian. *Black Elk's Story: Distinguishing Its Lakota Purpose.* Albuquerque: University of New Mexico Press, 1991.

Richards, Larry. *African American Films through 1959: A Comprehensive, Illustrated Filmography.* Jefferson, N.C.: McFarland and Company, 1998.

Riley, Glenda. "Airbrushing Western History (Eliminating the Notion of 'Frontier' in Western History)." *Journal of the West* 31:4 (1992): 3–5.

———. *The Female Frontier: A Comparative View of Women on the Prairie and the Plains.* Lawrence: University of Kansas Press, 1988.

Robbins, William G. *Colony and Empire: The Capitalist Transformation of the American West.* Lawrence: University Press of Kansas, 1994.

Roosevelt, Theodore. *American Ideals, and Other Essays, Social and Political.* New York: G. P. Putnam's Sons, 1897.

———. *The Americanism of Theodore Roosevelt: Selections from His Writings and Speeches.* Compiled by Hermann Hagedorn. Boston: Houghton Mifflin, 1923.

———. *Hunting Trips of a Ranchman.* New York: G. P. Putnam's Sons, 1885.

———. *Letters of Theodore Roosevelt.* 6 vols. Ed. Elting E. Morison and John M. Blum. Cambridge, Mass.: Harvard University Press, 1951.

———. *Ranch Life and the Hunting Trail.* 1888. New York: Century Co., 1904.

———. *The Rough Riders.* 1899. *The Works of Theodore Roosevelt.* National Edition, vol. 11. New York: Charles Scribner's Sons, 1926.

———. *The Rough Riders.* New York: Charles Scribner's Sons, 1905.

———. *The Strenuous Life: Essays and Lectures.* New York: Century Co., 1904.

———. *Theodore Roosevelt: An Autobiography.* New York: MacMillan Company, 1914.

———. *The Winning of the West.* 4 vols. New York: G. P. Putnam's Sons, 1905.

Rosa, Joseph G., and Robin May. *Buffalo Bill and His Wild West: A Pictorial Biography.* Lawrence: University Press of Kansas, 1989.

Ruiz, Vicki L. *Cannery Women, Cannery Lives: Mexican Unionization and the California Food Processing Industry, 1930–1950.* Albuquerque: University of New Mexico Press, 1987.

Rusco, Elmer R. *"Good Time Coming?": Black Nevadans in the Nineteenth Century.* Westport, Conn.: Greenwood Press, 1975.

Russell, Don. *The Lives and Legends of Buffalo Bill.* Norman: University of Oklahoma Press, 1960.

Sampson, Henry T. *Blacks in Black and White: A Source Book on Black Film.* 2nd ed. Lanham, Md.: Scarecrow Press, 1995.

Samuels, Peggy, and Harold Samuels. *Teddy Roosevelt at San Juan: The Making of a President.* College Station: Texas A&M Press, 1997.

Savage, W. Sherman. *Blacks in the West*. Westport, Conn.: Greenwood Press, 1976.

———. "The Negro on the Mining Frontier." *Journal of Negro History* 30 (1945): 30–46.

Sayre, Robert F. "The Proper Study—Autobiographies in American Studies." *American Quarterly* 29:3 (1977): 241–62.

———. "Vision and Experience in *Black Elk Speaks*." *College English* 32:5 (February 1971): 509–635.

Schell, Herbert S. *History of South Dakota*. Lincoln: University of Nebraska Press, 1968.

Schubert, Frank N., ed. *On the Trail of the Buffalo Soldier: Biographies of African Americans in the U.S. Army, 1866–1917*. Wilmington, Del.: Scholarly Resources, 1995.

Schwartz, Joseph. "The Wild West Show: 'Everything Genuine.'" *Journal of Popular Culture* 3:4 (1970): 656–66.

Silvio, Carl. "*Black Elk Speaks* and Literary Disciplinarity: A Case Study in Canonization." *College Literature* 26 (Spring 1999): 137–50.

Slotkin, Richard. "Buffalo Bill's Wild West and the Mythologization of the American Empire." *Cultures of United States Imperialism*. Ed. Amy Kaplan and Donald E. Pease. Durham, N.C.: Duke University Press, 1993. 164–81.

———. *Gunfighter Nation: The Myth of the Frontier in Twentieth-Century America*. New York: Atheneum, 1992.

Sorensen, Virginia. *A Little Lower than the Angels*. 1942. Salt Lake City: Signature Books, 1997.

———. "Mormon Wife, a Lively Family Story." Review of *The Peaceable Kingdom*, by Ardyth Kennelly. *New York Herald Tribune Weekly Book Review* 24 April 1949: 6.

Standing Bear, Luther. *My Indian Boyhood*. 1931. Lincoln: University of Nebraska Press, 1988.

———. *My People the Sioux*. Edited by E. A. Brininstool, with an introduction by William S. Hart. Boston: Houghton Mifflin Company, 1928.

———. *My People the Sioux*. 1928. Edited by E. A. Brininstool. Lincoln: University of Nebraska Press, 1975.

Statutes at Large of the United States of America, from Dec. 1885 to March 1887. Recent Treaties, Postal Conventions, and Executive Proclamations. Vol. 24. Washington, D.C.: Government Printing Office, 1887.

Stegner, Wallace. "Sorensen." Review of *A Little Lower than the Angels*, by Virginia Sorensen. *Saturday Review of Literature* 9 May 1942: 11–12.

Steward, T. G. *The Colored Regulars in the United States Army*. 1904. New York: Arno Press, 1969.

Stirling, M. W. *Three Pictographic Autobiographies of Sitting Bull*. Smithsonian Miscellaneous Collections 97:5. Washington, D.C.: Smithsonian Institution, 1938.

Swann, Brian, and Arnold Krupat. *I Tell You Now: Autobiographical Essays by Native American Writers.* Lincoln: University of Nebraska Press, 1987.

Takaki, Ronald. *Strangers from a Different Shore: A History of Asian Americans.* Boston: Little, Brown, 1989.

Taylor, Quintard. "Bibliographic Essay on the African American West." *Montana: The Magazine of Western History* 46:4 (Winter 1996): 18–23.

———. *In Search of the Racial Frontier: African Americans in the American West, 1528–1990.* New York: W. W. Norton, 1998.

Tompkins, Jane. "At the Buffalo Bill Museum." *South Atlantic Quarterly* 89:3 (Summer 1990): 525–45.

Trachtenberg, Alan. *Incorporation of America: Culture and Society in the Gilded Age.* New York: Hill and Wang, 1982.

Turner, Frederick Jackson. "The First Official Frontier of the Massachusetts Bay." *The Frontier in American History.* 1920. Mineola, N.Y.: Dover Publications, 1996. 39–66.

———. "Roosevelt: The Winning of the West." *American Historical Review* 2:1 (October 1896): 171–76.

———. "The Significance of the Frontier in American History." *Rereading Frederick Jackson Turner: "The Significance of the Frontier in American History" and Other Essays.* New York: Henry Holt and Company, 1994. 31–60.

Utley, Robert M. *The Indian Frontier of the American West.* Albuquerque: University of New Mexico Press, 1984.

———. *The Lance and the Shield: The Life and Times of Sitting Bull.* New York: Henry Holt and Company, 1993.

VannEpps-Taylor, Betti Carol. *Oscar Micheaux: A Biography . . . Dakota Homesteader, Author, Pioneer Film Maker.* Rapid City, S.D.: Dakota West Books, 1999.

Vexler, Robert I., ed. *Chronology and Documentary Handbook of the State of Utah.* Dobbs Ferry, N.Y.: Oceana Publications, 1979.

Vizenor, Gerald. *Manifest Manners: Postindian Warriors of Survivance.* Hanover, N.H.: Wesleyan University Press/University Press of New England, 1994.

Wald, Priscilla. *Constituting Americans: Cultural Anxiety and Narrative Form.* Durham, N.C.: Duke University Press, 1995.

Walker, Dale L. *The Boys of '98: Theodore Roosevelt and the Rough Riders.* New York: Tom Doherty Associates, 1998.

Walton, Edith. Review of *The Giant Joshua,* by Maurine Whipple. *New York Times Book Review* 12 January 1941: 6.

Washington, Booker T. "Boley, A Negro Town in the West." *The Outlook* 28 (4 January 1908): 28–31.

———. "Booker T. Washington Tells About Conditions of Negro in Northwest." *New York Age* 20 March 1913: 1ff.

————. *The Negro in Business.* 1907. New York: AMS Press, 1971.

————. "Negro in South Has Brightest Future," *New York Age* 10 April 1913: 2.

————. *The Story of the Negro: The Rise of the Race from Slavery.* 1909. 2 vols. Gloucester, Mass.: Peter Smith, 1969.

————. *Up from Slavery. Three Negro Classics.* New York: Avon, 1965. 22–205

Washington, Booker T., N. B. Wood, and Fannie Barrier Williams. *A New Negro for a New Century.* 1900. New York: Arno Press, 1969.

Watson, Elmo Scott. "The Photographs of Sitting Bull." *The Westerner's Brand Book* (Official Publication of the Chicago Corral of Westerners) 6:6 (August 1949): 43, 47–48.

Wax, Darold D. "The Odyssey of an Ex-Slave: Robert Ball Anderson's Pursuit of the American Dream." *Phylon* 45:1 (1984): 67–79.

————. "Robert Ball Anderson, Ex-Slave, a Pioneer in Western Nebraska, 1884–1930." *Nebraska History* 64 (1983): 162–92.

Webb, Walter Prescott. "American West: Perpetual Mirage." *Harper's Magazine* (May 1957): 25–31.

Welch, James. *The Heartsong of Charging Elk.* New York: Doubleday, 2000.

Wells, George. "Wives Gambit." Review of *The Peaceable Kingdom,* by Ardyth Kennelly. *The New York Times Book Review* 13 November 1949: 23.

West, Elliot. *Growing Up with the Country: Childhood on the Far Western Frontier.* Albuquerque: University of New Mexico Press, 1989.

West, Ray B. "Mormon Story" Review of *The Giant Joshua,* by Maurine Whipple. *Saturday Review of Literature* 4 January 1941: 5.

Whipple, Maurine. *The Giant Joshua.* 1941. Salt Lake City: Western Epics, Inc., 1976.

————. "Maurine Whipple's Story of *The Giant Joshua.*" *Dialogue: A Journal of Mormon Thought* 6:3,4 (1971): 55–62.

————. *This is the Place: Utah.* New York: Alfred A. Knopf, 1945.

White, G. Edward. *The Eastern Establishment and the Western Experience: The West of Frederic Remington, Theodore Roosevelt, and Owen Wister.* New Haven: Yale University Press, 1968.

White, Richard. "Frederick Jackson Turner and Buffalo Bill." *The Frontier in American Culture: An Exhibition at the Newberry Library, August 26, 1994–January 7, 1995.* Ed. James R. Grossman. Berkeley: University of California Press, 1994. 7–65.

————. *"It's Your Misfortune and None of My Own": A New History of the American West.* Norman: University of Oklahoma Press, 1991.

————. "Trashing the Trails." *Trails: Toward a New Western History.* Ed. Patricia Nelson Limerick, Clyde A. Milner II, and Charles E. Rankin. Lawrence: University of Kansas Press, 1991. 26–39.

Whitney, Orson F. "Home Literature." *A Believing People: Literature of the Latter-day Saints.* Ed. Richard A. Cracroft and Neal E. Lambert. Provo, Utah: Brigham Young University Press, 1974. 203–7.

Wickstrom, Gordon M. "Buffalo Bill the Actor." *Journal of the West* 34:1 (January 1995): 62–69.

Widtsoe, John A. Review of *The Giant Joshua*, by Maurine Whipple. *The Improvement Era* 44:2 (February 1941): 93.

———. Review of *A Little Lower than the Angels*, by Virginia Sorensen. *The Improvement Era* 45:6 (June 1942): 380.

Williams, Brackette F. Introduction ("Nat Love Rides into the Sunset of Slavery and Racism"). *The Life and Adventures of Nat Love, Better Known in the Cattle Country as "Deadwood Dick"* . . . Lincoln: University of Nebraska Press, 1995. vii–xviii.

Williams, Nudie E. "Black Men Who Wore the 'Star.'" *Chronicles of Oklahoma* (1981): 83–90.

Williams, Raymond. *Culture and Society.* New York: Columbia University Press, 1983.

Wilson, Elinor. *Jim Beckwourth: Black Mountain Man and War Chief of the Crows.* Norman: University of Oklahoma Press, 1972.

Wilson, John W. Review of *The Giant Joshua*, by Maurine Whipple. *Southwest Review* 1 (Autumn 1940): 262–65.

Wilson, R. L., with Greg Martin. *Buffalo Bill's Wild West: An American Legend.* New York: Random House, 1998.

Wister, Owen. *Owen Wister's West: Selected Articles.* Ed. Robert Murray Davies. Albuquerque: University of New Mexico Press, 1987.

———. *The Virginian.* 1902. New York: Pocket Books, 1991.

Wong, Hertha Dawn. *Sending My Heart Back across Years: Tradition and Innovation in Native American Autobiography.* New York: Oxford University Press, 1992.

Worster, Donald. *Rivers of Empire: Water, Aridity, and the Growth of the American West.* New York: Oxford University Press, 1985.

———. *Under Western Skies: Nature and History in the American West.* New York: Oxford University Press, 1992.

Wrobel, David M. *The End of American Exceptionalism: Frontier Anxiety from the Old West to the New Deal.* Lawrence: University Press of Kansas, 1993.

Zanjani, Sally. *Sarah Winnemucca.* Lincoln: University of Nebraska Press, 2001.

INDEX

Page numbers in **bold** represent illustrations.

Wax, Donald, 95
Webb, Walter Prescott, 55, 78–79
Welch, James (*The Heartsong of Charging Elk*), 146–49
West, Ray B., 127
Western Book Supply Company, 87, 224n12
Western (frontier) mythology, 1, 4, 8, 13, 55, 90, 103, 208–12; as false history, 11; as national story, 1–4, 52, 46, 207, 208–12; and New Western History, 11; in politics, 2, 21. *See also* Frontier; Frontier Thesis; Turner, Frederick Jackson
Whipple, Maurine, 16, 116, 136, 139, 150; *The Giant Joshua*, 116, 117–28, 229n12
White, Richard, 8, 10–11, 209–210; concept of the frontier, 9–10
White Bull, Joseph, 200
Whitney, Orson F. ("Home Literature"), 113
Widtsoe, John A., 127, 133
Widtsoe, J. P., 113
Williams, Brackette F., 100
Williams, Raymond, 4
Wilson, Woodrow, 208, 218n17, 218n22
Wind From Nowhere, The (Micheaux), 61–62, 66; and Exceptional Negro, 69–70; land acquisition 68, 71; and miscegenation, 70, 71–72; as racial uplift fantasy, 73–75; and Turnerian ideals, 72–75; white love interest, 71–72, 93, 225n15
Winnemucca (chief), 166, 172
Winnemucca, Sarah. *See* Hopkins, Sarah Winnemucca

Winning of the West, The (Roosevelt), 22, 26, 27; Frederick Jackson Turner's review of, 51–52
Wister, Owen, 7, 8, 41, 44, 75–76, 80, 151, 186; *The Virginian*, 75–76
Wood, Leonard, 28, 216n9
Wooden Leg (*Wooden Leg: A Warrior who Fought Custer*), 183–84
Woodruff, Wilford, 109–10, 117, 118; in *Children of God* (Fisher), 138–39
Woodruff Manifesto, 3, 7, 109–11, 116, 117, 118, 227n3; in *Children of God* (Fisher), 138–39; in *The Peaceable Kingdom* (Kennelly), 134–35; and Utah statehood, 111
World's Columbian Exposition, 3; and Buffalo Bill's Wild West, 152, 162, 231n5
Wounded Knee, 3, 7, 195, 196; Black Elk on, 195, 202; in *Heartsong of Charging Elk* (Welch), 149; Standing Bear on, 190–91
Wright, Solomon Alexander (*My rambles as east Texas cowboy, hunter, fisherman, tie-cutter*), 102
Wrobel, David W., 213n1

Yankton settlement (South Dakota), 61
Yellow Wolf (*Yellow Wolf: His Own Story*), 183–84
Young, Brigham, 117, 118; in *Children of God* (Fisher), 138; in *The Giant Joshua* (Whipple), 119, 124; in *A Little Lower than the Angels* (Sorenson), 130

Zanjani, Sally, 166, 167